Diana

An Intimate Portrait

INGRID SEWARD

CB

CONTEMPORARY BOOKS

Library of Congress Cataloging-in-Publication Data
is on file at the United States Library of Congress.

The photographs in this book are reproduced by kind permission of:

Alpha Photographic Press Agency Ltd: 2 (John Rigby), 3 above (Alan Davidson)
4 below (Jim Bennett), 6 (Jim Bennett), 9 above (Alpha/Agence Angeli), 9 below
13 below (Jim Bennett), 14 (Jim Bennett), 15 above (Jim Bennett), 16 below
(Jim Bennett), 18 (Jim Bennett), 21 (Jim Bennett), 22, 30 above (Tim Anderson).
Robin Nunn: 1, 3 below, 4 above, 5, 7, 8 (L. Brooks), 10, 11 above, 11 below (Γ
Connell), 12, 13 above, 15 below, 16 above, 17, 19, 20, 23, 24, 25 (Aasta
Børte), 26, 27, 28 (D. Connell), 29, 30 below, 31, 32.

Cover design by Kim Bartko
Front cover photograph copyright © 1991 by Patrick Demarchelier/Camera
Press/Retna Ltd.
Back cover photograph copyright © 1995 by Mike Dunlea/Express Newspapers

This edition published 1997 by Contemporary Books
An imprint of NTC/Contemporary Publishing Company
4255 West Touhy Avenue, Lincolnwood (Chicago), Illinois 60646-1975 U.S.A.
Prologue and Epilogue copyright © 1997 by Ingrid Seward
Copyright © 1988 by Ingrid Seward
All rights reserved. No part of this book may be reproduced, stored in a retrieval
system, or transmitted in any form or by any means, electronic, mechanical,
photocopying, recording, or otherwise, without the prior permission of
NTC/Contemporary Publishing Company.
Manufactured in the United States of America
International Standard Book Number: 0-8092-2860-2
18   17   16   15   14   13   12   11   10   9   8   7   6   5   4   3   2   1

Diana

To my husband

Contents

Acknowledgments

In compiling this book about the Princess of Wales I have drawn on my sources and experience gained from my involvement as editor of *Majesty* magazine. In that time hardly a day has passed without my witnessing some incident regarding the Royal Family or having it related to me. The problem, as always, has been to sort out the fact from the fiction, and I am grateful to the many people who have helped by giving their own account of circumstances as they actually happened.

I would also like to thank Jean Payne and Rachel Weller at Hanover magazines for their tireless help in transcribing the work onto the word processor and Harry Dalton for all his encouragement when things went wrong.

I owe special thanks to Derek Shephard, the publisher of *Majesty* magazine, who decided to employ me as editor, thus enabling me to be in a position to write this book; my mother for her painstaking efforts to file and record clippings about the Royal Family over the years; Alan Frame, who conceived the idea in the first place; and my agents at IMG for getting it off the ground.

Diana

Prologue

The last time I met with Diana, Princess of Wales, was shortly before she embarked on the series of holidays that was to lead to her tragic and untimely death.

It was one of those hot, sultry days of summer when she greeted me in the sitting room of her Kensington Palace apartment. It was eleven o'clock in the morning, and despite the early hour she was dressed as if she were about to attend a cocktail party. She was wearing an electric-blue Versace dress, and her jewelry was discreet but expensive—a thin diamond bracelet, a gold watch, and small sapphire-and-diamond earrings. She was lightly tanned and perfectly coiffed and manicured—as always—and, judging from her buoyant mood she was, for once, seemingly at peace with herself.

Diana was proud of the fact that her uphill struggle to call the attention of the world to victims of landmines was at last gaining international momentum. She felt that finally she had found a niche for herself. The campaign to achieve a worldwide ban on landmines, she explained, was giving her a real sense of purpose; she was determined to do everything within her considerable powers of publicity to see it through.

As we talked, the light in her eyes and the warmth of her replies gave me the distinct feeling that Diana was happier than she had been for years—since that fateful summer of 1987, in fact, when her marriage started its long and inexorable downward spiral. Keeping in touch with reality, something that Diana said she always tried to do but sometimes found difficult, requires character and nerve; she had plenty of both. What she found harder to deal with was the scrutiny with which her every action, however slight and insignificant, was relentlessly observed and quickly converted into the script for the next episode of fantasy.

"No one understands what it is like to be me," she said. "Not my friends, not anyone."

She admitted there was a positive side to her unique situation: she could use her high profile to bring attention to the causes she cared about. But it was the darker, negative aspect that she had to live with every day that profoundly troubled her. After all this time, she explained, it still upset her to read untruths about herself, and it was not her nature to be able to ignore them.

"It makes me feel insecure, and it is difficult going out and meeting people when I imagine what they might have read about me that morning," she said.

I sensed her enormous vulnerability in the way she absent-mindedly wrung her hands and furtively looked at me out of the corner of her startling blue eyes to gauge my reaction to what she was saying.

It seemed extraordinary that after seventeen years in the spotlight this child-woman was still caught between wanting to do the right thing and at the same time wanting to follow her instincts and her passions and do what she wanted to do.

What Diana was searching for was love. She knew it would be hard for her to find a man who could deal with her celebrity, which on occasions threatened to engulf her. Whether or not she had found it in Dodi Fayed, we shall never know. On that summer morning when I last saw her, however, the future, at least from where she sat, seemed brighter than it had been for a long time.

What she never fully grasped, of course, was just how loved she already was. Beautiful and confused, vulnerable but determined, emotional yet in many ways emotionally deprived, she never fully understood just how much she had come to mean to so many people around the world.

Only in death did she achieve all the things that she had wanted to achieve for so much of her life.

Her tragedy was that she was not there to witness it.

1

So Long as Ye Both
Shall Live

*T*he wind sweeps onto Lochnagar from the west, bringing with it the faint scent of stag on a day when the air
is crystal and the cloud wracks have blown through.
The Prince of Wales could see across the Grampians almost
to the Western Isles.

For much of September and for all of October but one day
he was there, a hillman with nature for his companion and
3,786 feet of what Byron called the "frowning glories" of
Lochnagar for his inspiration.

From first light until the sun surrendered itself to the
snow-tipped peaks in the west he was out on the "hill," as the
gillies call it, searching the crags and outcrops with his
binoculars, crawling up ravines, wading through rushing
creeks, and stumbling over rocks worn smooth by time's
eternity—all the time climbing higher and higher. It is a
place for caution and concentration, for the deer, the monarch of this land, is a wily and nervous creature that will take
flight at the first sight or smell of man, however princely he
might be.

For a man like Charles, who draws spiritual comfort from a

Highland majesty greater than his own, it is a place for reflection. And in the autumn of 1987 Charles, Prince of Wales, had much to reflect on.

Diana was not there to share his thoughts. She was in London, in Kensington Palace. She was having lunch with girlfriends, she was playing tennis, she was going to dinner parties, she was working, she was playing bridge, she was happy.

Prince Charles was not. It was more than physical distance that separated the Princess of Wales from her husband.

By now the marriage storm clouds had been gathering for some time, and toward the end of October concern over the marriage between Diana and Charles had reached as far as the echelons of the British Cabinet.

This was not how a romance that had begun as a fairy tale was meant to end. But to even the most casual observer it appeared clear that the threads of affection that bound the world's most famous couple were coming dangerously loose.

The experts were more specific.

Research psychologist Dr. David Lewis, casting his eye over a video of Charles and Diana together, remarked: "The emotional temperature is very, very cold. There's nothing there, not even at the most basic level.

"It seems as if she's trying to cut him out of the picture entirely, to pretend he isn't there. It's not the sort of behavior one would expect from a close, happily married couple living normally as man and wife."

As in all marriages, Diana's relationship with the man she had married had fluctuated. She had loved him, rowed with him, kissed him, borne him two sons, and squabbled with him again. And every change on the emotional barometer had been duly recorded.

And along the way there had been stories—some true, others the product of imaginations fertile with invention—of her breakdowns and threats of separation.

But this time it was different. This time the rumors came supported by a foundation of hard evidence. As the leader of the Rat Pack of newspaper reporters who make their living recording the Royal Family's every cough and sneeze remarked: "For once we don't have to make the story up."

One of the Royal Family's ladies-in-waiting agreed. "There is trouble," she said simply.

Publicly, ministers of the Crown were steering well clear of what the future held for Charles and Diana. Then in October a maverick Tory MP tried to force a debate in the House of Commons on whether the Prince of Wales should—by the right of primogeniture of being the eldest son—automatically succeed to the Throne. It was a sneaky way of trying to raise the Waleses' marital problem in Parliament, but the British government's front bench sat as impassively as ever. As it had to; Parliamentary procedure precludes such discussions of the Royal Family.

Privately, however, senior ministers—including Kenneth Baker, the Secretary of State for Education—were asking just what exactly was going on. It was a question of some constitutional importance. Charles will one day become King and head of the Church of England. Diana will be his Queen. And with the popularity of the Royal Family slipping in the opinion polls, there were those who wondered whether the British electorate would tolerate a separation—even a private one—or worse, a divorce.

A secret two-page "background paper" was passed down the corridors of Westminster Palace from MP to MP. Then, in the first week of November, the executive committee of the powerful 1922 Committee of Tory Party backbenchers concluded that the Royal Family was in urgent need of better advisors and that certain "younger members" should make strenuous efforts to avoid criticism in the future.

Certainly the Buckingham Palace press office's record in damage control is not an impressive one. In 1957 Sir Michael Adeane, the Queen's private secretary, tersely announced, "It is quite untrue that there is a rift." He was referring to the four-month separation of the Queen and the Duke of Edinburgh, who was aboard the royal yacht *Britannia* on a world tour. His statement, however, only fueled the gossip, and since then the Palace has followed the example of the ostrich and worked according to the principle that if it said nothing the problem would simply go away. It is a policy that has on occasion led to a breakdown of trust between the people who are the Monarchy's official spokesmen and the reporters they are supposed to be speaking to.

On this occasion, however, the Palace was not at fault. For thirty-eight days Diana had remained in London while Charles prowled the hills around Balmoral, gun or fishing rod in hand, and speculation about the rift had reached the elevated level of the Independent Television News. It had made the network news in the United States. It had even made the front pages of the usually staid *Sunday Times* and *Sunday Telegraph*.

On the advice of the Queen Mother, who had been so instrumental in bringing Diana and Charles together, it was arranged that the Prince of Wales would fly down from Scotland to join his wife in Wales to comfort the victims of a recent flood. They met at the RAF base at Northolt, just outside London, and flew together to Swansea and then drove on to the disaster area at Carmarthen on the river Twyl.

It was an opportunity, and one carefully stage-managed by the royal advisors, for the couple to show the world how happy they were. It was an opportunity Charles refused to take. They were together only six hours. That night, against the best advice of his household, which had expected him to spend the night with his wife at Kensington Palace, he insisted on flying back to Balmoral.

The reaction was predictable. "Charles Leaves Di Again," the front page of the *Daily Express* announced. The *News of the World*, never at a loss for a pithy phrase, simply announced: "Marriage IS on the rocks."

The Royal Family has many duties. But above all else its members are expected to be the embodiment of stability, of those finer virtues of family and home and parenthood, even if only for appearances' sake. It is a task the Queen performs brilliantly. It is her example that her subjects demand her son and his wife follow. "The royals," the *Sunday Times* wrote, "are not 'allowed' to have personal problems."

If that is the rule, then the Prince and Princess of Wales

were breaking it. So what, as those concerned government ministers were asking, was going on that autumn?

There is their oft-mentioned difference in age. It was something that caused Diana some concern in their courting days but that she had chosen to ignore.

"The gap just does not matter," she said on the day their engagement was announced. Charles joked, "Diana will certainly keep me young."

She hasn't. Nor, conversely, has he aged her. Now in her middle twenties, she has—despite all Charles's discouragement—a well-developed interest in rock music and discotheques and chatty lunches with girlfriends in the kind of designer-label restaurants her husband hates.

He, on the other hand, gives a convincing impression of sinking into a premature, cerebral middle age. He likes delving into books of philosophy and history (Diana prefers the less demanding entertainment of romantic fiction). He is a countryman at heart; Diana, like most people of her age, enjoys the bustle and adrenaline rush of the city.

And so the list adds up to build a picture that would suggest that they have absolutely no common ground at all. Indeed, when they were married, a team of marriage guidance counselors in Dallas, Texas, presented with "blind" personality profiles of the pair, concluded that they were in need of urgent professional help.

"If this was an ordinary couple coming to see me, I frankly don't think they'd have a very good chance of making it," said Maria Molett of the Marriage and Counseling Center. "I would recommend counseling immediately." The trouble, they said, lay in their disparate backgrounds. He, they pointed out, was a university graduate. She was a high school dropout.

She was expected to break away from her family, but he still sought his mother's advice and required her permission on just about every major decision he might have to make. He had set a prenuptial standard for her that he never declared for himself. And for the rest of her life she would be expected to walk through doorways *behind* him.

Then there was the fact that he had never held a proper

job—and neither, the counselors pointed out, had his father.

"Here is a man who has spent his whole life playing second fiddle to his mother," said Dr. Mervyn Berke, a Dallas marriage counselor. "He needs to examine that and how it is going to affect his relationship with other women—especially his wife."

It was never quite as bad as that of course. Like the rest of the world, Charles was captivated by his bride's beauty, her refreshing innocence and openness, and her easy, attractive charm. She also had a model's figure with excellent legs, and Charles, in his old-fashioned way, has never been ashamed— even in this feminist age—of being attracted by such things.

Diana for her part was in love with her husband. She admired his athleticism and his comparative intelligence and the sensible way he looked at life and its problems. And the fact that he also happened to be a prince with the means to provide her with the most gilded nest was not a handicap.

Her affection showed. She kissed him at polo. She embraced him tightly on dance floors. She held his hand. And when she looked at him it was with eyes that shone.

But in a way those American counselors were right. There were differences, and quite profound ones, and as the years passed they started to show. Diana can be willful. She is a woman who will demand her own way and can become obstreperous if she doesn't get it. That grated on Charles. He had lived all his adult life as his own epicenter. Remarked his former valet, "For the first time he had to consider someone other than himself," and he found the adjustment a difficult one.

He was easily irritated by his wife's demands. He was unhappy about the way she had taken over the running of what had been *his* household and the way retainers who had been with him for years were leaving the royal employ, adding to the disruption of his routine. He also developed the less than admirable habit of criticizing his wife in front of people—a habit he still has.

Says a friend, "He sometimes seemed to take pleasure in putting her down with little asides."

And sometimes Diana has taken pleasure in turning the tables on him. At a dinner party one night Charles was talking about Rudyard Kipling, the great imperialist author and poet.

"Do you remember the *Just So Stories?*" he inquired of his wife.

"Just so what, Charles?" she replied.

"You know, the *Just So* books by Rudyard Kipling," Charles said.

"Just so what, Charles?" she asked again.

All newlyweds soon discover their differences, especially if they have not had the opportunity or the inclination to develop an intimate relationship before marriage. It is part of the process of compromise, of fine-tuning one's reactions and personality to fit in with the other person. What made it difficult for Diana was that she was expected to do this in the full glare of the most intense scrutiny any couple has ever been forced to endure. Charles had been trained from birth to expect this, and although it could make him angry, he knew how to handle it. Diana did not, and by 1982 the word was circulating that the marriage was steering through troubled waters.

Said Stephen Barry, who was Prince Charles's valet for twelve years, "All the rumors in the summer of 1982 that Princess Diana was unhappy, and that the marriage was having problems, were quite true. Everyone at the Palace was worried that the fairy-tale romance was going to collapse.

"There was no question that Charles would do his duty. But the Princess—at that time volatile, happy and unhappy by turns, imperious and then pathetic—was the unknown quantity.

"It was not the Princess who had doubts; it was the Prince. He was concerned that he might have married someone who could not do 'the job' as he calls it, but he was also experiencing a disruption of his entire life."

The Queen too was concerned by the disturbing turn of events. Senior editors of Britain's newspapers were called to Buckingham Palace and kindly asked if, in consideration of

Diana's mental health, they would order their reporters to rein back on the intrusive attention they were paying her daughter-in-law. Most gladly agreed.

It was only a year since they had rattled back from Saint Paul's Cathedral in the 1902 State Landau to Buckingham Palace; only a year since they had stood on the balcony and kissed ("Go on, why not?" Diana had said) before a world-wide television audience of 700 million people.

It was only twelve months before that they had sailed off into the Mediterranean on a three-week honeymoon cruise aboard the world's largest private yacht, *Britannia*. A company of 21 officers and 256 ratings were on call to give the royal couple the most romantic, most memorable beginning to their life together. From the moment Prince Charles leant across his wife and pushed the dressing bell beside the double bed, the ship was on full alert.

They slept in Prince Philip's bedroom, in a special large bed Charles had ordered aboard, and Diana had the Queen's special permission to use her bathroom across the gangway. For the first time in his life Charles actually stayed in bed until past eight o'clock before they headed out to take their breakfast on the veranda deck.

Diana, full of energy, would rush around, sometimes putting tapes on the stereo, at other times consulting with the chef on the meals for the day.

Charles would laze on an old-fashioned sunbed, soaking up the rays. He used to use Bergasol sun cream until someone told him inaccurately that it caused cancer.

There were picnics of salad and lobster, cold meats and fresh local fruits and cheese carried in large old-fashioned wicker hampers and eaten on sandy beaches in secluded coves.

In the evening they dined by candlelight, alone or with some of the ship's officers, off beautiful old Irish linen brought from the old royal yacht, *Victoria and Albert*. A small orchestra played medleys of musicals for them, and Charles wore his tropical white uniform, Diana a simple long frock and some of her new jewelry.

"There were no rows on honeymoon," said Barry. "They

kept those for later . . . after the honeymoon it went down-hill."

Not beyond the point of redemption, however—nowhere near it. As the Queen's action with the editors acknowledged, those first few months of married life had been marked by traumas of one sort or another, and there were indeed times when first Charles, then Diana, wondered what they had let themselves in for. But there was no question then of their going their separate royal ways. She was young; he was understanding. She was also pregnant and suffering terribly from morning sickness. That, of course, exacerbated the situation. But when William was born, a vital bond was forged, and the marriage settled down into a steady and steadied routine.

Diana adored her young son. So did Charles. And when Harry arrived two years later, even the Rat Pack of royal watchers started talking with resignation about hanging up their binoculars and going back to the more mundane business of train crashes and court reports.

The early 1980s were good days. Diana was establishing herself as the world's most stylish woman, to be imitated and admired, who at the same time had the fulfillment of a young family to care for. Charles was getting on with the business of being the Prince of Wales, though it was, he sometimes complained, a role without definition.

What was defined, however, by the restrictions placed on a constitutional monarchy, was the rule of political neutrality all members of the Royal Family must obey. Charles was not always allowed to say exactly what he really felt for fear of breaking that rule, and this often frustrated him. He is a man with firmly held convictions whose politics are well to the left of Thatcherism. He would bring his concerns home to his wife, and she, it must be said, was not particularly interested. If Diana has any politics at all, they are of the High Tory kind traditional to the old land-owning class she was born into.

But if that was a cause of occasional stress, it hardly registered against the woes of unemployment and mortgages and urban despair many newly married couples were having to face. There were always nannies and cooks, valets and maids, gardeners and housekeepers to help ease the domestic strain. And not many young wives start their married life with a mansion in the country and a home in a palace in London, not counting the country retreats in Scotland and Norfolk and Windsor (even if the last lot did come with the in-laws).

Even by the standards of the landed aristocracy Diana had married well. In fact, she couldn't have married better—on paper, that is.

There is a price to be paid for membership in the most exclusive family in the world. There is the constant attention—at first fun and flattering, then annoying—and eventually the inducement of claustrophobic depression.

There are subtler club fees to be paid as well. The Royal Family is all-embracing. Upon joining, newcomers must surrender themselves to the protocols and habits already established. Old friends and old ways must be discarded, at least publicly. Holidays are preplanned by tradition, and for Diana to persuade her husband to take those summer breaks in Spain with King Juan Carlos constitutes a major breakthrough. Spontaneity is frowned upon except in the most carefully prearranged circumstances, like a visit to a children's hospital where Diana is expected to "spontaneously" embrace a child.

In older times, before the advent of the telescopic lens and the long-range microphone, the Royal Family could more or less do what it wanted, provided its members remembered to turn up for the requisite State occasions. They could hunt and shoot and drink and smoke and wear extravagant furs secure in the knowledge that their private life would remain private. They could maintain their mistresses; the Queen's great-grandfather, Edward VII, for example, maintained several.

Since the reign of George V, however, propriety in all things has been expected—indeed enforced—by weight of public opinion. Britain, like every other Western society, suffers its share of divorce and drunkenness and marital indifference. At the same time it has learned to accommodate the social trends of feminism and equal opportunity and gay rights and "liberation" in the sexual and intellectual sense of the word. They are movements that are supposed to have passed the Royal Family by. It is supposed to remain in a permanent time warp, a nice suburban middle-class family peering out at life from behind the net curtains of the 1950s.

To be cast in this role by the accident of birth has proved difficult enough. For Diana it has proved a strain that at times has verged on the intolerable. Glamorous and beautiful and just a little bit spoiled (and with at least twenty servants on call it would be hard not to be), Diana must have felt that her young life was passing her by in a labor of official banquets and boring dinner parties with an older husband who, as a friend says, "didn't or wouldn't" understand her urges and interests.

By some accounts Diana was an emotional disaster waiting to happen, and stories started appearing, in both Britain and the United States, telling of disharmony and tantrums and "malice in the Palace." They were an overdramatization. Diana, a wife and a mother almost before she became a woman, was simply growing up. The ingenue peeking out from under a schoolgirl fringe of hair had been replaced by someone more sophisticated, much more assured, who was no longer prepared to follow, doelike, where her husband chose to lead.

It was here that the "Fergie factor" came into play. Sarah Ferguson has approached marriage to Prince Andrew with a singular determination to maintain her independence, and it is an example that Diana followed. She began going out more—without Charles. She started inviting *her* friends back to Kensington Palace for late-night supper parties. She discovered, as if she didn't intuitively know it already, that she had much more in common with the crowd of "Sloanes" (preppies) that Fergie introduced her to than she had with the Laurens Van der Posts so favored by Charles.

Charles did not approve. But Diana had set her course. She and her husband would be going their own ways, she told a newspaper reporter who has known her for ten years, "more and more from now on."

The first indication of precisely what she meant by that

remark came in Klosters, Switzerland, in the winter of 1987. Charles and Diana were at a house party. At night Diana would go out to discotheques like Casa Antica while Charles, who was not impressed by the "Hooray Henry" antics (unsophisticated, often boisterous antics of the upper middle class) of some of his younger fellow guests, stayed behind and retired early.

There was, of course, an acceptable explanation for this. The Princess of Wales likes nightclubs and dancing. Charles does not. "I always end up paying the bill," he grumbles, "and I hardly ever drink anything."

When she returned to London, however, while Charles stayed on for a few extra days on the piste, he suddenly started turning up in the clubs he had refused to visit with his wife.

One night he was to be found buying £30 bottles of champagne for his party of fifteen and £4 bottles of beer for his security men at the Funny Room in the Aaba Hotel. And when he took to the dance floor to dance the rumba with a pretty girl, recalls the hotel's manager, Wolfgang Eisenhoser, "everyone in the room started to clap."

And on to this unsettled marital horizon strode the handsome figure of one Philip Dunne.

He is tall and dark-haired with a well-developed appreciation of his own good looks. Educated at Eton and a godson of Princess Alexandra, he is the son of the Lord Lieutenant of Hereford and Worcester, and his family home is stately Gatley Park near Leominster. He was a good friend of Fergie. And although ensconced in a live-in relationship with Katya Grenfell, the former wife of conductor Oliver Gilmour, he bore with him a reputation as a lady's man.

The Princess of Wales was smitten. And when the twenty-eight-year-old Dunne joined the royal party in Klosters, it was obvious that the two got on very well together.

Diana is naturally flirtatious and had become increasingly aware of her ability to interest very good-looking men. One evening after skiing everyone joined in an after-dinner party that culminated with Diana lying in the bottom of a large chest of drawers pretending to be asleep. She called out that the first person to kiss her would become a prince. Dunne stepped forward and obliged.

It was all good hearty fun. So was the visit Diana paid to Gatley Park. She was not there alone, for among the other guests was David Waterhouse, the major in the Household Cavalry who has known Diana "since she was a schoolgirl." The drumbeat of rumor had started, however. First in the better salons of London and then in the gossip columns, stories circulated of Diana's attachment to the young merchant banker.

Dunne turned up by Diana's side again at Royal Ascot.

Then came the wedding of the Duke of Beaufort's son, the Marquis of Worcester (a large, portly figure who is known as Bunter) to the actress Rachel Ward's sister Tracy. It was a splendid affair, held in a marquee in the grounds of the Ward family home in Oxfordshire. There was a discotheque and dinner and as much champagne available as the guests cared to consume.

Charles and Diana, accompanied by the Duke and Duchess of York, arrived early for the dance while their hosts were still having dinner. In certain higher reaches of the British aristocracy the Royal Family are regarded with an indifference that can border on contempt (they are regularly referred to as "the Germans" or "the Krauts" because of the Windsors' Hanoverian antecedents). And a number of the revelers failed to rise to their feet as protocol demands.

But if the royal arrival went almost unobserved, other events that evening did not.

One of the guests was Anna Wallace, the tempestuous Scottish landowner's daughter Charles had once courted. Their relationship had been ill-starred; on a visit to Windsor Castle some years before, for instance, Charles had scuttled away only to return a long few minutes later with a bottle of brown ale he had commandeered from one of the Guardsmen and the sad explanation, "Mummy's got the key to the drinks cupboard."

The two still keep in touch, however, and see each other occasionally when they are both out hunting with the Belvoir (one of England's most distinguished hunts). They saw each other that night and interior designer Nicki Haslem, who knows both Charles and Diana well, was dispatched across the canvased room to instruct Anna to prepare herself to dance with the Prince of Wales. Mick Jagger, who witnessed the scene, was heard to comment, "Don't think much of her 'weekend house party' style of dancing." Once back at his own table, Charles locked himself in conversation with Camilla Parker-Bowles, the wife of the colonel of the Household Cavalry.

There had been a time when Diana would have been enraged by her husband's behavior. Prone to jealousy, she had always shown signs of unease when Charles spoke to any woman with whom he had once been linked. And for the first few years of their marriage, Diana had pointedly excluded Mrs. Parker-Bowles—who, though married, had enjoyed more than a passing acquaintanceship with the heir to the Throne during his bachelorhood—from Kensington Palace and Highgrove.

Now Diana was unconcerned. Her husband could speak to whom he liked. And while he did, she went off to enjoy herself. She danced furiously with gallery owner David Ker. She dragged someone she had never met onto the dance floor and engaged him in fifteen minutes of frenetic arm wavings and leg kickings—much to the embarrassment of the young man, who did not find her "windmill" style of dancing aesthetically pleasing.

"She behaved rather badly," one of the guests remarked afterward.

Said another, "It was not the way you'd expect to see the future Queen behaving."

Charles left early and, by one salacious account, stopped on the way to tell Anna Wallace that he was not happy with his life. Diana carried on dancing until six o'clock in the morning, pausing only long enough to wipe her forehead on the hem of her gown.

And one of her dancing partners was Philip Dunne.

His name cropped up again when it was mistakenly reported that he had accompanied her to a David Bowie concert at Wembley. In fact her escort was Major Waterhouse, who took the muddle-up with gentlemanly good grace. "I find the whole thing amusing," he said later. Then, on a more serious note, he added, "There has been a lot of talk about the Princess and Philip. It is absurd to say they are having an affair. The allegation is totally untrue."

Diana's friend, newsagent heiress Kate Menzies, agreed. "It's nonsense," she said.

They were telling the truth. That Diana found Dunne an engaging and attractive companion, as many other women have, is not in question; nor is the fact that Philip was flattered by her flirtatious attention. And it was no secret among her friends that Diana was intent on enjoying herself and in her own way more than she had done previously.

But after seven years of marriage, she knew full well her royal parameters. To stray beyond them would have been all but inconceivable for a devoted mother who has the example of her own parents' marital disaster to remind her what the consequences could be. However, if Diana's friends were convinced of the propriety, Prince Charles was more circumspect.

He is a thoughtful man, aware of his destiny and resolved to fulfill it. Old-fashioned—and some would say old before his time—he has an inbuilt understanding of the need for "appearances," especially when it comes to the family business of royalty. He was appalled by the publicity the speculation of the state of his marriage had engendered. Some of that was the consequence of his own behavior; serious-minded, he was not always able to appreciate his wife's enthusiasm for what he dismisses as the "flighty" and at times could be unbending and severe when flexibility would have been a more productive tactic. Others were naturally inclined to place the blame for his deteriorating situation at Diana's doorstep (or "Diana's dancestep" as one wag referred to it).

But if all this was bad enough, worse was to follow. Since his earliest youth Prince Charles has gone out of his way to avoid confrontations. Brought up to contain his emotions, he allows his temper—which can be vile—to get the better of him only on the rarest occasions. He is unwilling to follow ire down its unchartered pathways, preferring orderly retreat to the dangerous ground of verbal combat.

On the 22nd of September he flew north to Balmoral. Diana remained behind in Kensington Palace. They were not to spend a night together under the same roof for well over a month. Such separations are fairly common to the Royal Family, and both Charles and Diana have very full agendas of official engagements that can take them hundreds and often thousands of miles away from each other. But as the *Sunday Times* observed, "What characterizes many of Charles and Diana's recent times apart—he is on his painting expeditions to Florence, she visiting restaurants, cinemas and clubs without him—is that they are avoidable."

The ensuing furor this separation generated was not. Like Ted Koppel counting up the days the American hostages had been held in Iran (and, in so doing, counting out the presidency of Jimmy Carter), the newspapers published a daily account of the time the royal couple had been apart.

"Just what is going on?" Sir John Junor, the authoritative and respected columnist for the *Sunday Express*, wanted to know. He went on to write, "Prince Charles is far too sensible not to be aware that a four week absence from his wife and children would be bound to arouse comment.

"Why then did he permit such a long absence to happen?

"His Press Secretary assures us that the couple are as much in love as ever they were.

"Really?

"In that case unless they wish to do lasting damage to the Royal Family, shouldn't they begin to show it?"

On the last Saturday in October Prince Charles came down from Lochnagar and flew south to attend the wedding of Earl Mountbatten's granddaughter, Lady Amanda Knatchbull, a woman who it had once been suggested would make him an ideal wife. The Queen was there. So were Prince Philip and the Duke and Duchess of York and Viscount Linley and Lady Sarah Armstrong-Jones.

The Princess of Wales was *not* there. And that night Charles did not return home to her, preferring instead to sleep over at the home of Prince Andrew's father-in-law, Major Ronald Ferguson.

Was this the end? Was Britain about to witness what the politicians feared it would not accept—the end of the royal marriage? That weekend, the couple flew off together, all smiles, on an official visit to West Germany. Had the royal goldfish bowl once again distorted reality to create an image of crisis when there was none? Not quite. The problems had been real enough, and the Queen herself—as reluctant as she is to interfere in the lives of her family—was forced to point out the dangers of the course her son and heir and his wife were following.

It was obvious that adjustments were going to have to be made in the relationship between Charles and the woman who will one day, God willing, be his Queen.

2
Charles Philip Arthur George

To understand Diana and the role she plays it is important to understand something of her husband.

It was Charles who made her a Princess and will one day make her a Queen. It is Charles, the tetchy, old-fashioned conservative with hair that was never long, in trousers that never flared or quite fit, who has taken the backseat as Diana set about—perhaps unconsciously but still definitely—reshaping the image of the Royal Family with her style and glamour and personality.

It is Charles who was born to be King, but it is Diana that the crowds turn out to see—as he readily admits. And it is a situation to which he acquiesces, by his nature and training.

To the public at large, he was forever parachuting out of airplanes and diving under polar ice caps and riding his polo ponies into breakneck confrontations, pausing only long enough to slake his supposedly prodigious romantic thirst with yet another leggy blonde.

The reality, however, never quite matched the image the media so determinedly bestowed on the prince they nicknamed "Action Man" (a sobriquet, incidentally, he detests).

Behind all the bravado, traces of the shy youngster who never really knew what to say to a girl are still discernible. The veneer is smooth and sophisticated, but the man behind it has an attitude and approach to women very different from the ones his list of so-called conquests would suggest.

Raised in a matriarchy where the men, even someone as overtly chauvinistic as Prince Philip, must defer to the women and most particularly to one woman, Charles was brought up to regard the female sex with deep respect. It did not make him a mother's boy—far from it. But it provided him with little preparation for the rugged, all-male world he encountered at Gordonstoun, Prince Philip's alma mater and the school to which Charles was sent at age 13. And Gordonstoun, in its turn, was no training ground for the princely lothario the popular imagination would brand him as.

His years spent there as a teenager, on the windswept coast of the Moray Firth, were not the happiest time of his life.

He had been put into Windmill Lodge where his housemaster, Bob Whitby, did little to make life easy for him. Brusque, opinionated, and seemingly always angry, Whitby made it a point of principle to shout loudest at the boys he liked best, especially new boys. He had been ordered by Prince Philip to treat the heir to the Throne as he would any other pupil, and it was an instruction he carried out with relish. It was not surprising that the first couple of years Charles spent so far away from the family he so depended on were lonely and fearful.

He was not academically exceptional, and it took him three attempts to pass math "O" level. Even history, the subject he is so fond of and the one of which he says, "I honestly believe that the only real way one can hope to understand and cope with the present is by knowing and being able to interpret what happened in the past," could prove perplexing. On one occasion his tutor, the exuberant Robin Birley, felt moved to shout at him, in front of the whole class, "Come on, Charles, you can do better than this—after all, it is the history of your family we're dealing with!" But it was an episode in history one must presume Charles would not want to see repeated;

his "A" level form was studying the reign of the executed King Charles I.

Nor did he shine on the sporting field. As a polo player he has worked and trained himself up to a creditable four-handicap player. At rugger and athletics and cricket, he was disappointing.

The London newspapers, already making their first stab at creating their action prince, would write how well he was doing at this sport or that and how it would be only a matter of time before he made the Rugby First XV.

Gordonstoun fielded four rugby teams that traveled the north of Scotland to engage schools like Strathallan and Aberdeen Academy in sporting combat. Charles never made any of them. Instead, he spent miserable, morose, wet afternoons with the infirm and unathletic playing for a motley Windmill house side. He cut a forlorn figure, often to be seen standing apart from his teammates with his hands clasped behind his back, taking little part in the unskilled action eddying around him.

His lot was not improved by the resentment his arrival had generated among many of his fellow pupils. Gordonstoun is peculiar to the British public school system in that it is, to a large extent, run by the boys themselves. The senior prefects, called *color bearers*, meet periodically to revise the rules. And, in theory at least, the headboy, called the *Guardian*, enjoys equal powers with the headmaster, being allowed to grow a beard and marry. (Practice, of course, was rather different; one of the Guardians who succeeded Charles as the appointed headboy was promptly expelled when he was found with a woman in his rooms.)

This independence was underscored by the kind of boys who went there. It has been called a reform school for expelled Etonians, and the boys who went there in Charles's day certainly tended to be wilder and more independent and more adventurous than the kind usually encountered in other public schools.

Charles's arrival, however, brought with it the introduction of a whole new and stricter set of regulations. The boys were now forbidden to go into the local town of Elgin without specific permission, for instance. This was hardly Charles's fault, but not all of his four hundred fellows were convinced. He made few friends, and anyone who did try to strike up a conversation with him was instantly accused of "sucking up." He also found himself the butt of the inevitable jokes. One—and one often repeated—concerned his marmalade.

To supplement their spartan diet of black puddings and porridge and a biweekly helping of haggis, the boys were allowed to order a few luxuries from the school suppliers, Gordon and McPhail. (Gordon and McPhail are also the bottlers of many of the finest Glenlivet malts, but they were never allowed on the list of food luxuries.) Charles would order Robertson's marmalade, and many was the morning when someone would pick up his jar and point to the "By Appointment to H.M. The Queen" on the label and proclaim, "Oh goody, mummy approves."

Charles resented the gibes. If he wanted anything other than to be away from the place, it was to be accepted, to be treated like everyone else. But no matter what Prince Philip may have ordered, and no matter how aggressively Whitby tried, Charles could never be just another boy. Gordonstoun was a school well stocked with sprigs of the aristocracy, but no one was allowed to use his title, and everyone was addressed by his surname—except Charles, who was always called "Charles," a title in itself.

To add to his sense of isolation, his father had the disconcerting habit of flying in to see him and landing his helicopter on the lawn of Gordonstoun House—and this at a school where even the richest parents would never dream of arriving in a Rolls-Royce for fear of embarrassing their son.

To widen the gap between Charles and his classmates, three of them who were in London together at the end of one term and had prankishly telephoned Buckingham Palace and asked to be put through to their contemporary found themselves "gated," confined to school grounds as punishment for their impertinence when they returned to Gordonstoun. It was around this time when Charles was nearly fifteen that the notorious cherry brandy incident took place.

Every year the boys went off on "expeditions," either walking through some isolated part of the Highlands or cruising through the Western Isles on the school yacht *Pinta*. It was a break from the normal routine and was greatly anticipated by the boys, who hoped to have the opportunity to meet girls or perhaps sneak into a local pub for a clandestine pint of beer. And the hills were alive with sight of master and boys playing an often farcical game of hide-and-seek as a result.

Charles got caught. The *Pinta* called in to Stornoway on the Isle of Lewis in the Outer Hebrides. There Charles walked into a hotel bar and asked for a glass of that sickly, sticky liqueur because "Having never been in a bar before, the first thing I thought of doing was having a drink. Being terrified and not knowing what to do, I named the first drink that came into my head—which happened to be cherry brandy because I had drunk it before when it was cold and I was out shooting."

By misfortune, a freelance journalist was sitting in the bar, and an innocent schoolboy transgression became front-page news.

"I wanted to pack my bags and go to Siberia," he recalls. He was exaggerating; where he really wanted to go was to Birkhall, the Queen Mother's Highland home—the home closest to Gordonstoun.

It was really only on stage that Charles came to life and into his own. He auditioned for the role of Shakespeare's Henry V in the school play and only just lost out to David Gwillim who went on to make acting his career and played the role again in the much praised BBC television production of the play. Eric Anderson, the master in charge who went on to become headmaster at Eton, explained that Charles was passed over because he did not want to be accused of favoritism and because it was just possible that the young Prince might have failed to live up to the promise he had shown in rehearsals.

Anderson had no such misgivings when he cast the future King as Macbeth. It was faith well justified; Charles was superb. And Anderson—a caring, intelligent man who encouraged the boys to express their thoughts and opinions and can be considered the first of the older "gurus" who have so influenced Charles—considers him to be the finest Macbeth he had ever seen. Only by playing someone else, it seems, was Charles truly able to play himself.

But then role playing has been the cornerstone of his life.

He has had to live up to the role model provided by his father, a hardy, athletic man always on the go and intent on instilling in his eldest son a sense of the machismo he deems so important. Prince Philip was a hard act to follow and one Charles was always uncomfortably in awe of.

Then there was the role forced on him by the British press. By the chance of birth, he was the "most eligible bachelor in the world," and the reporters employed to report on his activities were determined that he would live the part to the fullest.

Certainly he has an appreciative eye for a pretty face, and the well-rounded figure of an attractive woman can still excite his interest, but in neither his home life nor his education were the makings of the rampant bed-hopper the papers chose to present. Childhood had taught him to respect women in a way that is uncommon among the British upper classes. Gordonstoun, with its enforced separation of the sexes, had made him a little self-conscious in the presence of girls of his own age. He had never followed the example of some of his contemporaries, known as "shades," who used to sneak into Elgin to pursue clandestine romances with the local girls. And those he did pursue, during the production of Gilbert and Sullivan's *Pirates of Penzance*, remember him as a shy and self-conscious teenager.

His mid-school term in Australia at Geelong School at age 16 had rounded out his character. But it had also reinforced his inhibitions. Australia, in the days before improved air travel and immigration had eased the national psyche, was still a place where the men gathered on one side at a party and the women on the other, and any male who made the crossing was instantly labeled a "poofter," a homosexual.

It was therefore a distinctly old-fashioned attitude toward women that Charles took with him to Cambridge. One of his contemporaries at the university where he read history was quoted as saying, "When he first came up he was astonishingly naive about girls. He really thought that girls who slept with their boyfriends weren't 'nice.' "

Like most undergraduates, though, he soon discovered that university has more to offer than academic study. He became friendly with Lucia Santa Cruz. The daughter of the former Chilean ambassador to London, she was at Cambridge helping Lord Butler, the Master of Trinity College and Charles's university guide, to write his memoirs.

Exotic, foreign, Catholic, four years his senior, and with political opinions far to the right of Charles's own (it was only on Lord Butler's stern advice that the future King was dissuaded from joining the university's Labour Party)—she was an unlikely choice for a royal companion. But the attachment was serious enough. And according to biographer Anthony Holden, Lord Butler said, "The Prince asked if she might stay in our lodge for privacy which was a request we were very glad to accede to." The implication in that is obvious. Clearly the school of life was modifying Charles's view of relationships. And Earl Mountbatten of Burma was encouraging the change.

"I believe in a case like yours, a man should sow his wild oats and have as many affairs as he can before settling down," Uncle Dickie wrote to his favored great-nephew.

Charles's oats were never sown as wildly as they might have been, however. He is not a natural womanizer, and many of the girls he went out with were simply friends.

Georgiana Russell was one whose name was linked to his in those early days. The daughter of Britain's former ambassador to Madrid, she is bright, intelligent, and socially acceptable. She wore miniskirts and on occasion the see-through blouses fashionable at the time. Her hair was long and blonde. She was invited to spend the weekend up at

Balmoral, but that is as far as their relationship ever went. Some years later, when she married Baronet Sir Brooke Boothby, the Prince saw her wedding photograph in a society magazine and declared in astonishment; "Good God, her hair is black. She's not a blonde at all!"—a remark hardly revelatory of intimacies past.

It was the same with Fiona Watson, the attractive daughter of Lord Manton. She too was declared to be "the girlfriend," and according to legend it was only the unfortunate discovery that she had once displayed her ample figure in all its naked splendor in the girlie magazine *Mayfair* that ended their affair.

That was not what happened. Always "very cautious and very careful" about committing himself emotionally, Charles would often wait until the last moment before asking a girl out, and Fiona was not the kind to sit at home on the off chance that he might telephone.

She had other boyfriends. And when Charles did ring one evening, Fiona, after first dismissing his call as a prank being played by one of her friends, told him she had already made other arrangements. It was the end of the affair that had never started.

There were, of course, others who were prepared to cancel everything for an evening with the Prince of Wales. But as they soon discovered, a date with Charles was not the most exciting of occasions. An evening at the opera perhaps. Or a dinner in his chambers on the second floor of Buckingham Palace—which was not quite as romantic as it sounds. The girl would be asked to make her own way there, for Charles—excused the normal conventions—never picked up his dates himself and but rarely arranged for his bodyguard or valet to do the collecting for him. And once there she would find that there were always servants on hand, serving the food (usually a cold supper), clearing away afterward, hovering in the corridors, their ears always pricked for the faintest hint of gossip. There is also the point that as far as the Royal Family is concerned, the Palace is the Queen's home. That puts a brake on everyone's behavior, and having been smuggled in through the basement to avoid being spotted by the press, the girls usually found themselves on their way out again to make their own way home well before midnight.

Stephen Barry recalled, "If he was meant to be in his bed in the morning when I went to wake him up, he was in bed. Alone." Barry added, "Buckingham Palace was totally unsuitable for anything indiscreet to take place. It would have been impossible for a girl to have spent any time there without a footman or his bodyguard or me not being aware that she was there." They never were, which prompted Barry to remark, "I sometimes thought the limitations on his privacy were part of the reason for his participation in so many energetic activities."

That is not to say that Charles did not enjoy a private life. He did. He had his girlfriends, drawn from the utterly discreet stream of Britain's aristocracy and upper middle class, combined with an occasional exotic diversion like Laura Jo Watkins, the daughter of an American rear admiral.

They had met in California in 1974 at a cocktail party aboard HMS *Jupiter*, one of the ships Charles served aboard during his spell in the Royal Navy. She called him "sir," but in an offhand, lighthearted way, and Charles was enchanted by her outgoing American personality and her uncomplicated sense of humor. She visited him in London and went through the entrance-via-the-basement routine before exiting again and returning to the American embassy where she was quartered. She witnessed his maiden speech at the House of Lords where Charles addressed his fellow peers on the dangers of too much government interference in sport.

In the end, however, the romance died its inevitable death. Laura Jo returned to the United States, but continued to correspond with the Prince. He managed to see her again during one of his stopovers in America, and when he went to a big charity ball in Miami, she joined him. It was all very discreet and Charles went to the ball accompanied by his secretary Rosie Taylor, who acted as a decoy. Laura Jo was smuggled into the party in a flower delivery van and remained out of sight until all the Miami matrons had had the chance to have their photograph taken with Prince Charles. By ten o'clock they had all gone home. Charles and the rest of his group, including Laura Jo, then stayed on and had their own private party—it was quite a party. They ended up dancing on the tables before returning to the house of a rich American couple where they were staying.

Charles, she said, "is a great guy." The strictures of his life, however, were "unlivable for kids like us."

The same applied to his brief dalliance with actress Susan George, who had appeared in the violent and, for the time, sexually explicit *Straw Dogs*. She described him as "romantic and loving."

He was also very taken with the beautiful blonde singer Lynsey de Paul, whom he met a couple of times at charity dinners. Once again the situation proved difficult and in spite of press stories of a romance, they never progressed further than some witty banter in the full view of several hundred other people.

It would have been saliently out of character for the Prince who, unlike his brother Andrew, has never felt comfortable making flamboyant advances, to move away from his bevy of blue-blooded, British blondes. For if there has been a watch-word in Charles's relationships, it is discretion. And discretion certainly characterized his relations with Lady Tryon and Camilla Parker-Bowles.

Both are married to men he has known for years and who consider him their friend. Lady Tryon, the former Qantas air hostess Charles nicknamed "Kanga," is the wife of merchant banker Anthony Tryon; Camilla's husband Andrew is colonel of the Household Cavalry, the Queen's Silver Stick-in-Waiting (the honorary military officer who takes command over the Queen's personal bodyguards) and a former escort of Princess Anne. Neither has ever spoken publicly of her relationship with the Prince, but both in their way provided him with the companionship and feminine comfort he sought.

The object of courtship, of course, is to find a suitable mate. For the future King it was a necessity, and however close he may have been to Mrs. Parker-Bowles or Lady Tryon, they could never be more than a footnote in his romantic development.

So, to the entertainment of his future subjects, a succession of more or less suitable young women rolled into and out of his horizon, to be scrutinized and dissected and subjected to the pressure of being, if only for the moment, "the girlfriend."

Finding someone suited to the role of future Queen had its unique problems. As Mountbatten had advised, "For a wife [you] should choose a suitable, attractive and sweet charactered girl before she has met anyone else she might fall for.

"I think it is disturbing for women to have experiences if they have to remain on pedestals after marriage."

In other words, virginity was, if not exactly a prerequisite, a distinct advantage—no easy criterion to meet in this modern age, especially as Charles grew older and so inexorably did the age of any potential match.

It was her past that put the end to Davina Sheffield's chances. Although she always insisted, "I never had a relationship with him; it was a friendship," there is no doubt that at one time she was close to Charles. Blonde, elegant, with a worldly sophistication, she was exactly his type. The relationship ended, however, when her previous lover, Old Harrovian powerboat enthusiast James Beard, felt moved to reveal all about their live-in affair.

The pressures of the goldfish bowl of royal life put an end to Lady Jane Wellesley, the highly intelligent and very beautiful daughter of the Duke of Wellington. She would have made an excellent consort for the Prince but very quickly decided that the future Charles offered was not for her. "I have a title already—I don't need another one," she stoutly declared before setting off to make a career for herself in television production.

Temperament took Anna Wallace out of the frame. The vivacious, sexy daughter of a substantial Scottish landowner, she fit well into Charles's essentially rural lifestyle. She hunts (they met while out riding with the Belvoir), and she is a fine horsewoman. She could pass the "Craigowan test" as it was known to the royal staff—those weekends spent fishing in the cold and rain of the Balmoral estate. It was a test Georgiana Russell had failed; she had nearly died of boredom.

But Anna was never as close to the Prince as is now widely assumed. She had bought a flat in Chelsea, but Charles visited there only once. It was to attend a formal dinner party, and he left before midnight.

She had other boyfriends—a fact that did not go unnoticed by the policemen assigned to look after their royal charge. They saw it as part of their duties to check into the backgrounds of the young women Charles took an interest in.

Also, Anna has a mind of her own. She has very clear ideas about how she should be treated. And when Charles took her to a birthday party for the Queen Mother at Windsor Castle and then left her to go off and talk to the other four hundred guests—as his duty required—she became deeply irritated. Declaring that she would not be treated like that, she left.

Others were unsuitable in other ways and did not match up to the Royal Family's idea of what was suitable. No one ever passed a direct opinion on Charles's fancies. They didn't need to; they had other ways of making their thoughts known. Which they did most pointedly when Charles arrived at Balmoral with Sabrina Guinness, the freewheeling brewery heiress whose past had included a spell in Hollywood where she had worked for Ryan O'Neal as a nanny looking after Tatum.

The whole Balmoral experience, she says, was "terrifying." On arrival she remarked that the car that had collected her from the station looked like a "Black Maria." To which Philip unkindly replied that she should know all about Black Marias. She hardly ever saw Charles. And when she was about to lower herself into a chair, the Queen told her sternly, "Don't sit there. That's Queen Mary's chair!"

Sabrina was out.

There were also the ones who simply did not "fancy" Charles. One was the red-haired Lady Sarah Spencer, daughter of Earl Spencer and Diana's oldest sister. They got on well together and Charles gave his support when she was struggling with anorexia nervosa. But that, as far as Sarah was concerned, was as far as it went.

"He's a fabulous person, but I'm not in love with him," she firmly declared. "I think of him as the big brother I never had."

By now Charles was moving into his thirties, and there was a mounting undercurrent of concern, not least among his own family, about his continuing bachelorhood. Some supposedly "informed" members of society, pointing to the proliferation of gays among the staff at Buckingham Palace and the alleged bisexuality of Earl Mountbatten, even postulated that he would never marry.

That was nonsense, of course. Charles had had his girlfriends. He had plenty of what one called "Hanoverian enthusiasm." And girls did make it past the inquisitive eyes of the servants to his rooms—including, on one spectacular occasion, more than one.

But the Prince who had once written a book of phrases detailing how to pick up women could still be unsure of himself in their company. His relationships needed time to develop. And time, private time, was in the shortest supply. "People don't make it easy for him to marry, do they?" Lord Mountbatten observed. "I mean, what chance has Charles to woo a girl? He can't even stop to joke with one without being married off the next morning.

"You've got to get to know her—and that's not easy if you are a royal."

Charles didn't make it easy for himself. Determined to live a life as normal and out-front as possible, he insisted on conducting his romances in the full public spotlight with the predictable consequence that most of them collapsed before they had properly begun. The Prince did not, as has sometimes been suggested, have a secret "love nest" in Notting Hill Gate—or anywhere else.

Princess Margaret, for one, however, had little sympathy for his predicament. As his aunt would often remind him, the Royal Family does have at its disposal a large collection of houses and hideaways where he could take a girl with the world none the wiser. That he chose not to is a measure of his honesty—or his reserve.

Lord Mountbatten, his eye always on the lookout for a chance to promote his own dynasty, inevitably had his own solution to the problem—his granddaughter, Lady Amanda Knatchbull.

It would have been the realization of all his ambitions. And, but for his tragic death, blown up by an IRA bomb in 1979, the man who had succeeded in marrying his nephew to the future Queen might yet have pulled off the coup of marrying another member of his family to the future King. People who knew him and Charles well were convinced he would.

But with Mountbatten's powerful influence removed, the proposed union never got past the starting gate. Intelligent and pretty as Amanda was, she wasn't Charles's type. There was also the point that they had known each other since earliest childhood and were too much like brother and sister to make the quantum step to being husband and wife.

Amanda went on to work in estate agency. Charles went back to his circuit of tall, attractive blondes. And, in rejection of his aunt's counsel, he continued to conduct his courtships in public, turning up with the latest "Charlie's Angel" at polo or Ascot, setting off the next round of speculation.

As intrusive as that was, it did serve some purpose. As Charles once candidly admitted to a reporter, "You can afford to make a mistake, but I've got to get it right first time. If only I could live with a girl before marrying her. . . ."

But he couldn't. Instead it was left to the press to drag up her past, to test her character with their remorseless pursuit. Charles claimed that all the attention infuriated him, and he accused the press of "cheap sensational writing." He insisted, "It's got nothing to do with anyone else who I might want to marry or anything like that."

If Charles believed that, he was the only person who did. The people he will one day reign over had an understandable and justifiable interest in the identity of their future Queen.

So did his friends and family. If Charles was happy in his bachelor ways, they were not.

One account that made the London rounds was that a group of his chums, including his cousin the Earl of Lichfield and his equerry Nicholas Soames, grandson of Sir Winston Churchill, met one evening and drew up a short list of blue-blooded virgins to submit to him for his perusal.

In addition, the Queen Mother and her friend, Lady Fermoy, discussed the situation over afternoon tea.

And the name that emerged out of those romantic premeditations was one Lady Diana Spencer.

3

The Little Duchess

*T*he *Duchess of Marlborough* was determined that her favorite granddaughter, the first Lady Diana Spencer, would marry the Prince of Wales and offered him a dowry of £100,000, which he was glad to accept. The prime minister, however, objected. He had other plans for the Prince and forbade the marriage.

The Spencers of Althorp would have to wait another two-and-a-half centuries for one of their daughters to wed a Prince of Wales. And by a twist of historical coincidence, her name was also Lady Diana Spencer.

If that first union was kept unconsummated by the dictates of politics, it was the beginning of a long, occasionally scandalous association between the families Spencer and Royal.

Descended from a fifteenth-century farmer, who had bypassed the local butchers and wool merchants to sell his sheep directly to London and in so doing had set the foundations of a fortune that enabled them to buy their first peerage from King Charles I, the Spencers lived in the grandest of splendor in their Jacobean mansion in Northamptonshire.

The men spent their years in courtly, if low-key, attendance to the sovereign of the day. And their women—gay, beautiful, enchanting—regularly caught a succession of royal eyes.

This close and often romantic link to the Royal Family had begun with Sarah, Duchess of Marlborough, wife of the first Duke, who defeated Louis XIV's forces at Blenheim, and forebear of Sir Winston Churchill. She rose to become the richest and most powerful woman in England and Queen Anne's Lady of the Bedchamber in much more than name alone (the two women exchanged passionate love letters, which they signed "Mrs. Freeman" and "Mrs. Morley").

It was a love affair that profoundly shaped the course of British history. Anne had wanted her exiled half-brother, James Stuart, to succeed her. Sarah, a fervent Whig intent on securing a Protestant succession, was committed to the Hanoverians, and in the end she got her way. She may have failed in her ambition to marry her granddaughter to the Prince of Wales, but it was her action that ensured that Charles was Prince of Wales when he married his Lady Diana. And when she died she left the bulk of her vast estate to her grandson, the first Diana's brother Jack, father of the first Earl Spencer.

In the next generation Lady Georgina Spencer, daughter of the first Earl, became closest friends with Prinny, the Prince of Wales who succeeded to the Throne as George IV—so close that when she became pregnant his constant and suspiciously paternal visits caused her husband, the Duke of Devonshire, "some emotion."

It continued into this century; Diana's grandmother, Cynthia, had been seriously courted by the Prince of Wales (who abdicated as Edward VIII to become the Duke of Windsor) before she married the seventh Earl Spencer in 1919.

When they weren't being romanced by the Royal Family, the Spencers were usually to be found serving it and being honored in return.

Edward VII was godfather to Diana's grandfather. His wife, Cynthia, daughter of the Duke of Abercorn, was the Queen Mother's Lady of the Bedchamber. Diana's father, "Johnny," was equerry to King George VI and to the Queen, whose sister, Princess Margaret, he once dated.

On the maternal side the Spencer family was also closely linked with the Throne. Her mother's father, Lord Fermoy, was a shooting and tennis-playing friend of George VI. His wife, the redoubtable Ruth, who would play such an encouraging role during Diana's courtship by the latest Prince of Wales, is the Queen Mother's lady-in-waiting and best friend.

It is an association that prompted one cynic to describe the Spencers as "ten generations of Royal groupies." More kindly, it bestowed in Diana a natural ease in the presence of the Royal Family. When asked, back in her courting days, if she ever felt uncomfortable in the presence of the Queen, she replied, "No, why should I be?" There was no reason. She had known its members from earliest childhood. There had never been a time when she didn't know them; the first meeting with the man she would marry took place, she recalled, "when I was still wearing nappies. I've known him all my life."

Those nappy days and the years that followed were spent in Norfolk at Park House, a ten-bedroom Victorian mansion on the edge of the Queen's Sandringham estate. Built by Edward VII to accommodate the overflow of guests from Sandringham, it had come into the family through Diana's mother, Frances, whose father had rented the property from George V. Shortly after Frances married the seventh Earl Spencer's heir, Viscount Althorp, Lord Fermoy died and the newlyweds took over the lease. And it was here, late in the evening of July 1, 1961, that Diana Frances Spencer was born. She weighed seven pounds, twelve ounces, "a superb physical specimen," as her father recalls.

Park House was ideal for a young family, large and rambling, overlooking the royal parkland but hidden from the road by woods and shrubs. Like their mother before them, Diana and her elder sisters Sarah and Jane and, later, her brother Charles enjoyed a traditional country childhood with walks in the woods, building tree dens, and playing games of hide-and-seek.

There were always a lot of animals in attendance—horses

and ponies and rabbits and the hamsters and gerbils Diana was so fond of and, of course, their father's gun dog, Bray, and a springer spaniel named Jill and a cat called Marmalade. There was also a swimming pool that Viscount Althorp had installed for his children's amusement during the summer holidays. It was a rustic and, in the Spencers' minds, simple existence. "We are not at all grand," Diana's mother would say.

That depends on your definition of grand. Park House was certainly not as grand as Althorp (pronounced "Althrup" according to some, pronounced as it is spelled by Diana), where her crotchety grandfather lived in opulent splendor until his death in 1975. But there were six servants, including a full-time cook, and from an early age the children were fed pheasant for lunch. There was also a private governess, Miss Gertrude Allen, who had also taught Lady Althorp, who gave Diana lessons in what had once been the butler's pantry. And Janet Thompson, Diana's nanny for two-and-a-half years, recalls that "the Althorp children never tidied their rooms or made their beds."

Another nanny, Mary Clarke, felt that she was "seeing a bit of old England that was dying fast," and she was right—life at Park House was very much in the "Upstairs, Downstairs" tradition, almost Edwardian in its order and routine.

"The children were brought up in the old-fashioned way," Nanny Clarke remembers, "with ideals clearly stated. Manners were very important." However, they were something the Althorp children did not always find easy to acquire.

Sarah, six years older than Diana, was particularly wild, forever getting herself into scrapes. The overworked women who were charged with the duty of turning her into a young lady often found the task overwhelming, and nannies came and went with indecent frequency—a cause of some concern to her parents, who belong to a social class where nannies are regarded as an essential part of the family and often raise several generations, staying on past retirement and on to death. The turnover at Park House, however, was fast. "I can't remember exactly how many, but it was a lot," says Sarah with amusement.

Jane was much quieter, but Diana did her bit to make up for that. She locked one nanny in the bathroom. In a fit of mischievousness she threw another's clothes out onto the roof. And no amount of persuasion could ever make her do something she didn't want to do. There were numerous occasions when the "spirited" little girl was dispatched to her room as punishment.

"She wasn't easy," Nanny Thompson remembers. "Some children will do as they are told immediately. Diana wouldn't. It was always a little battle of wills." Obstinacy remains a characteristic of Diana's to this day—to the occasional embarrassment of her Royal relations.

She didn't like going for walks, much preferring to ride along on her bicycle. Nor did she like having her long blonde hair washed. "I had to talk her round each time," says Nanny Thompson, who had charge of Diana's upbringing until she was nearly six. "My method was to lay her down in the bath, leaning her on my arm with her hair trailing in the water. But it was always a bit of a struggle. She would say, 'Oh, not hair wash time again.' "

The young Diana didn't like horses much either. Riding is an essential part of country life. But when she was eight, Diana fell off and broke her arm, which took three months to mend. She again fell off her bay, Romany, a couple of years later when the pony caught its foot in a rabbit hole and tripped. "We walked the rest of the way home, and the doctor checked her and said she was fine," Nanny Clarke relates. Psychological damage had been done, however, and it was only very recently, and under pressure from her husband and mother-in-law, that Diana could be persuaded back into the saddle.

But if life had its occasional bumpy downs, it also had a lot of ups.

There were romps with their father in the nursery, "a wonderful room for playing bears in. We used to play bears there on our hands and knees," Lord Spencer recalls. There were bedtime stories from nanny with animal and school tales, Diana's favorites. In the summer there would be trips to the seaside at Brancaster to build sand castles on the beach. There were shopping expeditions into King's Lynn, which Diana adored. Even at that young age she had a passion for clothes. There was also the round of children's parties. "The children were socializing all the time, and Diana loved parties," says Nanny Thompson.

One was at Sandringham. Neatly washed, her hair brushed, and wearing a new frock, five-year-old Diana and her brother Charles set off for the "big house" for tea with Prince Andrew and Prince Edward, who succeeded in covering himself with honey. And when the tea was finished, Nanny Thompson found her young charge and six-year-old Andrew engaged in a frantic and completely informal game of hide-and-seek in the corridor—with the Queen.

There were times, though, when mood won out over even Diana's love of parties. When she was ten, for instance, and had been invited to a post-Christmas tea party at Sandringham with the royal children, she emphatically refused to go, claiming that she had a headache.

By then, however, Diana's childhood idyll had come to a savage and heartbreaking end. Her parents had separated, and Lady Althorp had left home.

In the summer of 1966 Frances had met wallpaper heir Peter Shand Kydd. He was everything her husband was not.

Lord Althorp was quiet and kind and unassuming and preferred animals to people. He was, as far as his wife was concerned, something of a bore who spent too much of his spare time attending to the various local charities he was involved in and not enough time with his wife, who liked parties and the theater and people.

Shand Kydd, a graduate of Edinburgh University and a former naval officer, was an extrovert, attractive with an uncanny ability to make people laugh. He also happened to be married with three children, but that proved no impediment to the desire of the heart. According to the first Mrs. Shand Kydd, the two became lovers at an address in South Kensington.

Lady Althorp moved out of Park House and into an apartment in Cadogan Place in Belgravia, taking her two youngest children with her. Diana went to day school, Charles to a nearby kindergarten.

Lord Althorp was devastated. His wife's decision to leave him, he says, came as a "thunderbolt."

The couple had married in considerable pomp in Westminster Abbey. The Queen and the Duke of Edinburgh and the Queen Mother were among the fifteen hundred guests who attended at the Abbey and at the reception at St. James's Palace afterward. They had appeared the ideal couple. But how many of the fourteen years they had spent together had been happy ones? Lord Althorp wondered. "I thought all of them—until the moment we parted. I was wrong."

Lady Althorp returned to Park House with her two youngest children for a "family" Christmas. It was the last one they would share together. Lord Althorp also put his foot down on the matter of Diana and Charles. "He refused to let them return to London," said her mother.

In all the freewheeling morality of the sixties, marital breakups had become increasingly commonplace, and by 1978 even the Queen's sister, Princess Margaret, made it into the divorce court. The old strictures, which even fifteen years before had denied a divorced person entrance into the Royal Enclosure at Ascot, were gone.

The Althorp divorce was different, however. Frances was branded an adultress. Worse, she was perceived as having deserted her young family, and when the matter made its sad way into court, she was refused custody of her children, which was awarded to their father. Even Frances's mother, Lady Fermoy, had turned against her, lending her moral support to her son-in-law and the comfort of her physical presence to Sarah and Jane and Charles and Diana. When Prince Charles said, as he often used to, "I was told that before you marry the daughter you should first look at the mother," he clearly did not have Lady Althorp in mind.

Diana in particular was "seriously affected" by the split, Nanny Clarke says. The young girl, once so lively, became introverted and developed her nervous blush and the habit of always looking down. This was when she started locking the women employed to look after her in bathrooms and throwing their clothes out of the window. And she would say to Mary Clarke, "I'll never ever marry unless I really love, really love, someone. If you're not really sure you love someone, then you might get divorced. I never want to be divorced!"

So was her father, who suddenly found himself as the head of a single-parent family and without the skills to cope. He would join his children for tea in the nursery, but it was, says Mary Clarke, "very hard going. In those early days after the divorce he wasn't very relaxed with them."

He tried to break through the barrier by asking them questions about what games they had been playing, about how their schoolwork was going, and about their pets, "but they only answered his questions. They never started a conversation," adds Miss Clarke.

After a few weeks Miss Clarke suggested that it might ease matters if the children, rather than being confined to the top of the house, were allowed in future to join their father for lunch in the dining room. Lord Althorp readily agreed, and according to Clarke, the children became more relaxed.

The confusion would remain in their young minds for some time to come, however. The Althorp divorce became absolute in April 1969, and within a month Lady Althorp had married Shand Kydd. They moved into an old farmhouse near Itchenor in Sussex, where Diana would go to visit her mother on the odd weekend and during vacations. When she returned to Norfolk, she was always "awkward." And she would test her nanny's loyalty by making "unfavorable remarks about her father. I knew she meant none of it and would always change the subject."

It was after one such visit to Sussex that Diana had stamped her stubborn little foot and refused to attend the royal children's tea party at Sandringham. She had become more solitary and was spending long hours in the nursery, dressing her teddy bear in her little brother's old baby clothes.

The change was not a dramatic one, but it was there; the

little girl the staff had affectionately nicknamed "Duchess" for her imperious manner had been deeply upset by the sad, irreparable turn her short life had taken. Both her parents had done their best to shield their offspring from the malice that inevitably marks a marriage breakup, but this divorce had been a particularly nasty one. It had set Lady Fermoy against her daughter, it had separated Lady Althorp from her children, it had virtually ostracized Lady Althorp from society, and it had left Diana confused and unhappy. The feuding and the legal haggling had also dragged on for two bitter years, and no matter how hard Johnny Althorp and his former wife tried to confine the bitterness to their solicitors' offices, the children had inevitably caught its strong scent, and it sickened them emotionally.

Diana did not talk about it except to say, over and over again, that she would only marry for true love because she never, never wanted to get divorced.

4
School Days

When Diana was nine years old, her parents decided that it would be in her best interest if she went to boarding school, which was not uncommon among young girls of the upper class.

It was, her father recalls, "a dreadful day." The little girl was driven those forty miles from Sandringham across the flat, monotonous Norfolk countryside and left at Riddleworth Hall near Diss with her pet guinea pig Peanuts and her trunk marked "D. F. Spencer" packed with her uniform of pleated dresses and white shirts and the "Sunday best" cherry-red dress, which her mother had bought for her at Harrods, the school outfitters.

It wasn't such a good day for Diana either.

She had been to school before. After being tutored at home by her mother's old governess, Ally Allen, she had spent two years at Silfield in nearby King's Lynn. But that had been a day school, and every evening she had the warmth and familiarity of Park House to come back to. Now she was away from home with lots of other little girls who were away from home, many for the first time, and for the first few nights the dormitory was filled with the sound of them weeping quietly into their pillows.

And school, even at the best of times, was not an institution in which Diana would shine, at least not academically. Ally had called her a "real trier" and a "conscientious worker" who was interested in history (she liked stories about kings and queens). At Silfield the headmistress, Jean Lowe, who had given evidence on Lord Althorp's behalf in the custody battle, had been impressed with how well she could read and how clear her writing was, at the same time noting that she dedicated all her pictures and drawings to "Mummy and Daddy."

But she had been young then. At Riddlesworth her education moved on from the nursery games of infancy to the harder curriculum of grammar and arithmetic and history lessons that were about dates and facts, not fairy-tale kings and queens. She was, Miss Lowe remembers, "extremely average."

The British boarding school is, however, a strange institution. It can be a horror. Yet by its very routine and insistence on rules and order it can give a sense of security. Diana, like many other children from broken homes, found a stability there she might otherwise have missed.

She soon settled in, and her mother and father would come to visit her on alternate weekends, bringing with them the ginger biscuits and Twiglets and cream eggs she was so fond of. She never did rise to any noticeable academic heights, but she came to excel in other ways.

"The things that particularly stand out in my memories," Miss Lowe recorded in the school's magazine in 1981 when Diana became, by marriage, the most famous of her old girls, "are kindness to the smaller members of the community, her general helpfulness, her love of animals, and her excellence at swimming and indeed her considerable prowess in general physical activities."

Riddlesworth had taught her enough to pass the Common Entrance Examination that gave her passage to her next school. With the inevitability of family tradition, she went to

West Heath, the all-girls public school near Sevenoaks. Founded in 1865, its aim was to "train the students to develop their own minds and tastes and realize their duties as citizens."

Prince Charles's great-grandmother, Queen Mary, had been a pupil there. It was also where Diana's mother had been educated and had risen to become "captain of everything." It was where Mrs. Shand Kydd had decided to send her own daughters—with mixed success.

The middle girl, Jane, who was a senior girl when Diana first arrived, enjoyed it. Not so her eldest sister, Sarah.

An excellent tennis player like her mother, who had qualified for junior Wimbledon only to be struck down by appendicitis, Sarah was an excellent sportswoman. She had played lacrosse and netball and cricket and tennis. She had captained the swimming team and was famous for her prize-winning dive, the Spencer Special, which left barely a ripple in the pool.

But she was also headstrong and rebellious. Though now a teetotaler, she also developed a youthful taste for strong liquor.

"I used to drink because I was bored," Sarah recalls. "I would drink anything. Whisky, Cointreau, sherry, or most often, vodka because they couldn't smell it on my breath."

One day they did, and Sarah was firmly told to pack her trunk and depart the school—and not to return.

Diana was never in that league, but she did have her moments.

The headmistress, who retired recently, was Australian Ruth Rudge, and her intention was to "develop character and confidence" in her girls. They had to wear a uniform or navy jumper, pleated skirt, and black stockings ("Oh look," said Diana enviously when she went back to open a new sports hall in 1987, "I see you are allowed to wear colored tights now"). They slept in dormitories they nicknamed "cowsheds." Diana's was decorated with a portrait of Prince Charles, though it was Prince Andrew her contemporaries would jokingly say she was going to marry.

As part of their "duties as a citizen" everyone was expected to take part in community work, and Diana would visit an old lady in Sevenoaks every week to sit and chat, do some shopping, and help tidy up. She also paid a weekly visit to a nearby home for handicapped children.

Music and sport were also emphasized, and Diana was good at both. She played tennis well enough, though not as well as her mother or eldest sister. She won the diving prize. She excelled at netball because, as she says, "it was much easier for me to get the ball in the net because I was so tall."

She danced tap and ballet and went for long walks through the attractive grounds that surround the Georgian mansion that is the main school building.

And like all children at boarding school, she had her holidays to look forward to. Diana's were particularly pleasant. Whatever her father may have thought of his former wife (and not surprising in the circumstances, it wasn't a lot), they were still determined to spare their children from as much of the lingering bitterness as possible, and vacations were divided among Norfolk, Sussex, and, later, the Isle of Seil on Scotland's West Coast, where the Shand Kydds had bought a thousand-acre sheep farm.

Scotland was an idyllic retreat for a teenager who was still rather young for her age. There was swimming in the warm waters of the Gulf Stream that sweep into the Firth of Lorn and lobster pots to be baited and occasional trips to the cinema in Oban where Frances Shand Kydd ran a small gift shop.

From the age of fourteen onward, Diana also had the rather grander alternative to Althorp, the Northamptonshire seat of the Spencer family.

In 1975 her grandfather, the seventh earl, died, and her father succeeded to the house, a magnificent mansion a two-hour drive out of London set in two thousand acres of rolling countryside. Portraits of Diana's ancestors, including works by Sir Joshua Reynolds, hang in the 115-foot gallery. There is a library stocked with some of the rarest books in Europe. On the ground floor is the china collection.

Lord Althorp was now Earl Spencer. Diana was fifteen

years old when Johnny Spencer fell in love and found someone to replace his first wife, Frances. It was almost a reenact-
ment of the bitter marital troubles of the previous decade. For
the woman in question was Barbara Cartland's daughter,
Raine—and she was married to the Earl of Dartmouth, one
of Spencer's friends.

She left her husband, divorced him, and she and Spencer
were married two months later in a five-minute ceremony at
London's Old Caxton Hall register office in 1976.

It was a case, says Spencer, "of two very lonely people who
found each other and found happiness together."

His daughters did not share in that happiness. When
Raine moved in, the girls, led by Sarah, would sing, "Raine,
Raine go away." They resented her grand airs and graces and
the imperious way in which she had supplanted their mother
in their young minds.

The first time Lady Dartmouth, as she still was, came to
lunch at Park House, nanny Mary Clarke feared trouble. "I
remember feeling tense and trying to distract Diana without
success. Sarah was sent from the room and Diana followed
her. We did not lunch together again with Lady Dartmouth."

As the new Lady Spencer, Raine is credited with effecting
a rapprochement between her husband and his cantankerous
father. That, however, did not improve her relations with his
children. Lord Spencer, who still tries his best to paper over
the cracks, has been forced to concede; "No step-relation-
ships are easy. It was hard on my children and hard on Raine,
moving into a family as close as we are.

"You couldn't expect it to work wonders at the start."

Upon Lord Spencer's elevation to the peerage, his daughter moved up from being plain Miss to become Lady Diana
Spencer. This social elevation did not curtail her stubbornness and occasional naughtiness. Back at school, if she didn't
like a particular sporting activity, she had been known to
smear blue eyeshadow on her knees and pretend they were
bruised. And there were, she remembers, dormitory romps
and pillow fights and midnight feasts and custard pie throwing.

When she was caught, she was punished by being made to

"run six times round the hall, which has to be preferable to the lacrosse pitch or weeding the garden, which I became a great expert at."

This expertise did not extend to her schoolwork. At Silfield she was awarded a prize for trying hard. At Riddlesworth she won the Pets Corner cup, the prize for the best-kept pet.

West Heath rewarded her social work with a "special award for service," which, as Miss Rudge emphasized, was given only to outstanding pupils.

The examiners who marked her "O"-level papers were not so charitable. She failed them all. And when she went back to take them all again, she failed them all again.

When she returned to the school in 1987 to open a new £250,000 sports hall, she said, "In spite of what Miss Rudge and my other teachers may have thought, I *did* actually learn something." It was not enough, however, for Diana to continue her education at the age of sixteen. Without any tangible qualifications, she left West Heath.

There then followed a brief, though not highly productive, stay at the Institut Alpin Videmanette, an expensive Swiss finishing school. She was supposed to improve her French. Instead she spoke English with Sophie Kimball, another English girl, and became desperately homesick. The school imposed a reign of terror, forbidding anyone to utter a word of anything but French. Pupils were supposed to learn a bilingual secretarial course and acquire cooking skills, but if they failed to understand anything that was going on, it made their lives very miserable indeed. At night they were locked up, and the only boys they ever saw were the ones from the local village. Young for her age, Diana did not fit in well with the European and more worldly pupils, and although she enjoyed the skiing, she hated everything else. One day, and after many tears, she left and flew home to her mother's London apartment in Chelsea.

But Diana was not the only pupil to leave. Melanie Greene, who attended the school a short time after Diana, recalls, "I hated it. I can quite understand why she left. I have never been so miserable in my life, and I left too."

For many youngsters so underqualified, the future would have offered nothing but a wasted life on the dole queue. Diana was spared that indignity. She was born an aristocrat with a cushion of family money to support her. She moved into her mother's home and attended a cookery course and took dancing lessons.

And when Mrs. Shand Kydd decided to sell the house, Diana's family trust, supplemented by a tidy bequest left her by her American great-grandmother, Frances Work, bought her a flat at number 60 Colherne Court on the borders of Kensington and the rather more low-rent area of Earl's Court.

Sophie Kimball moved in as a flatmate. And when she moved out she was replaced by Carolyn Pride, a school friend from West Heath, who was studying at the Royal College of Music. Joining them were Ann Bolton, who is now married to Australian Noel Hill, and the extrovert Virginia Pitman, who has hitchhiked through Africa.

They got on well together, buying their groceries at the little Indian-run shop on the corner, eating at the local bistros, occasionally entertaining friends at supper (Virginia usually did the cooking; Diana, ever the tidiness fanatic, did the washing up).

There was also money that had to be earned. Ann Bolton, for instance, was an estate agent's secretary. Diana had to make do with more lowly employment—for a year she worked as a daily maid and a baby-sitter!

Her sister Sarah was also living in London, in an apartment she shared with Hampshire landowner's daughter Lucinda Craig-Harvey. Lucinda is now a West End theater producer. She recalls, "She worked for me as a 'daily' three days a week. She did everything. She dusted. She cleaned. She did the washing up. She cleaned out the bathroom. She scrubbed out the loo. She did the lot. And she was very good. Well, good enough. She lasted a year, and Sarah, as her older sister, would have soon got rid of her and got someone else if she hadn't been. I'd mark her a good eight out of ten."

In the evenings the world's most successful charwoman— not many cleaners rise to become Princess of Wales—would baby-sit. Her clients included an American couple, Patrick and Mary Robinson, who remember her as "refined—and wonderful with children."

It was working with children that gave Diana the most satisfaction. Her ambitions to become a dancer having ended when she grew too tall, she had nurtured the hope of becoming a ballet teacher instead. For a short time she had worked at the Vacani School of Dancing round the corner from her flat in Kensington, teaching infants their first rhythmic steps. She did not, however, have the dedication to make a career out of it. "She had rather a full social life," Miss Vacani recalls.

She had, however, been popular with the children. And when Kay Seth-Smith, a contemporary of her middle sister Jane at West Heath, offered her a job at the Young England Kindergarten she helped run in Pimlico, Diana jumped at the chance.

"She got along very well with the children, and the parents liked her," Kay recounts.

Her job was to help the children with their pictures and picture books and bricks, to give them simple dancing lessons, to comfort them when they cried, to change them when they wet themselves. It was work she did well. As her mother had once remarked, Diana was a "positive Pied Piper with children."

But that full social life Miss Vacani had been talking about was getting much fuller. For a young man had come onto her horizon, and the man was the Prince of Wales, the "most eligible bachelor in the world."

Diana was flattered and charmed. Her flatmates were quickly caught up in the excitement of the romance and became involved in the subterfuge and the plots and the plans that went with it. And when it became clear that Diana's friendship with Charles was more than just a passing thing, the excitement grew and acquired a life and momentum of its own. Would Charles call tonight? Would Diana be invited to Balmoral? Was Charles too old for her? Diana asked the girls who shared her home. Did he love her? Did the girl who had sworn that she would never marry someone she didn't truly love, really love him?

In this frenzy of royal courtship there was little time for clear or introspective thought. That would come later.

In 1987 Carolyn Pride was interviewed for Australian television. What, she was asked, did Diana and Charles have in common? Her mouth dropped open and stayed there as she stumbled for a reply.

It never came. Diplomatically, Carolyn's reaction was cut off the tape and never broadcast.

5

The Courtship

*B*efore the days of daily hairdressers, high fashion, and expertly applied makeup, Diana looked her best when she was wearing her least. No frilly blouses concealed her elegant neck, carefully cut skirts her long legs, or bulky sweaters her well-rounded figure. She was young and not fully aware of just how attractive she could be. But if she wanted to impress a young man, any young man, she always made it a point to go swimming or sailing or, at the very least, play a game of tennis.

When Prince Charles saw her aboard *Britannia* at Cowes in the late summer of 1980, however, he wasn't particularly interested. She belonged to his younger brother Andrew's set and had come aboard not by his invitation but with Lady Sarah Armstrong-Jones, his cousin and sixteen years his junior.

Diana was three years older than Sarah, but still almost a generation away. And besides, Charles had his mind on other things—most particularly the breakup of his romance with the beautiful but oh-so-self-willed Anna Wallace. There was also the fact that if he noticed Diana in anything more than passing, he thought about her as the sister of one of his former girlfriends—Lady Sarah Spencer—who had recently married (he hadn't attended), and whatever others might have been plotting, he most certainly was not thinking of renewing his romantic links with the Spencer girls.

But if Charles was not instantly enchanted by the fresh, gamboling nineteen-year-old who spent some days aboard the Royal Yacht, his staff members were. "She was so unassuming and so natural," one recalls. And in the manner of all servants, particularly ones who are in the employ of the bachelor Prince, they inevitably started speculating among themselves if she was the one for what they called "The Job."

So, it seems, did Diana. At the age of sixteen she had jokingly told a friend that she was "out to get" Charles. That may have been just romantic fantasizing on the part of a young girl whose main reading was the soapy romances penned by her step-grandmother, the redoubtable Barbara Cartland. The Prince's late valet, Stephen Barry, insisted, however, "She went after the Prince with single-minded determination. She wanted him—and she got him!"

She had, of course, met him many times before, in the years of her childhood spent as a near neighbor of the Windsors at Sandringham. Charles used to pop his head round the nursery door where she was having tea with Andrew and Edward. There had also been the shooting party on Sandringham estate where, at the age of sixteen, she was reintroduced to him by her sister Sarah. More recently she had encountered him at polo. But then he had always been busy or had a girlfriend in tow. This time he was alone.

She made sure Charles was watching in the choppy and not too warm waters of the Solent Channel. Naturally flirtatious, she made sure he noticed her long slim legs and trim figure. And he could not fail to start to take an interest—if only a comparative one—in the beautiful younger sister of Sarah.

Accounts of this first meeting vary. Some claim that it is where the famous romance began. Others insist that his interest was but a mild one, that with Anna still in mind he simply regarded her as a new and pretty addition to his surprisingly limited circle of friends, and that the timing was wrong.

But she had certainly impressed him enough for him to invite her up to Balmoral shortly afterward. Diana accepted with alacrity.

At this stage of her development the young woman whose life was soon to go the way of a fairy tale was inclined to lapse into a world of fantasy.

Undereducated, without a proper career to interest her, and with an imagination fueled by the Mills and Boon-style novelettes she was so addicted to, she was—like a Barbara Cartland heroine—simply marking time until she married and had children. And there were times when she could not but feel that her life was uninteresting and, above all, desperately lacking in the kind of romance she was seeking.

She did have admirers among her set of well-connected young Sloanes. They included Old Etonian Simon Berry, a member of the family of St. James's wine merchants, and George Plumptree, six years her senior, who now writes books on gardening. They would dine out together in one of the Chelsea restaurants favored by her set. Occasionally they would eat in, and Diana, who had attended a Cordon Bleu cookery course, would make scrambled eggs. She went skiing in France with Berry and sixteen other friends. But for whatever reason, none of the men she met quite matched the "identikit" Diana had mentally drawn of her dream mate.

The Prince of Wales, on the other hand, fit her romantic notions perfectly, and the more he dismissed her in person as a "little sister," the more intrigued she became.

There were no obvious signs, however, that her interest was being reciprocated during that first stay at Balmoral. And her second trip north in October also passed without any romantic incident that anyone who was there can remember.

Diana was not without her supporters, however. The staff was very taken with her. And on that second expedition to the Highlands she stayed with the Queen Mother at Birkhall on the Balmoral estate. Her grandmother, Lady Fermoy, was also there. Both ladies had always been fond of her, and in the enclosed and female-dominated world that Charles lived in, the approval of those two grand dames was certainly no handicap to a young woman with a romantic interest in the Prince.

And Diana, it must be said, played the part demanded of her to ingenious perfection. These days, she can hardly bring herself to visit Balmoral. Then she was cheerful and obliging. While Charles was out on the hill stalking stags, she would get on with her needlepoint until it was time to join the returning men for afternoon tea followed by evening drinks and dinner and perhaps a game of charades. She had sat for the "Craigowan Test" that other girlfriends had failed, and she passed with honors.

In August 1980 Charles and Diana's relationship changed up a gear. Once back in London, Charles invited her to join him for what he called "cozy" dinners in his rooms at Buckingham Palace. He then paid her the enormous compliment of inviting her down to Gloucestershire to take a look at Highgrove, the eighteenth-century manor house he had bought in 1980 for £800,000 out of his income from the Duchy of Cornwall.

If Diana was not overly impressed (and she wasn't) with the sparsely furnished and rather stolid house whose rooms in a failure of imagination Charles had painted all white, she did her best not to show it. The fact that she was there was enough. It could mean only one thing—that Charles was beginning to take a serious interest in her.

It was in many respects an odd romance. Throughout his courting years Charles had kept within his own age group. Diana was almost young enough to be his daughter, a still unformed woman barely out of school. She shared none of his obvious interests. (He likes opera, she didn't; she likes ballet, he could not abide it.)

There was also the contrast in their educational backgrounds. Diana, as the Americans say, is a high school dropout. Charles, on the other hand, is a university graduate who likes nothing better than settling down with an intellectually taxing book on psychology or history.

Nor—and this was a rarity indeed among Charles's serious girlfriends—did she share his love of equestrian sports.

For all their differences, however, the two were developing an obvious and genuine affection for each other—perhaps even *because* of their differences. Diana had an ingenuous freshness that Charles found captivating. She was unspoiled and good-humored, and even the vociferous press attention she quickly attracted failed on all but the rarest of occasions to disturb her unduly—unlike Lady Jane Wellesley, who had been reduced to near hysteria by the hordes of paparazzi who had attached themselves to her when she had first started walking out with the Prince of Wales.

Another factor too worked in Diana's favor: time was running out for the "world's most eligible bachelor."

Some of his friends believe that, left to his own devices, Charles might never have married. He enjoyed his bachelorhood, and as the years passed he was becoming ever more set in his own self-centered routine. He had his sport, and an army of servants was always on hand to tend to his needs. He had his foreign travel. There was usually a pretty girl available to join him for dinner or accompany him to polo. He is a man who enjoys his own company, who indeed becomes irritable and depressed if deprived of the chance to spend time alone with only his own thoughts for company, and the compromise a marriage demands did not entirely appeal to him.

But Charles was under pressure. When the press started worrying about his continued reluctance to take a bride, they were merely reflecting a public concern—and one that was growing. The Queen too was becoming unhappy with the situation. She is a woman whose whole life has been dedicated to upholding the Crown, and one of the fundamental responsibilities of monarchy is to secure its own succession. On a more personal level she was growing increasingly uneasy about the way her son and eventual successor was ending romantic escapades and eroding the dignity of the Royal Family.

This was hardly Charles's fault. If he had been born as few as thirty years earlier, he could have dated whom he liked, secure in the knowledge that his romances would have been allowed to mature in private and not on the front pages of the tabloids. But the old barriers that hide the Royal Family from public view had fallen, for the press no longer followed the unwritten rules of discretion, and Charles's lovelife was looking disconcertingly like an episode out of a soap opera. The Queen was not amused.

Nor was his father, Prince Philip, who had made it his lifelong habit to remind his son of his royal responsibilities. He reminded him of them now and kept pointing out that if Charles didn't make his choice soon there would be no one left to choose.

He was also concerned that Charles should not be seen to be leading a nineteen-year-old up a garden path to a still-born romance. It was a worry shared by Diana's mother, Frances Shand Kydd. In a letter to the *Times* she complained.

In recent weeks many articles have been labelled "exclusive quotes" when the plain truth is that my daughter has not spoken the words attributed to her. Fanciful speculation if it is in good taste is one thing, but this can be embarrassing. Lies are quite another matter and by their very nature, hurtful and inexcusable.

May I ask the editors in Fleet Street whether, in the execution of their jobs, they consider it necessary or fair to harass my daughter daily, from dawn until well after dusk? Is it fair to ask any human being, regardless of circumstances, to be treated this way? The freedom of the press was granted by law, by public demand, for very good reasons. But when these privileges are abused, can the press command any respect or expect to be shown any respect?

Mrs. Shand Kydd had underestimated her youngest daughter. Diana quite enjoyed the chase and with the connivance of her friends and Charles's private staff made a game out of outwitting the pursuing Rat Pack of reporters assigned to cover her every move.

She would sometimes slip off to her grandmother's apartment in Belgravia's Eaton Square and then slip out again into a waiting car driven by Charles's valet, Barry, who would whisk her away to a rendezvous at Buckingham Palace or Highgrove. She would sometimes say she was going to one place and then double back and head off in another direction in her Mini Metro. And if, as sometimes happened, the journalists succeeded in double-guessing her, she always took the trouble to drop her head in that familiar way and award them the prize of a demure smile.

For despite what her mother might have thought, she had been giving quotes—and quite genuine ones—to a number of royal reporters. She had established a friendly rapport with several and had sought the private, off-the-record advice of at least one journalist and had told him that she disagreed strongly with what her mother had written.

She also happened to enjoy the attention. Every morning she took delivery of the newspapers and would sit for hours with her flatmates, giggling over the morning's quota of pictures and stories devoted to her.

The press in their turn adored her. She had won them over through a combination of charm and subtle cooperation, and they had become her unquestioning allies in what in truth had become a courtship by newspaper.

It was weighed down with this backpack of public and private pressure that Charles entered the New Year of 1981, and whatever his private thoughts might have been, the roller coaster was speeding toward what was now looking like an inevitable denouement.

In keeping with royal tradition, he went up to Sandringham in Norfolk for the New Year celebration. Diana went too. So, of course, did her fan club of royal reporters. The Royal Family was becoming very tetchy. Prince Edward fired a shotgun over the heads of photographers. Charles shouted to the waiting journalists that he hoped their editors had an unhappy New Year. Even the Queen was irritable and, in an unprecedented break of temper, shouted at the Rat Pack, "Why don't you all go away!"

They didn't, needless to say. For by now just about everyone who could had entered into the plot. It was reported that Kanga Tryon and Camilla Parker-Bowles had "vetted" Diana and found her acceptable. Questions were being asked in the House of Commons.

And the matter of "experiences" once addressed by Lord Mountbatten became a major issue—at least in the eyes of the public and the press. Barbara Cartland declared, "Prince Charles has got to have a pure young girl. I don't think Diana has had a boyfriend. That is marvelous. . . . " Giving more explicit expression to what people had come to believe was a prerequisite for any bride of the Prince of Wales, Diana's uncle, Lord Fermoy, went so far as to announce, "She, I can assure you, has never had a lover."

The Windsors, contrary to accepted opinion, have never held physical purity in quite the high esteem they are supposed to, as witnessed by the unproblematic way Sarah Ferguson was accepted into the Royal Family. And Lord Fermoy, who was never as close to his niece as he liked to think he was, was hardly in a position to know with true certainty what a young woman living unchaperoned in the center of London might or might not have got up to.

But if purity is a public virtue, then Diana could provide. No ex-boyfriend emerged from the woodwork of the past to talk about love trysts in "rose-covered cottages." All that anyone managed to dig up was that she had once taken a shine to a handsome young lieutenant in the Scots Guards called Rory Scott and used to take his shirts back to her flat to wash—but all in perfect romantic innocence, as everyone was at pains to point out. There simply was no past to expose because, as Diana herself observed, she simply didn't have one. She had sat for another test, this time before the jury of public opinion with the press presenting the evidence, and passed again with flying colors.

Whatever reservations Charles may have harbored, whatever excuses he may have given himself, had run out. Diana had captured the greatest heart of all—the heart of the British public.

At the end of January, Charles flew off for his annual

skiing holiday in Klosters. Diana had hoped to go with him and had been looking forward to the break. In the end, however, it was agreed that with the constant attention it would be better if she remained behind in Britain.

On February 2 Charles flew home. Two days later he made Diana an official proposal of marriage. Not on his knees, "not on either of them," he says, but over dinner in his private sitting room at Buckingham Palace just before she flew off for a vacation in Australia with her mother and stepfather.

"I chose the moment so that she would have plenty of time to think about it, to decide if it was all going to be too awful," he recalled.

Diana decided it wouldn't be and promptly said yes—as he knew she would. For the couple had already discussed marriage, in a roundabout way, (Charles would pose hypothetical questions, such as, "If you were to marry someone thirteen years older than yourself, do you think it would be a difficult adjustment?") over "picnic" dinners of eggs and spinach eaten off a card table in the still-to-be properly decorated discomfort of Highgrove. Charles can have been left in no doubt that the young girl all of thirteen years his junior was deeply in love with him. And when a television interviewer asked her, "Are you in love?" she answered instantly, "Of course."

Charles was more circumspect. Asked the same question, the Prince hesitated for a moment and then answered, "Yes, whatever that may mean."

It was not a dramatically romantic response. But then, for the man born to be King, marriage is as much an act of state as a declaration of the heart. For him there would be no going back, no divorce, no second chance. Love, whatever that may be, could all too often prove to be only infatuation, he had said. "Creating a secure family unit in which to bring up children, to give them a happy, secure upbringing—that is what marriage is all about," he once explained. "Marriage is more important than just falling in love."

Indeed, marriage to the Prince of Wales entailed much

more—as Diana was about to discover. To win a prince is one thing. To become a princess is something very different. In becoming engaged, Diana had made a reality out of every lovelorn schoolgirl's fantasy—including, it is fair to say, her own.

She was to discover what the price was. The engagement was announced at 11:00 A.M. on Tuesday, February 24, 1981. (The *Times* had the story on its front page that morning, leaked to its editor, Charles discovered to his profound anger, by former prime minister Edward Heath.) At that hour Lady Diana Spencer became, for all practical purposes, a member of the Royal Family.

She was assigned a detective who from now on and forever would accompany her everywhere, even into the Bond Street lingerie shop where she went to buy her silk knickers. She moved out of her flat in Colherne Court—not into Clarence House with the Queen Mother as was stated by the press at the time but into Buckingham Palace, into a suite of rooms a tiptoe away from Charles's own chambers.

There was a very good reason for this. Charles and his wife-to-be had been walking out together for six months, but it had been a courtship conducted in a goldfish bowl.

"They hardly ever had a moment when they could be alone together," one of Charles's aides told me. "The time between the engagement and the marriage was the time when they could get to know each other—absolutely vital for two people who, after all, are going to have to spend the rest of their life together."

Again this might seem odd. Most people get engaged *after* they have got to know each other, not before. But that, even in this day and age, is not the royal way, not if the royal in question is the future King.

On a more mundane level, Diana also had to learn how to behave.

"We had a lot of problems with Diana at the beginning," one of Charles's closest aides explains. "She had come straight out of the nursery school into the Palace, and she sometimes got carried away with it all.

"The most important thing we had to do was to calm her down. She got very excited. She was always waving and smiling—like a film star. But there is a difference between being a film star and being a member of the Royal Family. Everything has to be more discreet."

The task of guiding her through the unseen pitfalls fell to Charles's closest aides and to Lady Susan Hussey, wife of the director general of the BBC and lady-in-waiting to the Queen. It was Lady Susan who would quietly and discreetly advise her to wave now but not to wave then and how to execute the royal handshake (always brief and never too firm; the exercise gets very painful over the course of a day after hundreds of hands have been shaken).

Oliver Everett, Charles's assistant private secretary, taught her how to walk. For a while each day he would parade the future Princess up and down the palace ballroom with yards of tissue paper attached to her head and dragging along the floor behind her. This was how she was prepared to walk down the aisle at Saint Paul's with her wedding train. Everett, a polo player and seventeen years Diana's senior, formed an immediate bond with the Princess. She was lonely, and he was around far more often than Prince Charles. He was later appointed her private secretary but left in 1983—some say because Diana was embarrassed by the close friendship she had formed with Everett and threw him out after her marriage.

She was given a selection of royal biographies, books describing the lives of other women who in times past had married other princes of the realm, and she was expected to read them. "It was a fast lesson in recent royal history," an advisor explains.

There were inevitable hiccups and mistakes. Explained Charles's late valet Stephen Barry, "There isn't a charm school for princesses. Diana had to learn by example."

And if the example proved insufficient, subtle action had to be taken. As in her dealings with the household servants.

The Royal Family are as a rule most polite to the people who look after them, and Charles always ends his orders with the words "if you don't mind?" But there is always a distance between them, a chasm that is never crossed, and the relationship is never more than that of master and servant.

In those early days, however, Diana was too familiar. Lonely and left alone for long hours each day, she was forever popping down to the kitchens, looking for company or engaging young footmen in conversation.

It was the senior staff members who objected and took the matter in hand. They did not approve of these "Scandinavian" practices. The British do not have a bicycling Royal Family, and their employees, whose own lives are governed by a servants' caste system, do not want one.

Barry admonished a footman who was becoming too friendly with her. The Yeoman of the Glass and China gave her a sterner reminder of the social divisions of her new role as the future Princess of Wales.

One day when the court was at Sandringham, Diana again arrived in the kitchens. The yeoman saw her. He bluntly pointed to the door and said, "Through there is *your* side of the house—and through here is *my* side of the house." Diana blushed a deep red and fled, never to return.

It was an ivory tower from which there was no escape. One day she decided to go out. The moment she got into her red Metro, which was parked in the quadrangle of Buckingham Palace, Paul Officer, one of the policemen from the Royal Protection Squad, climbed in beside her. She said she could manage by herself, thank you. He replied, "I'm sorry, but we're part of your life now."

The staff called her the Princess in the Tower. The Prince, returning from a day of royal duties, would anxiously inquire, "Is Lady Diana all right?"

True to the old theater adage, of course, it was all right on the day of the event, and it was a radiant and beautiful Diana who arrived on the arm of her father at St. Paul's Cathedral that glorious summer's morning in 1981.

There were the little confusions, of course. She got his names round the wrong way. ("Well, with four names it's quite something to get organized," she explained afterward.)

He stumbled over the words "all my worldly good with thee I share," and instead endowed her with just "all my goods." "But it added a certain amount of amusement into the proceedings," Charles said.

The night before, tens of thousands of people had gathered in the Mall and sung "Rule Britannia." Remembers Charles, "It really was remarkable, and I found myself standing in the window with tears pouring down my face."

Weddings are a moment for hope and optimism. They represent a commitment to the future, and when Diana and Charles married, a whole nation joined in the celebration.

"I found we were carried along on a wave of enormous friendliness and enthusiasm," Charles recalls. "It was remarkable. And I kept telling myself to remember this for as long as I could because it was such a unique experience."

He added, "Inevitably these things don't always last very long. But I think it made one realize that underneath everything else, all the rowing and the bickering and disagreements that go on the rest of the time, every now and then you get a reason for a celebration or a feeling of being a nation."

Diana shares all those feelings. She also has one more private memory. She says, "It was terrifying."

A worldwide television audience of 700 million people had watched Lady Diana Spencer marry the Prince of Wales. They would be watching to see how the marriage would work. Diana was right. It was terrifying.

6

In-Laws

The Queen, senior members of the Royal Household assure me, "thinks the world" of Diana.

So she does, though in her own regal way.

For all that stern public persona, the Sovereign is in fact easygoing with a witty and—at times—wicked turn of phrase. She enjoys a joke, a glass of wine, and her children. She adores her grandchildren. And she is very taken with both her daughters-in-law.

She knew instinctively how to treat the young coltish aristocrat who married her eldest son and brought such glamour into the family business of monarchy.

One day when Diana came into her private sitting room in a state of high agitation, the Sovereign took one look and remarked, "She's like a nervy racehorse. She needs careful handling."

And the Queen has handled her carefully, encouraging her with her genuine affection and the occasional encouraging word.

There is, though, another side to the woman who has spent almost all her adult life reigning over a fifth of the world's peoples. She is always regal, always a little reserved—even with her closest kin.

In the popular imagination she is a woman who is always worrying over the behavior of her offspring, forever calling them to account—an ermine-plumed mother hen forever fretting over her brood. In fact she is far too busy with her works of state, work she approaches seriously and with a single-minded dedication, to overconcern herself with the normal ups and downs of day-to-day life that might afflict other members of the Royal Family. And for all the talk about the "young royals," it is worth remembering that they are in fact adults, often with children of their own, and they are expected to deal with their own problems themselves. If there are any sharp words of advice to dispense, it is usually Charles—already on the threshold of middle age—who does the dispensing.

Indeed, there have been times when the Queen's own staff wondered if she was expecting too much independence from her family. There were certainly times right at the beginning when Diana was in some need of the Queen's guidance but never got it. The Queen does not visit the part of the building that houses the modest suite that was Diana's before her wedding. It was by appointment only that Diana would visit her future mother-in-law in her private suite a mile of Palace corridors away. The appointments were few and far between.

It was confusing and not a little disconcerting to a young girl who was used to the companionship and informality of her own family. She was lonely and felt isolated. Her confidence, as yet uncast by the mold of experience, began to erode. Diana, initially so relaxed and at ease in the Queen's company, went through a period when she was "petrified" of the Sovereign. She felt herself under scrutiny, and she was. There were several occasions before the wedding, she admits, when she cried. There were similar occasions afterward, and at one point the Queen had cause to wonder if Diana was going to "make it."

It is easy to say the Queen should have done more to help. But the Queen, by natural shyness and a lifetime's training, is no doting grandmother capable of giving tactile comfort and motherly love at the drop of a tear. And besides, the Royal Family has always held that you are either royal or you are not, and if Diana was going to "make it," as they put it so colloquially, she had to make it herself.

To everyone's delight and the Sovereign's particular pleasure, a marked warmth now characterizes the relationship between the Queen and the woman who will be a Queen herself one day.

Over time Diana came to realize her power and her position, and she began to feel more and more relaxed in the presence of her mother-in-law.

The Queen in turn is "delighted" with the way Diana has developed. The Princess of Wales still joins the Queen for lunch or tea or a light evening meal, though still "by appointment" only. (No one, not even the Prince of Wales, drops in on the Queen, a member of her household points out.) Such exigencies of royal life notwithstanding, however, the relationship is "first class."

There are moments of exception as there are in all families. But it was more in sadness than in anger that the Princess and her husband were summoned to Buckingham Palace in October 1987. It was the time of the Balmoral estrangement, and the estrangement was degenerating into royal crisis. Even the Royal Family, which lives most of its life cocooned in an ivory tower of indifference high above the speculations of the rabble, had come to realize that something had to be done to quench the bushfire of speculation and that only the Queen was in a position to do so.

Her Majesty does not like confrontation. In fact she detests it and goes out of her way to avoid it, as does her son. But eventually, after Diana had attended a fashion show and Charles had been to the opera, the Waleses left Kensington Palace and drove the few short miles across London to the Monarch's London HQ. Twenty minutes later they were on their way back home again.

It had been a terse exchange. But it had been at Charles and *not* Diana that the Queen's displeasure had been directed.

It is not easy to apportion blame when a relationship hits

the skids. As far as the Queen saw it, however, Charles was the one who had to take the larger share of responsibility for that altogether unseemly situation. Having been trained from birth to handle problems, Charles was clearly at fault.

"The Queen did not think Diana had done anything wrong," says a member of the household.

It is a measure that illustrates just how far Diana has come since her marriage and in what affection the Queen now holds her. She is no longer a newcomer. She is a fully integrated and immensely important member of the family and one whose side the Queen will take, even against her own son if the situation so warrants.

Perhaps more surprisingly, Diana is also on the best of terms with Princess Margaret. Bohemian but at the same time *very* royal, the Queen's sister can be somewhat tricky. If she wants to stay up until three o'clock in the morning leading a singsong from the piano, she does so—and everyone has to sing along with her until she grows tired. No one departs her royal presence until she retires herself. And that includes the servants. It even included the Queen's servants until, up at Sandringham one year, the Queen asked why her retainers were looking so tired. On being told that it was because they had been on duty almost till dawn, the Queen ruled that when she retired her staff could retire too. (Those houseguests without the necessary stamina for Margaret's all-night sessions now follow the servants' example and make a discreet bolt for the door when the Queen gets up to go to bed.)

Amusing and a splendid mimic, Margaret can also exercise her tongue to withering effect. She does not suffer fools or bores lightly, and many poor souls, talking on into tedium, have found themselves cut off in mid-sentence with the word "Quite," which she uses as incisively as a surgeon uses a scalpel.

Princess Margaret likes to be entertained—and she is not an easy woman to please. Yet she is very fond of Diana. She was most impressed when the Princess of Wales took the trouble to send her butler, whom she hardly knows, a handwritten note and a potted plant when he was hospitalized with jaundice in 1987.

Diana also makes the point of bringing her aunt-in-law small baskets of fresh raspberries she has picked herself on the Highgrove estate.

Margaret rarely entertains her royal relations, much preferring the company of actors and handsome property developers. The Waleses however, are an exception. They are regularly invited to walk across the courtyard at Kensington Palace from their own apartment to hers for a fine gourmet dinner, and in turn Princess Margaret will be asked back for a rather simpler repast of fish and fruit.

It is an easygoing, informal interplay between two disparate women, and Diana must take much of the credit for it.

The only time Princess Margaret really disapproved of anything Diana did was when she put her hair up in a classic chignon for the State Opening of Parliament in November 1984. She thought Diana upstaged the Queen and should have been sensible enough to realize what an uproar the new style would cause. Diana's former hairdresser, Kevin Shanley, who had refused to do the style and left it to his assistant, Richard Dalton, agrees "I knew it wouldn't suit her," he said. "Her hair wasn't long enough, but Diana got her own way— and at what a cost. That one hairstyle ruined everyone's fantasy of her."

Diana's relationship with her sister-in-law, the Princess Royal, is much more complex. On the face of it they have absolutely nothing in common. Anne can be brusque to the point of rudeness; Diana, if not the Shy Di of the tabloid headlines, is always trying to put people at their ease. Diana is very aware of how she looks. Anne doesn't care. Jeans and jumpers and artificial-fiber shirts are her preference, and more than one grand lady has been astonished by her chipped and unvarnished fingernails.

It is only on the most special of occasions and then only in the company of the most special of friends that she can be persuaded out of the country she loves and into a West End restaurant. Diana adores her girlie lunches in such fashionable London eateries as San Lorenzo and Launceston Place.

Anne had earned international respect for her work for the Save the Children Fund. Diana's work is simply to be the Princess of Wales—just being Diana is a job in itself.

There is also the eleven-year age gap. Anne was a fully formed woman secure in the role she had created for herself when she first met the gamboling filly who was destined to be her sister-in-law and, one day, her Queen.

"I am *not* Diana Spencer!" she shouted angrily at a photographer who tried to take her picture one day.

Inevitably, stories started to circulate in the salons of Belgravia and Chelsea that the two did not get on, that Anne regarded Diana with something approaching barely disguised contempt.

The notable absence of Anne and her husband, Mark Phillips, from the christening in 1984 of Prince Harry did not help matters. Buckingham Palace described it as unfortunate and explained that it was because of a "longstanding engagement that had been fixed far in advance."

The longstanding engagement turned out to be a rabbit shoot, organized by Mark Phillips's parents.

Diana did not feel it was necessary for Anne to be made a godparent. But she was nonetheless upset when Anne could not be bothered to attend the ceremony.

The situation is not quite as bad as it may appear, however, and recent months have seen a distinct improvement in their relationship. They could never be called best friends (BF, as Diana says). But friends they are.

In a television interview with Sir Alastair Burnet, Diana, in reference to the estrangement, acknowledged, "The story arose obviously as she wasn't chosen perhaps as a godmother for Harry, which, had our child been a girl, was a possibility. But Harry arrived, so we went to a man."

She emphasized, "Princess Anne has been working incredibly hard for the Save the Children Fund, and I am her biggest fan, because what she crams into a day I could never achieve. And we've hit it off very well, and I just think she's marvelous."

That is something of an overstatement. But Diana *is* to be heard loudly praising Anne's indefatigable work for the world's underprivileged children to her friends. And when Anne is abroad, which she so frequently is, Diana will drive the eight miles to Gatcombe Park to keep a surrogate mother's eye on little Peter and Zara Phillips or invite them over to Highgrove for tea. What strains there were have been alleviated as the two came to accept each other's finer points—a compromise all families make if "Dallas"-style feuds are to be avoided.

There were never any problems between Diana and Princess Margaret's daughter, Lady Sarah Armstrong-Jones. Ever since Sarah extended Diana the fateful invitation to the Royal Yacht *Britannia*, the two have been close friends. And in those early days, when Diana was still intimidated by the stuffy formality of royal dinners, they would slip away and take their supper together in the kitchens at Balmoral.

Of course, once she had overcome her initial insecurity, Diana's natural stubbornness quickly reasserted itself. She can fight her corner—and loudly. She remains reluctant to do what she doesn't feel like doing. She cheerfully admits that she is no intellectual athlete, but if she believes in something, however flimsy the foundations of her argument might be, it takes a considerable effort to change her mind.

These are traits that can be something of a handicap in her relations with her husband. As far as Prince Philip is concerned, they constitute a virtue.

The most outspoken member of the Royal Family, the Duke of Edinburgh, has spent his royal lifetime putting his foot neatly into his mouth just about every time he opens it—to the constant irritation of the politicians who serve his wife and the subjects she reigns over.

If he is angered, he will use expletives. If he is kept waiting, he will complain. When annoyed, he can display an unsavory disregard for the feelings of others.

At the Royal Windsor Horse Show one year, for example, he stood in line to receive his prize for four-in-hand driving, nodding and smiling to his fellow competitors. But the moment he returned to the sanctum of the Royal Box, he declared in a stage whisper that all the other prize winners were "such snobs." What had generated such royal opprobrium? Simply that the "snobs" had actually bothered to dress up to receive the medals they had worked so hard for, and therefore Philip had had to treat them with deference.

The Queen Mother does not get on with him and they regularly pass each other on the staircase without exchanging so much as a nod. The Queen's dresser, friend, and lifelong confidante, Margaret MacDonald, whom the Sovereign calls Bobo, has little time for him and has been known to walk out of a room when he walks in.

It is not surprising that at times relations between Philip and Charles have been fraught. It was the currency of the Palace servants' realm that Anne and not Charles was the child whom Philip most identified with and who most lived up to his expectations. They were right. Philip's strengths— and for all his failings they are still considerable—lie in action and practicality. He has little sympathy and less time for intellectual navel contemplation, and Charles's Laurens van der Post—inspired contemplation leaves him cold.

He was always insisting that his son could "do better"—at sport, at shouldering his share of royal responsibility (Philip is one of the hardest-working members of the Firm). And when he didn't, Philip was quite capable of reducing his son to tears with his invective.

"My father is very wise about how one should look at life," Charles has said. "As I got older I began to realize that he was probably worth listening to. Then again, sometimes I disagree. It happens, you know."

Those disagreements came to a head one day in an astonishing confrontation at Buckingham Palace. The two men were shouting at each other. Suddenly Charles rounded on his father and said, "Just you remember whom you are talking to. You are talking to the future King of England!"

He then turned on his heels and stormed out of the room—past a senior Palace advisor who had witnessed the whole incident through the open door.

This is where Diana comes into play. She is the peacemaker

and, during particularly fractious moments, the go-between. Her own father can be difficult. Her grandfather, the seventh Earl Spencer, was a real old grouch who would declare "I don't like people" and would greet unwelcome guests at the door of Althorp holding a shotgun. Diana is used to difficult older men and knows how to handle them.

Philip is extremely fond of her. He has a notorious eye for a pretty woman, especially one with blonde hair, and he was charmed by her femininity and, of course, by her stubbornness.

"The Duke of Edinburgh gets on much better with the Princess of Wales than he does with his own son," says a Palace advisor bluntly.

He also has a certain sympathy for the role marriage has forced on her. He sees in her situation a mirror of his own—an outsider marrying into the most difficult family in the world and then having to carve a niche for herself within the rigid confines of the royal protocol. And he approves of the way she has gone about that daunting task.

So too, naturally enough, does the Queen Mother. It was she, after all, who with the connivance of her friend, Diana's grandmother, Lady Fermoy, brought Diana together with Charles. An earl's daughter herself, the Queen Mother does love a good title and regards Diana as an eminently suitable consort for her favorite grandson. They speak frequently, and the Queen Mother is always delighted when Diana brings round her great-grandchildren for the royal ritual of afternoon tea, which, by Windsor family tradition, is always served at five o'clock.

It was the Queen Mother, rather than the Queen, who gave Diana some elementary advice when Diana was in training to be a princess. She had told her, over one of her many gin-and-vermouths that a princess does not display plunging décolletage, like the black silk taffeta dress Diana wore to a poetry reading at the Goldsmith Hall in the city of London in 1981.

It had been a daring declaration of her independence. But there are royal rules, and Diana has to adhere to them. She is now a member of the Family. That does have its advantages, of course. There are castles and limousines and servants and jewels beyond the dreams of a young girl who came into married life with just a necklace with a gold D hanging on it. But there are restrictions.

There is also sacrifice. Those who marry into the House of Windsor may gain a family, but they also lose one—their own.

Inexorably their lives become consumed by and taken over by the business of being royal. There are duties to perform and official engagements to attend and security to worry about. There is no longer time available to spend with the people one might want to spend time with, and the process is as poignant as it is inevitable.

The attitude of the Royal Family does not help soften the separation. They are *the* Family, close-knit, self-contained, secure in their position, and content in their own company. They are also isolated; as Charles warns, only members of the Royal Family can ever fully trust each other. There is little room in their self-sufficient round of holidays and high days for outsiders, and new in-laws remain always the out-laws.

It was little noticed at the time, but Diana's father, Earl Spencer, was not invited to attend the marriage in Westminster Cathedral of his daughter's brother-in-law, Prince Andrew, to his daughter's best friend, Sarah Ferguson. Nor were Mr. and Mrs. Peter Phillips, parents of Princess Anne's husband, Mark, and grandparents of the Queen's two eldest grandchildren.

After the Duke and Duchess of York had departed on their honeymoon, the Royal Family attended a supper party held by Lady Elizabeth Anson, the Queen's cousin, at Claridges to look at a video of the ceremony and eat smoked salmon and scrambled eggs.

Fergie's stepmother, Susan, attended. So did Fergie's sister, Jane, and her half-sister, Alex. Major Ronald Ferguson, Fergie's father, however, left as soon as he could.

"I took the young children home as soon as I could from the hotel, because I knew that the children had to get home, obviously—and secondly that night the village of Dummer were going to have a barbecue," the Major explains. "Having been in the village since 1939, and they having supported Sarah enormously throughout the entire wedding and had great fun, my place was in the village that night—not at Claridges hotel. That didn't go down terribly well with one or two people. But that's what I decided, so that's what I did. And I'm very glad I did because of the reaction from the Dummer village, who had no idea that I was coming. When I turned up, it made everything worthwhile. It was wonderful. They were amazed as they'd heard that there was a big party at Claridges, and they'd assumed that was where we were going to be."

It was where everyone assumed Major Ronald would be. But after an adult lifetime of royal service, Major Ferguson knows his place—and it was with the villagers at Dummer and not with the Royal Family.

This separation of families is not spoken about or defined. There are no written rules. It happens naturally. And it is not total.

Diana does see a lot of her sisters, particularly Jane. It would be hard not to—Jane's husband is Sir Robert Fellowes, the Queen's deputy private secretary, and with their three children they live almost next door to the Waleses in the royal housing estate better known as Kensington Palace.

Earl Spencer does not fare so well. An old man and infirm, one of his greatest pleasures is to see and play with his two grandsons. He does not see them as often as he would like. At Christmas, for instance, the Waleses follow the Queen's court, first to Windsor and then on to Sandringham for the New Year and January. Lord Spencer is not invited.

It makes the visits he does make to Highgrove all the more touching. One day William proudly showed him around Charles's farm—William excitedly running ahead, Spencer puffing along behind. They came to a five-bar gate.

"I can't open it, Grandpa, you've got to climb it; otherwise the animals will get out," William ordered.

And Earl Spencer did just that, remarking afterward, "William lectures me."

He always tries to make sure that Harry, so much quieter than his elder brother, is not left out and says, "They're basically very affectionate children who get on well together."

Sometimes they come to visit him at Althorp, where they race down the long elegant corridors in their pedal cars. But the visits are infrequent.

A courtier of the old school, Earl Spencer understands the all-embracing grip of royalty and says, "I'm just very happy that my daughter is happily married."

So he is. But that, unfortunately, does not make communication between the Earl and his daughter and her new family any easier.

In September of 1978, when Diana was seventeen years old, Lord Spencer suffered a severe stroke. He went into eight comas and very nearly died.

Diana and her sisters were grateful for the love and care Lady Spencer lavished on their father and her ironwilled determination to pull him through.

"Raine saved my life," he says simply. "Without Raine I wouldn't have lived to see Diana married, never mind walking up the aisle of St. Paul's. Raine sat with me for four solid months, holding my hand and even shouting at me that I wasn't going to die because she wouldn't let me."

The girls, however, were not so impressed with the way Raine had set about putting her imprint on stately Althorp, their family's home and their brother Charles's birthright.

Lady Spencer, a determined woman and a former member of the now defunct Greater London Council went through Althorp, where they moved after the death of the seventh earl, like a whirlwind.

On the Countess's instructions, eleven of the twelve Van Dycks were sold and replaced by a gushy chocolate box portrait in pink of Raine herself. The Old Master drawings and "quantities of rare, eighteenth century china, books, music, and furniture" were also dispersed.

In all it is estimated that some 300 irreplaceable works of art are now gone from the house since Raine's reign began. And not always at a price commensurate to their real value.

The Spencer sisters return to their
old school, West Heath, and pose
on the steps with former
headmistress, Miss Rudge. Left to
right: Lady Jane Fellowes, Miss
Rudge, the Princess of Wales and
Lady Sarah McCorquodale.

Diana's mother, the elegant
Frances Shand-Kydd, attending
Prince William's school play, with
Prince Charles in the foreground.

Diana's stepmother, Raine Spencer, holds tightly on to Earl Spencer's hand, in their gift shop at Althorp. The house is open to the public and they have a thriving business selling china and small luxury items to visiting American and Japanese tourists.

Diana's brother, Viscount Althorp, in his new role as a reporter for NBC, discussing tactics with Bo Derek and her husband, John Derek, at the Cannes Film Festival.

Sharing a joke with the Queen, during the Queen Mother's birthday celebrations at Clarence House.

A pensive Diana with Prince Philip as they watch a polo match.

The Duchess of York shielding Diana and Prince William from the typical British summer weather with a large umbrella. Polo matches are much more fun for Diana when she has Fergie for company and to lend a helping hand with the two boys.

Diana often invites her friends to the Royal Box at Ascot and here she is with Dave Ker making her way through the Royal Enclosure. Dave, who runs a successful art business and is happily married, hit the headlines when he danced with Diana at 'Bunter' Worcester's wedding ball; he was described as the mystery 'fat man'.

Kate Menzies, one of Diana's closest friends, enjoys an afternoon at Wimbledon with the Princess. A seat in the Royal Box is one way in which Diana can entertain her girlfriends without being harassed by the press.

One of Diana's former flatmates, Caroline Bartholomew, gives her friend a kiss on her wedding day in August 1982. Diana keeps in touch with all her former flatmates, but sees more of opera singer, Caroline, who lives in London with her husband William.

Diana at the wheel of the family Range Rover during a shooting party at Sandringham. Diana is careful never to be seen with a gun in her hand and although she has a very stylish shooting suit, restricts her activities to following the guns and transporting the ladies to the lunch, often held at one of the lodges on the Sandringham estate.

Horses are not Diana's favourite animals, but being a member of the British Royal Family means they are unavoidable. Here she makes friends with one of the polo ponies, while spending yet another afternoon watching Prince Charles play.

After a social day at Royal Ascot, Diana watches her husband play polo at Smith's Lawn, Windsor, from the bonnet of his Aston Martin. When she realized that photographers were getting more than their fair share of her shapely legs she quickly leapt off and Prince Charles teased her, claiming she had made a dent in his beloved car. She hadn't, of course, but went along with the joke.

A quick visit to Catherine Walker's shop, The Chelsea Design Company in London's Chelsea, is a far more interesting way to spend an afternoon. Diana's ever-present detective opens the door for the Princess as she emerges from the shop empty-handed, but happy.

Another pleasant way to vent her frustrations is on the tennis court, and Diana, looking very elegant in her short skirt and trainers, applauds the winners of a charity tennis match in aid of Birthright. Standing next to her is photographer Terence Donovan's attractive wife, Diana.

Before the tragic skiing accident which killed one of their friends, Major Hugh Lindsay, Sarah and Diana enjoy their annual visit to Klosters.

Nanny Ruth Wallace and Diana hold tightly on to the little Prince's hands as they arrive at a polo match. Bringing up the rear is detective Ken Wharf.

While on holiday at King Juan Carlos's summer palace in Majorca, Diana, the loving mother, helps Prince Harry put on his shoe.

Prince William emerges from his first day at nursery school with teacher Mrs Mynors. With him is his detective, who sits in the classroom with all the children.

Like mother, like son. Princess Diana and Prince William, in their matching blue coats, go to church.

Prince Harry emerging from his first day at Mrs Mynors' school. To foil the watching photographers he has constructed some home-made bins, out of toilet rolls!

Prince Charles plays his part in looking after the children and here he is on the banks of the River Dee in Scotland, watching them while they throw stones into the river.

The Princess Royal, the best rider in the Royal Family, loves taking the children out during the Sandringham holiday. Prince William looks quite confident on his little pony and is followed by his cousin, Anne's daughter, Zara Phillips.

Not quite so experienced a rider, Prince Harry feels safer when his mummy's holding his tiny pony's head.

Diana, who feels nervous on horseback, goes out riding with the Queen and Prince Edward during the long winter break at Sandringham.

Another bit of fun during the New Year's holiday at Sandringham is playing on the old fire-engine in the grounds. William, Harry and Peter Phillips try on the antique helmets for the benefit of the photographers, who promised if they had one picture they would leave the Queen and her family alone to enjoy their holiday.

Six months before she left her royal employers, Nanny Barbara Barnes, accompanied by detective Alan Peters, guides Prince William towards a waiting car.

For example, Andrea Sacchi's picture "Apollo Crowning the Musician Pasqualini," which had been purchased by the first earl in 1758, was sold in its original frame to Wildenstein's, the international art dealers, for £40,000. Wildenstein subsequently resold it to the Metropolitan Museum of Art in New York for $270,000.

The Earl Spencer defends his wife's actions. He insists; "We had to sell. We had no money, just a huge overdraft." The Countess says the 40,000 visitors Althorp generates a year has topped 400,000, "which is a pretty big jump from the 2,000 a year it was in my father-in-law's day."

That fact, however, has not placated her critics. In their damning catalogue of the Reign of Raine, Alexandra Artley and Thomas Dibdin wrote, "If it were not so tragic, what has happened at Althorp would be . . . high comedy." It explains why many people have come to regard Johnny Spencer's second wife as the Wicked Stepmother who sold the family silver.

This is not how the great families like to operate. It is a tenet of the British aristocracy that beautiful things like houses and paintings and furniture are held in trust for succeeding generations. The dispersals for which Raine is so largely held responsible cannot have helped her standing with the younger members of the Spencer family.

Nor can the remarks attributed to her. Regarding the future Queen, Raine is said to have remarked to a friend, "How can you have an intelligent conversation with someone who doesn't have a single 'O'-level?" "It's a crashing bore."

Prince Charles is, however, quite taken with his step-mother-in-law. Whatever her faults, she is intelligent and dynamic, which he finds appealing.

Diana does not. As Charles's late valet Stephen Barry recorded, "There is not a great deal of love lost between the Princess and her stepmother." And should Charles dwell too long in conversation with Raine, Diana will find an excuse to drag him away, and out of the house.

While Diana may have been born a Spencer, she is now a Windsor. With her two children and her husband, she has a new family now.

7
Homes

*A*s *they rounded the bend,* the house that was to be
Diana's future home came into view. The sand-
colored stone building, with its pillared porch and
tall windows, was a disappointment for the girl whose head
was full of fantasy and whose heart was hoping her dream
man would have a dream house.

That was eight years ago, and Highgrove, the nine-bed-
room Georgian house with 350 acres of land, had only
recently been purchased by the Duchy of Cornwall for Prince
Charles from Maurice Macmillan, son of Harold Macmillan, late Earl of Stockton, the former prime minister.

Inside, Diana's mood failed to improve. The house was
only partly decorated and furnished with all kinds of weird
and wonderful bits of furniture rescued from the basement of
Buckingham Palace, where Charles had stored the collected
booty from his many foreign trips.

Diana had been expecting, and hoping for, something a
little more impressive from the first home of the heir to the
Throne, but she didn't say anything. Her face remained
impassive as she went from half-furnished room to half-

furnished room. For the girl who divided her time between her father's stately home—Althorp House in Northampton-shire, one of the grandest houses in England, boasting a 115-foot gallery and acres of beautiful parkland—and a cozy, elegant flat near Earl's Court, Highgrove was a letdown. Her flat, part of a large block, 60 Colherne Court, was an impressive apartment for an eighteen-year-old to own. It had been purchased for £50,000 by her father with monies from a family trust. Situated on the ground floor of the Brompton Road entrance to the block, it has two large bedrooms, a sitting room, a bathroom and separate loo, and at the back a beautiful pine kitchen with a round table, perfect for the small dinner parties that Diana used to cohost with her flatmates.

For a girl whose home and family are her most cherished possessions, the disarray of Highgrove was an immediate challenge. During the solitary hours she spent waiting for Prince Charles to return from hunting in the early days of their courtship, she formulated plans and ideas for improving the house. Even if she would never be mistress of it, she hated the thought of Charles living there in discomfort. He, on the other hand, quite enjoyed what he called "camping" at High-grove and was perfectly happy sitting on the sofa in the sitting room over a plate of scrambled eggs thinking of ideas for the garden—which, he claims, was the reason he pur-chased the house in the first place.

"It was a challenge," he says, "to create something, and I did rather fall in love with it. The big cedar tree in the front and the walled garden finally made up my mind."

It was also near his sister. The Princess Royal's estate at Gatcombe Park is only eight miles away, set in the heart of the Gloucestershire countryside inhabited by his hunting cronies and close friends such as Andrew and Camilla Parker-Bowles. But, if Charles had had marriage on his mind when he first saw Highgrove, it is doubtful he would have bought it. Although it has four large reception rooms down-stairs, a large kitchen area and extensive staff quarters, nine bedrooms on the upper floors, and a nursery wing, it is small by royal standards. (For the Royal Family there is always security staff to be housed along with all the necessary domestics such as cooks and housekeepers.) But this was the house immediately available. And when Charles and Diana married, they made the decision to move in, at least until something larger caught their eye.

The Queen, who once joked that Highgrove "sounded like something in Wimbledon," would like her son and daughter-in-law to live closer to her at Windsor Castle so that she can see more of her grandchildren. But, for the present time, this seems unlikely. Seven years later they are still there. And Charles, through his Duchy of Cornwall estates, has spent considerable sums improving everything at Highgrove, from installing the elaborate security system of closed-circuit cameras that scan the grounds to planting a wildflower border down the front drive. Recently he has even improved the outside of the building. And five months' work, completed at the end of 1987, gave a splendid new look to the eighteenth-century mansion. Decorative Ionic columns have replaced the plain ones in front of the house, and a balustrade has been added to the roof. The front of the building now boasts a classical pediment—a low-pitched gable—with a round ornamental window in the center.

Charles was anxious to move in as soon as possible and dispatched his various staff to get the necessary furnishings to make the house habitable. His valet was sent scurrying to Heal's, a furniture store on Tottenham Court Road at the time, to buy beds. He didn't get anything too expensive, though; the Prince didn't quite know what interior design he wanted for the house and, being engaged, also wanted to wait for the wedding presents.

They were worth waiting for. At last Diana was able to have her dream kitchen (a German design), a swimming pool (from the estate workers at Althorp), wrought-iron gates from the village of Tetbury, and more china and glass than they knew what to do with.

Meanwhile, Diana was doing her best to sort out the interior of Highgrove and engaged the assistance of South

African designer Dudley Poplak. Diana's mother, Mrs. Shand Kydd, had used Poplak on both her London homes, and both she and Diana liked his attention to detail and traditional style. The soft pastel hues and country chintzes that dominate the color scheme at Highgrove today are the result of Poplak's influence.

Downstairs there are still the four reception rooms mentioned in the original estate agent's particulars. These include a comfortable sitting room for Diana where she can escape from the activities of the household, a large formal drawing room for entertaining, furnished with the most tasteful antiques, and a study for Prince Charles. The study is painted beige and has a matching sofa with scatter cushions. On the side tables are piles of magazines, books, and family photographs. There is also a dining room with a large table, which they use when they have guests. Dinners in the country are informal by royal standards. The staff waits on table, and the finest delicate dishes are prepared by the cook, but the men don't wear black tie, and as a rule the ladies wear simple dresses and low-heeled shoes. The conversation might be about the day's hunting or polo or sometimes, when Sir Laurens van der Post and his wife come to stay, takes on a more serious note.

The peach entrance hall of the house is wide with polished wood floors. It runs from the front door right to the back where French windows lead to the garden. There is a grand piano and a wide staircase leading up to the bedroom suites on the floor above. The staff quarters and the large kitchen area lead off the hallway, and an intricate pattern of back stairs joins them up with the nursery suite on the top floor, where the windows are barred to prevent any accidents like the one at Windsor Castle when Prince William unwittingly dangled his little brother out of the window "so he could have a better look."

Sometimes Andrew and Fergie come for the weekend, which brightens things up considerably for Diana, and while the men are swapping stories over the port Diana and Fergie will retire to the sitting room and have a good giggle (Sloane habits die hard). Diana finds Fergie's company exhilarating, and it gives her an excuse to have a good gossip without the ever-constant fear of having what she says repeated. These country dinners do not linger long into the night, and the assembled company are usually in bed by midnight at the latest. Charles sometimes works for a couple of hours in his study before retiring, but Diana has tried to dissuade him from this, explaining that he must have a break from his work or he will never be able to relax.

Weekends at Highgrove are relaxed affairs. When the Prince and Princess are alone, they rarely use the dining room, preferring to eat in Diana's sitting room in front of the television, though the folding table is always laid with a beautiful linen cloth and the best silver. In the early days of Highgrove life Diana spent a great deal of time watching television while Charles was out hunting or working on his papers, which go everywhere with him. "Wales works very hard," one of his cronies complained. "Those bloody papers even accompany him when he comes to stay for the weekend."

The Prince and Princess try to organize their life so that they can be at Highgrove from Friday afternoon, after William has been picked up from school, to Monday evening. Any staff from London who are on weekend duty leave Kensington Palace early, and butler Harold Brown, cook Mervyn Wycherly, one of the Princess's dressers, and a valet will travel together with the car piled with provisions. Sometimes Charles and Diana have a late engagement on Friday and will let some of the staff go ahead with the children. They will drive down with their bodyguards either late in the evening or early the following morning.

Charles hates London and is always keen to get out as quickly as possible. If he is playing polo in the summer or hunting in the winter, he will snatch an extra night in the country. Neither Charles or Diana will avail themselves of the red helicopters of the Queen's Flight unless they can combine the trip with an official engagement. Charles is reluctant to use any of the Queen's transport that is funded out of the civil list unless he has a thoroughly valid reason.

Princess Michael of Kent once pointed out to him that his life would be made a lot easier if he used helicopters instead of traveling by car. Charles thought for a minute and said, "But I can't do that; they are funded by public monies." "But," insisted the outspoken Princess, "haven't you thought about buying one yourself? You're easily rich enough." It seems Charles hadn't, and he continues to battle with the traffic on the motorways when he has private engagements.

The day at Highgrove starts a little later than at Kensington Palace, and if Diana wishes to take an early swim she asks the gardener, Dennis Brown, to remove the cover from the heated outdoor pool. She usually waits, however, until the family has had breakfast together, Charles buried in a copy of the *Times* while she attempts to bring some semblance of order to William and Harry's table manners. Both children are very well brought up and well mannered, but like many children their age they do get excited and insist on talking and trying to distract their father from his newspaper instead of eating. Perhaps the children also sense that reading the newspapers makes their father somewhat irritable.

Charles has been going through one of his periods of hostility toward the press, which is hardly surprising, as he says, "considering the amount of rubbish that is printed about my wife." Since 1986 he has had more than his fair share of criticism, and it annoys him that the quality newspapers have stooped to the levels of the tabloids. During a visit to Brixton he was forced to admit, "I don't believe much that I read in most newspapers. In fact I have great difficulty in reading them at all."

After breakfast, which is always something simple and healthy such as grapefruit, bran flakes, and toast or croissants with honey for Charles and Diana and cereal and milk for the children, Charles will often visit his farm, Broadfield, which the Queen loaned him the money to buy and where he practices organic farming methods and keeps a herd of dairy cows and sheep. Prince William loves to accompany his father on these visits and look at all the animals.

A few years ago it was the garden, not the farm, that

absorbed most of Prince Charles's time, but now the garden is almost completed. In June 1987 Charles invited members of the Worshipful Company of Gardeners, who had just elected him a Liveryman, to a tree-planting ceremony at Highgrove. It was a chance for him to show off to fellow enthusiasts his most prized possession and his favorite part of the whole thing—the walled garden.

Thigh-high grass filled with wildflowers interspersed with narrow-mown paths leads to the walled garden, a few hundred yards from the main house. It was once accessible only through a hole cut in the wall to get a tractor through, but now it is a masterful creation of fruits, flowers, and vegetables—designed by Charles himself with the help of a couple of gardeners.

The tranquility of the beautiful garden is the perfect atmosphere for Charles and Diana to escape to from the pressures of the royal existence. Charles has even been known to land a red helicopter of the Queen's Flight in an adjoining field during a busy working day—just for a couple of hours between engagements—to enable him to sit under the trees and work or do some weeding. "Very therapeutic, weeding," he claims, "and it's marvelous if you can do enough to see the effect."

"The thing I remember most about the garden," a visitor said, "was the beautiful scent and the way the paving in front of the French doors had little wildflowers growing in between the stones. It was done so beautifully, it all looked perfectly natural."

The garden is a paradise for the children. They have a pet rabbit who lives by the swimming pool, two little ponies who are stabled in the yard next to the main house, a climbing frame, a swing and a playhouse, and acres and acres of land to play in. Both William and Harry love meeting visitors and showing off their little ponies. Prince William is very polite and will come up and say, "Good morning," while Harry sits shyly in the background. One visitor who had parked her car in the stable yard was talking to William when he noticed she had a little puppy in her car. "Let me see the doggy," he said, squealing with delight, and rode up to the car where he took hold of the little puppy and held it close to his chest. As soon as the dog started to struggle he got bored and trotted off on his pony into the long grass. He then played hide-and-seek with Harry, who was not nearly at home on horseback and still needed the assistance of groom Marion Cox and the leading rein.

Beyond the walled garden and the stables are huge greenhouses filled with tropical flowers and scented plants for the house. These are out of bounds to William and Harry unless someone accompanies them. Charles knows the children would rather be in the swimming pool or picking runner beans than in his greenhouses, but if anyone shows an interest he will rush them off for a tour. He knows all the botanical names for the plants and is not shy about revealing his knowledge to fellow enthusiasts. Besides the visual beauty of the garden, the prince is keen to enhance the tranquility with suitably restful sounds such as running water and tinkling bells, sounds he loves.

During a trip to Italy he was entranced to see cows grazing with bells around their necks. He purchased some antique bells to try to simulate the effect and tied them round the necks of some of his cows. The experiment was not a success, as the cows were terrified of the noise. Diana is not so keen on the water, complaining it makes her want to go to the loo all the time.

"I have endless plans to do new things," Charles says. "Slight *folie de grandeur*—but I like to leave something better than I found it."

Many of the things in the garden have been gifts from friends. The Sultan of Oman presented them with a dovecote that stands at the far end of the main garden behind the back drive; musician Yehudi Menuhin presented them with a pond full of carp; and a woman's institute gave them an herb garden. Diana finds her husband's fascination with organic farming and old-fashioned gardening a trifle eccentric, and she heartily wishes he hadn't made the remark about talking to his plants during a "20/20" show in 1986.

Charles, for his part, couldn't care less. If people wish to make him out to be a weirdo, so be it. And during the visit by the Liverymen of the Worshipful Company of Gardeners, he tested them out for a reaction as he planted a young sapling. "I must give it a rub to wish it luck," he said, looking at the assembled company and adding wickedly, "I sit here talking to the plants."

An avenue of apple trees, a bank of shrubs and trees, and the wildflowers he has planted apparently have all benefited from a few words from the Prince of Wales. He has created a sanctuary for himself, his wife, and his children and for the variety of tiny wild creatures that choose to inhabit the peaceful setting of the Highgrove garden. When so much time and trouble has gone into a project, it is hardly surprising that Charles and Diana like to spend as much time as they can outdoors.

In the summer, meals are taken in the garden, weather permitting. Lunch is either a simple buffet of quiches, flans, salads and fruit-salad or a delicate offering of poached eggs in tartlets, cold salmon, and some of Charles's homemade soups followed by fresh apple pie, summer pudding, or homemade ice cream. Cheese and biscuits are offered at lunchtime, never in the evening.

Armand Hammer, head of Occidental Petroleum and the man whose financial contributions have kept Atlantic Colleges, one of Prince Charles's main interests, going, was frequently a guest at Highgrove with his wife, Frances. He describes a typical summer lunch with great relish: "Charles was tremendously proud of everything we ate. Fruit, vegetables, meat, dairy products had been grown or prepared in his gardens and on his farm. We ate on a table on the lawn, and Prince Charles was at his most informal and unregal.

"When we were about to leave, Prince Charles suddenly disappeared and returned to present us with several boxes of plump, sweet strawberries, which he had picked himself. He was more delighted to give us berries he had grown, and picked with his own hands, than if they had been jewels from the family vault."

Now that both the children are at school—William is at Wetherby in Pembridge Villas, and Harry is at Mrs. Mynors in nearby Chepstow Villas—Monday mornings are a time both Charles and Diana can have to themselves. Sundays are not a day of rest in the Wales household because from May to September Charles usually has a polo match at Windsor or Cowdray. More often than not Diana will accompany him, following in her own car with the children and nanny Ruth Wallace. Although she confesses "to enjoying polo," it does rather break up her weekends, and there is always the posse of photographers anxious to get photographs of her and the children in those offguard moments. Sometimes the match is held in aid of one of her charities, such as Birthright, and then it's another day's work for the Princess as she chats to the sponsors in the hospitality tent after the match, longing to get back to Highgrove and have a dip in the pool.

I have watched Diana at these polo matches on some hot Sundays and felt sorry for her, for, although Fergie is sometimes there to brighten things up, polo is not really a spectator sport unless it is at top level, and Diana would often rather be relaxing in the garden at home. As soon as she alights from her car, parked behind the pony lines, a crowd of photographers follows her to the Royal Box, running backward to get a good, informal picture. Depending on her mood, she either cooperates by smiling and posing for the picture or if she is feeling fed up, keeps her eyes downcast and hurries to the Royal Box as quickly as possible. Once there, it's another round of cocktail party conversation, and she will delight in any distraction.

During the 1987 Cartier International, for example, she was chatting to a paraplegic in the ambulance car when actor John Hurt sidled up to her and poked his head into the vehicle. Somewhat the worse for the excess of free drinks dispensed by Cartier, he struck up a conversation with the Princess, seemingly without realizing who she was. Diana was delighted. Not only does she love show business personalities, but the hilarity of the situation appealed to her. "Anything for a change of routine is fun," she tells people. "I love it when something unexpected happens." John Hurt's visit to the ambulance was certainly unexpected.

During the polo season Prince Charles will play at least a couple of times during the week as well as on weekends. During the week he leaves from Kensington Palace in his convertible blue Aston-Martin—he also has a new £80,000 model, a gift from the Amir of Bahrain—with his bodyguard in the back and one of his favorite operas blasting on the car stereo system. He has been criticized because polo seems to consume so much of his time, but his polo manager, Major Ronald Ferguson, father of the Duchess of York, springs to his defense.

"It's unfair criticism. He's like any other young person who is physically fit and who happens to enjoy a game. It doesn't mean that he cuts down on his public engagements. It means that he has more to do in one particular day than before. It's my job to see he gets the maximum number of matches in." The Major goes on to explain, "If he didn't play polo, he might want to play golf or tennis—he'd get into something. He'd never become a lump; he's not that sort of person."

When Charles hasn't got any sporting activities, he will work out to a routine of exercises devised by the Canadian Air Force. These take only a few minutes a day and gradually build up strength and stamina, the joy of them being that the Prince can do them anywhere, even in his cluttered study at Kensington Palace.

Kensington Palace, the London home of the Prince and Princess of Wales, is situated in an attractive part of central London between Kensington High Street and Bayswater Road and adjacent to Kensington Gardens. A field, convenient for helicopters, divides the rambling palace from a private road of embassies. You can walk up the private road but drive up only if you are going to one of the embassies or Kensington Palace.

Built nearly four hundred years ago of warm red brick, it was the home of William and Mary and the birthplace of Queen Victoria, and today it is a royal village—"the aunt heap," Charles once dubbed it, the home of no fewer than fourteen members of the Royal Family.

To gain access to any of these private apartments, the visitor has to pass a police sentry box where there are always two policemen on duty. They ask the visitor's name and, if the visitor is expected, surprisingly know his or hers. Then the security comes into full swing. A telephone call is made to the apartment that is the visitor's destination, and he or she is allowed to drive through. Closed-circuit television cameras monitor the visitor's route up the gravel drive, passing the Duke and Duchess of Gloucester's apartments on the right— they have a thirty-five-room apartment for themselves, their three children, and the Duke's mother, eighty-seven-year-old Princess Alice. A clocktower guards the entrance to 1A Clock Court where Princess Margaret now lives alone in the courtyard of the old stables, and then finally at the top north end are apartments 8 and 9, which belong to Charles and Diana. Their immediate neighbors are the Prince and Princess Michael of Kent, who live in apartment 10, and the Kents' cars share the partly walled courtyard with the Waleses and a police sentry box.

Because several intruders have been found within the enclave of Kensington Palace over the past year, security has been stepped up. Well-trained armed policemen sleep in the Waleses' apartments, so, in the unlikely event that an intruder gains access to the apartment, he would get no further.

Once the car is parked out of the way by the police sentry box (with the keys left inside in case the police want to move it) the visitor has the impression of being in a beautiful old village, complete with the old-fashioned gas street lamps of which Charles is so fond. In summer roses climb the walls of the courtyard, and in autumn the country smell of burning leaves hangs in the air. It is hard to believe one is only a few minutes' walk from the hustle and bustle of Kensington High Street.

Once inside the Waleses' three-story L-shaped apartment—having climbed two stone steps to the front door or, if unknown to the Prince and Princess, having entered via the side door under the stone arches at the back of the house—the visitor feels as if inside a country mansion. Vast oil paintings dominate the walls, and vases of flowers fill every available corner, including some very stylish dried flower arrangements, which Diana gets from Pulbrook & Gould. A sweeping staircase leads from the entrance hall to the rest of the house, the carpet is green with a gray Prince of Wales feathers motif. When Bob Geldof visited Prince Charles at Kensington Palace to discuss his Band Aid project, he noticed the carpet and typically remarked on it: "Don't think much of the carpet." Prince Charles, amusingly enough, agreed with him. "Yes, it is rather garish, isn't it ?" he replied.

As early as 1975 Prince Charles was given two apartments at the north end of the building by the Queen, to use as his London residence. The apartments in Kensington Palace belong to the Queen and are known as "grace and favor" (i.e., rent-free), but the occupants have to pay some of the upkeep, and the rates, since the apartments are in central London, are high.

Princess Margaret pays about £10,000 per annum for her apartment, her chauffeur's cottage, and a flat for her cook and butler. The others pay similar rates, depending on the size of the residence. Diana's sister, Lady Jane Fellowes, has a cottage in the complex with her husband, Sir Robert Fellowes. Sir William Heseltine, the Queen's private secretary, also has an apartment, as do the various staff members that the running of the palace necessitates. Those not so lucky are housed in apartments in Kennington, South London, part of the Duchy of Cornwall estate.

When they became engaged, Diana was anxious to get Charles out of his bachelor apartments in Buckingham Palace as soon as possible and employed the services of Dudley Poplak to supervise the interior design. She kept changing her mind as the building took shape and decided to have an extra bathroom in the master suite so that she and Charles would not trip over each other in the mornings. At one time moving both Charles's and Diana's offices into Kensington

Palace was considered, but there was no room, so for many years they commuted between Buckingham Palace and Kensington Palace, larger meetings involving both Charles and Diana being held in Kensington Palace.

Sadly, for the casual visitor and people involved in running the royal couple's various interests, those days are over. Diana found that the house was always full of strangers, so much so that she could hardly set foot out of her own suite of rooms without bumping into someone. So the Waleses moved their office and office staff into St. James's Palace, into the suite of rooms formally occupied by the Lord Chamberlain. Now the twice-yearly engagement meetings, lunches, and audiences with politicians and captains of industry are held there, where there is ample room for everyone and a dining room for official lunches.

So KP, as Diana calls it, is a home again. Charles still has his first-floor study, which is dominated by a large desk covered in a profusion of papers and pens and where he works late at night and early in the morning. Diana still has her sitting room with the wallpaper specially commissioned by Poplak to include the Prince of Wales feather motif, where she watches her favorite television programs and videos. Dress designers still visit her here, and it is her favorite room for the very small informal suppers she sometimes hosts. And, for larger gatherings, there is the dining room with a circular mahogany table that can seat sixteen and the beautiful drawing room that holds at least sixty people.

The drawing room, with its yellow wallpaper, marble fireplace, and collection of antiques and tapestries, has been the setting for occasions as diverse as a meeting with Indian prime minister Rajiv Ghandhi to the more recent party hosted by Charles and Diana for pop stars who had played at charity concerts in aid of the Prince's Trust, one of Charles's pet charities. The magnificent rug that covers most of the floor area was rolled back, and Diana persuaded some of the talented guests to play the grand broadwood piano. Elton John, who never needs any persuading to play at a party, gave a rendering of some of his hits, and even the shy Labi Siffre did a turn. Diana, who is a good player herself (her grand-mother, Lady Fermoy, was a concert pianist), was too shy to take part. She did, however, give a small recital during their 1988 visit to Australia when a wily old professor of music encouraged her to play a few bars of Rachmaninoff's Piano Concerto Number 2.

"All my side of the family are very music-oriented," Diana says, "and that's where I picked it up. I love it."

It was also in this room, under the large tapestry, that the Royal Couple gave their television interview to Sir Alastair Burnet—something that is unlikely ever to be repeated. Charles and Diana were disappointed with the results of the two separate films that were made and shown all over the world, and Charles found the television cameras, which followed them for a year, too intrusive.

The bedroom suite on the first floor is the most private area in the house. Here Charles and Diana have a large bedroom with a four-poster bed, brought from Charles's old quarters at Buckingham Palace, and a separate dressing room and bathroom each. Charles also has a uniform room where his valet, Ken Stronach, keeps his many uniforms and a brushing room where minor repairs are made. Diana's dressing room and bathroom are smart but functional with floor-length mirrors, antique chest-of-drawers, and, of course, the huge walk-in cupboards that house her wardrobe.

Above the bedroom is the nursery suite—William and Harry's little kingdom. There is a day nursery or playroom and a night nursery with bedrooms for the boys and a bathroom. All the furniture is scaled down, and the nursery is very smart with a beige and red carpet. Childlike drawings together with cowboy hats (souvenirs from foreign trips) decorate the walls, and Diana insists that all the toys be neatly stored away in cupboards or the bright red toy racks at the side of the room. Charles cares a great deal about the nursery and has fond memories of his at Buckingham Palace.

A few months before he met Diana, Charles was horrified to discover that Andrew had redecorated the wonderful old nursery with its open fire. "Why did you have to do that?" he exclaimed in horror. "Why not?" Andrew retorted. "You won't be needing it." As it happened, Andrew didn't need it either because shortly afterward Charles got married and moved out of his quarters, vacating them for Andrew. "Such a waste," Charles kept muttering.

Charles insists on dealing with the running of Kensington Palace, leaving Diana only to supervise meals or any redecoration. Charles communicates with his staff and neighbors by memo. Princess Michael, who lives next door, has been the recipient of many a short note, signed with a curt "C." Her outgoing nature was offended when he asked her to stop interfering with his staff—she had admonished then butler Alan Fisher for the bad language he had used in front of her two children—and Fisher went to Charles and complained. "Why doesn't she complain to me?" Charles said. She replied, "Why doesn't he pick up the telephone and complain to me if I have done something to upset him instead of sending a memo?" She added defiantly, "I didn't think it worth bothering the Prince of Wales with a minor complaint about his staff, but in future I will." The relationship between the two, never one of much respect since the time he told his then girlfriend, Anna Wallace, "not to curtsy to that woman," worsened when he entertained Robert Maxwell in the walled garden of his apartment. Maxwell's newspaper, *The Daily Mirror*, had been responsible for exposing the story that Princess Michael's father had been a member of the Nazi party, and caused her great distress. She couldn't understand why Charles, of all people, should choose to entertain the man right next door.

The truth of the matter was that Maxwell was presenting a large check to a charity parachute jump performed by the crack parachute team, The Red Devils, and Prince Charles, ever anxious to perform his Robin Hood act and extract money from the rich, had agreed that they could make the presentation in his garden. So Prince Michael's pleas on behalf of his wife, not to entertain Maxwell, fell on deaf ears.

Diana's relationship with the flamboyant Princess is much better. She has even persuaded Charles that Marie Christine is simply someone who says what she thinks and, therefore, rather refreshing to have about. In the early days things weren't quite so good however. One morning Princess Michael woke up to see a group of noisy schoolchildren outside her bedroom window. Horrified, as she had no idea how they got there or what they were doing, she telephoned the sentry at the gate to find out. Several more telephone calls ensued before she discovered that they were there specially to sing Diana "Happy Birthday" on her twenty-first. By the time Princess Michael had discovered this the word was about that she was complaining again, and even Princess Michael's attempts to put things right by sending Diana a present round by hand did little to improve relationships.

Prince Charles has a few other things that provoke his memos. He can't abide plumbing that gurgles in the night or overheated rooms. A member of his staff who turns up a radiator or the central heating will receive a curt note telling him or her to please leave the heating alone—signed "C." He also can't stand smoking and even has the ashtrays removed from his car. And woe betide anyone who should smoke in Kensington Palace. His staff says he can smell smoke "a mile off," and if he does so yet another memo is provoked.

It is probably Charles's dislike of cities that promotes his irritation when he is residing at Kensington Palace. "I am a countryman at heart," he says, and he can't wait to leave the confines of Kensington Palace for some peace and quiet in the countryside. Prince Charles has, however, found a new interest at Kensington Palace. He has played a crucial role in the drawing up of designs for a new £780,000 block in the Palace grounds to house his ever-increasing staff and will follow the construction through. He has insisted the design should be in harmony with the rest of the 300-year-old Christopher Wren original, and all the materials must be hand-made multistock bricks, green Cumberland slates, and stone sills. Each of the eight staff flats will have access to its own private garden, and there is a delightful clocktower in the center to harmonize with the one already there.

The Kensington Palace staff members, who are at present

housed on the nursery floor, where they have to be careful not to make too much noise as the Prince and Princess's bedroom is directly below, are naturally delighted. They will be able to smoke, drink, and make merry with their friends without fear of disturbing or being disturbed. It is also a bonus for their meager salaries—even butler Harold Brown has to make extra money by moonlighting at cocktail parties to supplement his wages, a practice not uncommon among royal staff. The Queen has often been confronted by one of her footmen at some grand house or other, which she doesn't mind at all. She likes to see a friendly face, and it usually means she will get better service!

Besides Highgrove, the Waleses have other country retreats. Tamarisk, a tiny house on the Scilly Isles, is one, and Craigowan, a five-bedroom house on the Balmoral estate is another. When the Queen Mother dies, they will probably inherit Royal Lodge at Windsor and Clarence House in the Mall, but naturally Charles can't even bear to think of such a thing, although he once remarked that he thought Clarence House would be "far too expensive to run."

Tamarisk belongs to the Duchy of Cornwall and is a tiny house with only two main bedrooms, overlooking the sea. As it is rather small for Charles, Diana, and their children, and the staff necessary to look after them, they hardly use it—although they did spend a few days there before William was born. Instead Charles lends it to various staff members, and every summer Freddie and Ella, Prince and Princess Michael of Kent's two children, spend a week there accompanied by their nanny.

Craigowan, the five-bedroom house on the Balmoral estate, does not belong to Prince Charles, but he still uses it for the odd weekend, and he and Diana spent the Scottish part of their honeymoon there, so it has fond memories. The younger members of the royal family, Andrew and Fergie and Prince Edward, have first call on it these days as it is far cozier than the draughty castle.

Nowadays, when Charles and Diana are in Scotland, they usually stay at the Queen Mother's house, Birkhall, which she has left to them in her will. Not long ago she had the entire kitchens redone, at no small cost. But the Queen Mother will spare no expense when it comes to her home comforts. Prince Charles adores his grandmother and throughout his life has turned to her when things have got difficult. He doesn't expect her to take sides—she won't, always sitting on the fence—but she offers a great comfort and solace. "She has seen everything before," he says.

In spite of the many houses available to them, Highgrove is the place that Charles and Diana consider their real home. Diana echoes that sentiment. "There's no place like Home," reads the cushion she embroidered.

8

Motherhood

In her effort to be a thoroughly modern mother, Diana has broken away from generations of royal tradition. When Buckingham Palace announced on November 5, 1981, that she was pregnant for the first time it was assumed the baby would be born within the privacy of a royal home—either Kensington Palace or Buckingham Palace.

There were good grounds for this supposition. Diana had not been born in a hospital, but at Park House and in the same bedroom as her mother, twenty-five years before. And Charles, Andrew, and Edward had all been born at Buckingham Palace, while Anne was born at Clarence House. In the late fifties and sixties it was not unusual for women to have babies at home, especially if they belonged to rich upper-class families where there were plenty of staff members to assist.

Diana had plenty of staff, but she also had a slavish devotion to the wisdom of her doctor, fifty-seven-year-old George Pinker, surgeon-gynecologist to the Queen. Pinker has a certain reputation as a high-tech doctor and draws the line at home deliveries even with someone like Diana, who was both young and healthy as the announcement that November morning confirmed.

"The Princess is in excellent health," it read. "Her doctor during the pregnancy will be Mr. George Pinker, surgeon-gynecologist to the Queen. The Princess hopes to continue to undertake some public engagements but regrets any disappointment which may be caused by any curtailment of her planned program. The baby will be second in line to the Throne."

It was the last line of the announcement that served as a reminder that this was no ordinary birth, and the Spencer family, the Royal Family, and especially the Queen assumed the baby would be born at home. But right from the start Diana knew this would never be the case. Highly nervous about the Queen's reaction to her plan, she implored Pinker to explain the situation to her mother-in-law.

Apart from the medical problems, she couldn't imagine anything worse than the prospect of having her baby in Buckingham Palace, with its ornate furniture and acres of red carpet, and Kensington Palace was not yet finished—they did not move in until May 17, 1982, almost a month before the birth. No, she would have her baby in St. Mary's Hospital, Paddington, where George Pinker kept his National Health patients and where his private patients had their babies on the fourth floor of the Lindo Wing. It was the first time an heir presumptive was to be born in a public hospital, albeit in the private sector.

On Sunday evening, June 20, 1982, former nurse and midwife Betty Parsons received a call from Diana.

"My contractions have begun," Diana said.

Betty Parsons, who was with the Queen when Prince Edward was born, has assisted almost every Duchess within the pages of *Debretts* with her philosophy of childbirth. She claims that there is no such thing as an unnatural birth and teaches relaxation by breathing, with different breathing for each stage of labor.

Diana knew what to expect. She had attended Betty's classes on relaxation and had her come to Kensington Palace regularly in the last month. Prince Charles, who had been devouring books on natural childbirth, was also a pupil of Betty's. He read her amusing guide, *The Expectant Father*, which told him to help and encourage his wife. She explained all the medical equipment that would be used to monitor the baby's heartbeat and Diana's contractions. And she answered a host of intelligent questions the Prince posed.

"I think it's a very good thing for a husband to be with a mother when she is expecting a baby," he had told well-wishers at the beginning of Diana's pregnancy. He had no intention of being left out now, and when Diana's contractions became more acute he leaped out of bed, helped her dress, and with a bodyguard in the back of his car drove her to St. Mary's.

They arrived at 5:00 A.M. Monday morning, entered through a side door, and took the lift to the top floor of the Lindo Wing. Everything was in readiness for the Princess. The adjacent three rooms had been cleared of any patients, a screen put up by Diana's room, which was at the end of a corridor at the back, and a private telephone line installed by her bed.

For a future Queen, the surroundings were not impressive.

Her room, with its metal hospital bed, small standing wardrobe, fridge, television, and wash basin, was functional rather than pretty. Although it is the largest in the maternity wing, it measures only about twelve feet by fourteen feet and would easily have fit into her dressing room at Kensington Palace. It has no private bathroom, but a screen was placed outside the door, and the shared bathroom opposite with its two baths and two loos was made exclusively available to Diana during her brief stay.

Diana didn't care. She hardly noticed the ugly floral wallpaper or the pink curtains with their tatty fringes. She knew she was in the best hands and in the best place to have her baby. Above all, she felt safe. She had total confidence in her doctor, the Welsh sister Delphine Stevens, who made her laugh when she rushed off down the corridor for a smoke, and the nursing sisters, Sister Kirwin and Sister Suarez. She also had Betty Parsons to help her with the contractions.

"Pick up your surfboard and ride it like a whale," Betty told her when she started the contractions and then, later on, "doggy, doggy, candle, candle" (pant, pant, blow, blow). Prince Charles was present throughout the day, holding her hand and whispering words of encouragement. After several hours Diana was given an epidural injection to relieve the pain. She had wanted to try to have the baby without an anesthetic but swiftly changed her mind when the pain became too intense.

Betty Parsons's opinion that there is no such thing as an unnatural childbirth was being given medical proof.

At 9:03 P.M. that Monday Diana delivered a son. He weighed seven pounds, one-and-a-half ounces, and had "a wisp of fair hair, sort of blondish, and blue eyes," beamed the proud father, Charles. Motherhood, for the Princess of Wales, had begun.

Diana had definite ideas on how any child of hers was to be raised, and she took charge right from the start. Determined to breast-feed her baby, she also vetoed the suggestion that he might be circumcised, although there is no official record of whether the procedure was done. The only record of that kind that exists is for Prince Charles, who was circumcised five days after he was born.

Diana also insisted, less than twenty four hours after the birth, she was ready to go home. Even for someone with as many staff members to help her as she had, this was somewhat unusual with a first child. After such a long labor her doctor knew what a big effort it would be for Diana to walk and move with ease. But Mr. Pinker made a statement to the effect that he was perfectly happy with the arrangement, concealing any doubts he might have had.

Charles was thrilled with his baby son. He was delighted with his wife. In the choice of godparents, however, tradition and Charles's wishes reigned. When William was christened in the Music Room at Buckingham Palace on the Queen Mother's eighty-second birthday, August 4, 1982, the only godparent Diana's age was the Duchess of Westminster, known as "Tally." A couple of years older then Diana, she had

married the Duke of Westminster, Britain's richest landowner, in 1978. Tally had a baby daughter, Lady Tamara, and
she and Diana had long telephone conversations about childbirth and the merits of breast-feeding. (Tally had also been a
pupil of Betty Parsons and had her baby in the Lindo Wing
under the care of George Pinker.) Today Diana confesses she
finds Tally "too grand" and prefers the company of her more
risqué friends, but six years ago Diana was new to the scene
and was pleased to have at least one of her contemporaries
represented. The other two female godparents, Princess Alexandra, a first cousin of the Queen and nicknamed "Pud" by
the Royal Family, and Lady Susan Hussey, one of the Queen's
senior ladies-in-waiting, were both close to Diana, Susan
Hussey having guided her through the royal ropes in those
lonely early days at Buckingham Palace and Princess Alexandra being the light relief at the many family gatherings. They
were, however, both much older than Diana. So was the most
surprising choice of all, author and philosopher Sir Laurens
van der Post, who was seventy-six at the time, a mere six years
younger than the Queen Mother. Sir Laurens comes from a
wealthy South African family and during the war survived
three years in a Japanese POW camp. He met Prince Charles
through the late Earl Mountbatten of Burma and has remained the Prince's friend and mentor since the Earl's untimely death in 1979 at the hand of the IRA bombers.
Charles has been greatly influenced by the ideas and exam-
ples of van der Post and later explained in an interview why he
had chosen him as a godparent.

"His thoughts and experiences mean a great deal to me,"
Charles said. "One of the reasons I asked him to be a godfather to my son was because he is one of the best storytellers
I have ever come across. I want my son to be able to sit at his
godfather's knee and listen to his wonderful stories. That's
really the best way to learn, through story telling. It was the
ancient way, through stories handed down from generation to
generation. We've lost the art today. All the mystery and
excitement, romance and imaginativeness have gone—mainly,
I think, because of television."

It wasn't Sir Laurens's stories that silenced William Arthur Philip Louis that day in the Music Room at Buckingham Palace, but the comfort of sucking his mother's finger. He cried noisily and resisted any attempts to stop him by the Queen, Charles, or either of the two other godparents, former King Constantine of Greece and Lord Mountbatten's grandson Lord Romsey, a Gordonstoun contemporary of Charles's. No, it was his mother's finger he wanted, and Diana, who hates the use of plastic pacifiers, provided it.

When Diana returned to Kensington Palace after the birth of William, she immediately put into practice all the things she had been taught, read, and done herself. She was used to children, having looked after her young brother Charles when he was a baby, helped with her two sisters' children, and, of course, had experience as a nursery school teacher.

One of the first things she had decided was that no child of hers was going to be reared by nannies, seeing his parents only for short periods during the day, as she had. Both she and Charles agreed that their firstborn must have "as normal a life as is possible," and they wanted their children brought up in a close family unit where the parents involved themselves with all aspects of bringing up baby, including changing diapers. Unlike in Diana's childhood, when the nursery was very much the nanny's domain, William's nanny was there merely to assist, not to take charge.

It was that very issue that brought on Diana and Charles's first disagreement about the upbringing of their son. Diana was terrified of employing one of the dyed-in-the-wool traditional royal nannies, who are used to having servants to cater for them, while their duties revolve solely around the care of the child. She wanted a modern, more progressive nanny whom she could control. Charles disagreed. He thought a royal nanny should know the royal ropes. He wanted to employ his old nanny, Mabel Anderson, who looked after him for most of his young life and to whom he was strongly attached.

Mabel Anderson along with another Scottish nanny, Helen Lightbody, joined the royal nurseries soon after Charles's christening. Helen had been nanny to the Duchess of Gloucester's two boys, William and Richard, and Mabel answered an advertisement in the "Situations Wanted" column of a nursing magazine only to discover to her amazement that her application was answered by Buckingham Palace.

Their nursery duties followed a regular pattern. They would wake the children (Charles and his sister Anne) at 7:00 A.M., dress them, and give them breakfast in the nursery. Then, at 9:00 A.M., Nanny Lightbody would take them downstairs to play with their mother for half an hour before taking them for their morning walk.

When the Queen and Prince Philip left on a six-month tour of the Commonwealth in 1953, the two Scottish nannies were left in sole charge of the two royal children. Naturally, they became closer to their nannies than their parents, and until she died in 1987 at the age of seventy-nine, Nanny Lightbody received regular visits from Charles at her grace-and-favor flat in Kennington. On the day of her funeral Charles sent a handwritten note on a wreath that read: "For Nana, in loving memory of early childhood—Charles."

Nanny Lightbody left royal service in 1956, and Mabel continued to look after all the Queen's children—Anne, Andrew, and Edward. In 1977 she went to Gatcombe Park, Anne's home, to take charge of her first child, Peter Phillips. But life at Gatcombe was nothing like the days at Buckingham Palace when Mabel had the nursery floor to herself. Although Mabel didn't wear a uniform—she stuck to a blue blouse and skirt, a white cardigan, and flat sensible shoes—she was in every respect the epitome of the traditional royal nanny. She had an assistant, a nursery maid, a chauffeur, and two nursery footmen and shared the duties of looking after the children with governess Miss Catherine Peebles, known to her young charges as "Mipsy." Unable to adapt to the informality of Gatcombe Park, Mabel eventually left to be replaced by a less formal nanny, Pat Moss.

No way, Diana thought, would she fit into any home of hers and firmly put her foot down. Mabel wasn't coming. Charles swallowed his disappointment. He had to. Diana would not have allowed him the "quiet life" he craves if he had insisted on Nanny Anderson.

Instead the job went to the daughter of a forestry worker,

forty-two-year-old Barbara Barnes, who found herself the first royal nanny to a probable heir not to have two footmen and two housemaids to help her. She did, however, have a nursery maid, Mrs. Olga Powell, an experienced nurse in her late fifties, to assist her and all the comforts of the nursery suite at Kensington Palace with its scaled-down furniture, open fireplace, and tasteful decoration, inspired by Dudley Poplak. (The Highgrove nursery is equally attractive, and Diana went to the trouble of having some characters out of nursery rhymes painted on the walls as a mural only to discover, to her horror, they looked far too frightening for children and so had them painted over again.)

Barbara Barnes, with her informal manner and no-nonsense approach, seemed just what Diana was looking for. She didn't wear a uniform, have any formal training, or regard the royal nursery as her private domain and herself as a mother substitute. Echoing the Princess's desires, she said, "I'm here to help the Princess, not take over." But her methods of bringing up children, which had so delighted her former employer, Lord Glenconner, husband of Princess Margaret's lady-in-waiting, Lady Glenconner, did not meet with quite the same enthusiasm from Prince Charles, who believes in "simple old-fashioned values for survival," not in the changing fashions in child rearing.

"There were some experts who were very certain about how you should bring up children," he says. "But then, after twenty years, they turned round and said they'd been wrong. Well, think of all the people who followed their suggestions!" One of those experts is Dr. Benjamin Spock, a distant relation of Diana's.

At the beginning, however, Charles was quite happy with the setup. Lord Glenconner's praise of Nanny Barnes seemed quite justified. "She has a natural way with children," Glenconner said. "She has a genius for bringing out the best in them. They are never bored. She has all the traditional values to the highest degree but is perfectly up-to-date."

She was also very careful not to interfere with Diana's upbringing of baby William. Nanny and mother did things together, such as walking in nearby Kensington Gardens or shopping for baby clothes (not that William needed anything, but Diana could never resist a shop).

Diana became so involved with the baby that she thought of little else. Her husband, as husbands often do in these circumstances, found that he was no longer the center of his wife's attention. But Charles, who Diana sometimes thought was "rather stuffy," took a delight in bathing his son and heir and helping change his nappies.

Diana was forever worrying about William's health and listened carefully to his breathing at night. "Is he all right, Baba?" she would say, looking anxiously down at his recumbent form in the crib. " Is he breathing properly?" Both Barbara and Prince Charles understood her natural anxiety and had friends who had suffered from the tragic occurrence of crib deaths—when the baby stops breathing and dies for no apparent reason.

It was not William's health that should have worried Diana at this time, but her own. She had lost a huge amount of weight very soon after the birth and seemed unable to get enthusiastic about anything. Charles was worried and consulted several expert doctors. They assured him she did not have anorexia, as her sister Sarah once had, but was suffering from a form of postnatal depression. She was thoroughly exhausted. Giving birth can be a huge strain on a woman's body, and it can take up to a year to return to normal, the doctors assured him. It was not the pressures of her own home or the baby that bothered her, Diana insisted, but the outside world. She had been under the microscope of public scrutiny for almost two years, and instead of letting up it appeared to be getting more intense.

Barbara Barnes suggested that she be allowed to take over more of the responsibilities of looking after William, but Diana was adamant. "A mother's arms are so much more comforting," she said. "He comes first . . . always."

He came first on the night Charles and Diana were both expected at the Annual Festival of Remembrance at the Royal Albert Hall, two minutes' drive from Kensington Palace.

Diana was exhausted from her sleepless nights and didn't want to go. Charles insisted, and they had a heated row. He finally arrived alone and flustered.

"Diana's not well," he told the rest of the family gathering. She wasn't; she was unhappy, fraught, and depressed.

"I'm exhausted," she told her then hairdresser, Kevin Shanley, "but how can I let people down?"

She decided she couldn't and finally went to the Albert Hall—arriving fifteen minutes late and after the Queen, which is against royal protocol. The royal party ignored the obvious coolness between the couple, and when they got home later that evening Charles decided that Diana needed a holiday, not at Balmoral or the Scilly Islands but somewhere abroad.

In January 1983 they had that long-awaited vacation, as guests of Prince Franz Joseph II of Liechtenstein in his castle perched high on the cliffs. It was not a success. There wasn't enough snow locally for skiing, so the royal couple were forced to travel to different venues every day and failed in their attempts to thwart the attendant press. Diana was miserable about leaving William, miserable about the weather, and thoroughly fed up with the photographers, so much so that she refused to pose for them.

"Please, darling, just one picture," Charles pleaded. She refused and was close to tears. It was the last thing she needed at this stage. Charles hoped that if Diana agreed to pose the photographers would leave them alone. They didn't.

It was a difficult time for Diana, but she had made her choice. She had married the Prince of Wales, and she had to put up with what went with that role. She would have to cope as well as she could.

It was for this reason the Queen agreed with Diana's suggestion that William accompany her and Charles on their six-week tour of Australia and New Zealand. The Queen felt, quite rightly, that Diana was close to the breaking point and that the presence of her baby, even if he was not with her the entire time, would have a stabilizing effect on the Princess, both mentally and physically. She also knew it would present the troubled couple in a happy light to the Australian people and help make their trip a success.

Diana had broken another royal tradition—never before had a member of the Royal Family undertaken an overseas tour with such a young child. But if Diana wanted something badly enough, she always got her own way—even with the Queen.

When they arrived in Australia, Nanny Barnes, complete with nappies, clothing, special food supplements, fluoride drops, and multivitamins for William, headed for their temporary home in the tiny town of Woomargama. Diana and Charles returned there every few days to break their trip and be with him. Apart from having his routine and sleeping pattern disturbed, William, the experts agreed, was far better off close to his mother than left at home in the Kensington Palace nursery.

The experiment was a success. But it was not to be repeated: when Charles and Diana went to Canada two months later, they left William behind—missing his first birthday. Diana didn't enjoy the trip nearly as much as the visit to Australia and claimed on her twenty-second birthday, ten days after William's, "My perfect birthday present is going home. I can't wait to see William."

It wasn't just Diana who missed William. So did Charles. Having devoured dozens of books on child rearing and baby care, he became an authority on the subject, which prompted Diana to remark in irritation, "Charles knows so much about babies, he can have the next one." But they both agreed all the attention they lavished on William was worth it. "Babies like being talked to," Diana said. She and Charles believe a baby left alone in his cot without lots of kisses and cuddles can become bored and may well turn out to be a slow developer, something William certainly wasn't. When he was just over a year old and Nanny Barnes had left him unattended for a few minutes in the Balmoral nursery, his natural curiosity got the better of him, and he pushed a button on the wall, unwittingly sending a direct signal to the police headquarters in Aberdeen, some fifty miles away. The police raced to

Balmoral and sealed off the grounds before it was discovered William was the culprit. A couple of months later he toddled through an infrared alarm beam in the walled garden of Kensington Palace and brought another couple dozen policemen to the scene. Nanny Barnes was highly embarrassed, and the Prince had to apologize to the amused policemen for his son's mobility.

"You couldn't take your eyes off him for a second," Diana's former hairdresser, Kevin Shanley, remembers. "He was into everything." Not only was William into everything, but he broke everything and developed the habit of flushing everything he could lay his hands on down the loo—including his toys and his father's shoes. Diana nicknamed him "her mini-tornado" and delighted in telling the people she met during her official duties little snippets about her son. She described, for instance, how Prince Charles encouraged William to get used to the bath by getting in the tub with him. One night when they were both due to go out for an important engagement, she couldn't find Charles anywhere. She discovered him in the bath with William.

"They were having a great time," she said. "There was soap and water everywhere."

9

Rearing the Royal Progeny

O   *ne of the most important* roles any woman could ever perform is to be a mother," Prince Charles says. Diana had fulfilled this role for her husband with great success, and when she discovered she was pregnant for the second time in January 1984 Charles was delighted. Just before the official announcement was made, Diana flew to Norway on her first official solo trip. She returned to a love note written by her husband, which read "We were so proud of you," and was signed with the nickname Charles gave to his son at the time, "Willie Wombat and I."

For whatever reasons of state Charles may have married, affection had now developed into something much stronger. The man whose position had ensured him center stage of his own universe had adjusted to having a wife and child to care for. He was enjoying the change in his routine and was taking pleasure in the new responsibilities.

Prince William was twenty months old, and Charles felt by the time the new baby was born he would be ready to accept the new addition to the family without jealousy. Diana was not quite so sure. William was used to being the center of attraction and had toddled into the limelight at the age of eighteen months in the garden of Kensington Palace to speak that time-honored word "Daddy." Six months later he was again in the walled garden, this time to celebrate his second birthday with an increased vocabulary. The media noted he weighed twenty-eight pounds and was three feet high. Diana noted he loved their attention and was fascinated by the lens of a television camera. Photographer John Scott remembers Charles at the same age. "He was precocious too," he says, "and when he was hardly three years old he could pronounce my Yugoslavian name, Colonel Voynovich, as well as if he'd been brought up in Belgrade."

Diana was worried William was developing too fast, but circumstances were overtaking her and her inquisitive, self-possessed little child. She hoped the new arrival would teach him to share not only his possessions but also his position at center stage.

Although Diana loved children and babies, being pregnant did not suit her. Again she suffered from morning sickness and complained of feeling rotten "since day one." She joked with friends about Charles's excitement and added, "If men had babies, they would only have one each."

During the long months of her pregnancy Diana did her best to remain cheerful. The only time she let her feelings show was when Prince Charles left on a two-week tour of Africa; photographs taken then show her looking thoroughly miserable. She was tired, William was still teething, and her nights were often disturbed by his cries. Nanny Barnes was experiencing problems as Diana still refused to allow her to do very much, but she hoped the arrival of the second child would allow her more control. From her very first trip without Prince Charles at her side, immediately before her pregnancy was announced on St. Valentine's Day, and right up to the birth, Diana continued with her public engagements, the last of which was, fittingly enough, to open the Birthright Centre at Kings College Hospital in London.

On Saturday morning, September 15, Diana's contractions began. This time she really knew what to expect. Her suitcase was already packed with a cotton nightgown, earplugs, lip salve, water spray, and all the other things Betty Parsons recommends expectant mothers take to hospital. Diana wanted everything done with as little fuss as possible. It was—almost. Outside the Lindo Wing the police had already erected the crash barriers to hold back the crowds, and inside the screens were up and the room next to Diana's had been converted into an office, complete with a telephone and lady-in-waiting in attendance. Positioned in the corridor outside Diana's room was one of her two personal bodyguards, who had been alerted that the Princess was on her way. At 7:30 A.M. Charles and Diana arrived and the hospital staff sprang into action.

At 4:20 P.M. on Saturday afternoon Diana gave birth to a second son. And when Prince Charles emerged from the hospital a couple of hours later, he told the waiting crowd, "My wife is very well. The delivery couldn't have been better. It was much quicker this time." It was, however, a full nine hours, and he admitted, "She's very tired. I reckoned it was time she was left alone to recuperate." He then added, "As for me, what I think I need is a celebration drink."

Throughout the nine-hour labor Charles had once again been at Diana's side. When she was thirsty, he gave her ice cubes to suck; when she needed comfort, he held her hand. He admitted he had fallen asleep briefly while waiting for the birth but said it was only a "little doze." Once again Diana was determined to leave the hospital as soon as possible, but first she insisted William must visit his baby brother to establish an all-important bond between the two children. Diana had already told friends that she wanted William to take a keen interest in the baby and would do everything to ensure that he was included in the celebrations. She did, and on Sunday morning William was driven to the hospital with Prince Charles and Nanny Barnes. There was so much excitement inside the hospital that Diana's bodyguard knocked over the screen outside her door with a resounding crash. A few seconds later William and Charles arrived in the lift and William ran down the corridor looking for Mummy. Diana heard the commotion and popped her head around her door, scooping William into her arms so she was holding him when he first saw his baby brother. Meanwhile, Nanny Barnes was waiting politely outside in the corridor, anxious that the family should be left alone, but after a couple of minutes Charles beckoned her in to see Harry before she took William back to Kensington Palace.

At 2:30 P.M. Diana left the hospital, less than twenty-four hours after the birth. This time she was prepared for the crowds that awaited her and had taken care with her hair and dressed in a smart red coat. Charles drove her back to Kensington Palace and then drove to Smith's Lawn polo ground in Windsor, where he had a friendly polo match organized to mark the big event. Sipping champagne, which he rarely ever touches, he held an impromptu party, using the back of a Land Rover as a makeshift bar. His polo-playing pals drank many toasts to the baby, already named Prince Henry Charles Albert David, to be known as Harry. Back at Kensington Palace Diana was sleeping, the tiny baby in the care of Sister Anne Wallace, who had looked after William for the first weeks of his life. She was happy, and above all William was delighted with his little brother.

Indeed William was so delighted with the baby that he wanted to play with him and hold him at every opportunity, and when Harry was christened in St. George's Chapel, Windsor, on December 21, he couldn't understand why he wasn't allowed to hold the baby as he had done during Lord Snowdon's photographic session some six weeks before. But the delicate christening robe, which had survived for 143 years, would have been shredded if William had got his hands on it, so Diana turned to Lord Snowdon, who was taking the official photographs, for help. Snowdon came up with the perfect solution to keep William in the picture and out of mischief—an antique bird cage, which held the excited little boy's attention just long enough for Snowdon and his assistant to shoot the pictures. His assistant remembers being surprised by the attention William was getting from the assembled godparents and the Royal Family. "Every time he did something naughty they roared with laughter. No one admonished him, and he was being a thorough pest."

His antics were, however, something of a relief to the Royal Family. Formal photographic sessions have a habit of being very stilted, and William provided the distraction they all needed. The christening celebration was televised and shown as part of the Queen's Christmas broadcast that year. Naturally enough, Prince William's antics, including chasing his cousin Zara Phillips round the legs of the Archbishop of Canterbury, stole the show. In one sequence Diana is shown explaining to young William how many generations of the Royal Family had worn the valuable christening gown. "Great-granny was christened in it," she said, causing Charles to give her one of his quizzical looks and add, "And I was christened in it." Diana had slipped up on her history, as Palace officials explained later: "Great-granny's husband was christened in it. Great-granny wasn't." Great-granny is the Queen Mother, who later married the Duke of York who became King George VI, and it was he who wore the robe as a baby.

By her own admission Diana is no scholar, and she often tells jokes against herself to explain her lack of knowledge. "I'm as thick as a plank," she once admitted to a group of youngsters, and on knocking her head when passing through a low doorway during a visit to Italy she quipped, "Don't worry—there's nothing in it." Empty-headed or not, she did have a little more say in the choice of godparents for Harry than she had for William. Her former flatmate, Carolyn Pride, married to brewery heir William Bartholomew who runs Juliana's discotheques, was one, and Lady Sarah Armstrong-Jones was another. Lady Cece Vestey, second wife of meat baron Lord Sam Vestey; Prince Andrew; artist Bryan Organ, whose informal portrait of Diana was vandalized in 1981; and Old Etonian farmer Gerald Ward completed the group. Her sister-in-law Princess Anne was not there. Her sister Lady Jane Fellowes was.

Jane was especially supportive. Her two older children, Laura and Alexander, are playmates of William and Harry,

who often walk down the drive with their bodyguard to have
tea at the Felloweses' house. Having three children of her
own and a husband who was in a senior position within the
royal household, Jane's proximity and sensible advice has
proved invaluable to Diana, who was already thinking of
possible schools for William. She considered having a governess, as she and Charles did at an early age. They both
agreed, however, it would be better for William if he were to
mix with ordinary children rather than remain in the hal-
lowed atmosphere of Kensington Palace with a few carefully
chosen playmates. The problem was brought home to Diana
when she started looking at nursery schools and visited the
school where she herself once taught, Young England Kindergarten in St. George's Square, Pimlico. While she was chatting with the headmistress, Prince William, never one to sit
on his laurels, joined in with the other children's game.
"Prince William couldn't do galloping horses," one of the
tiny pupils explained to her mother when she returned home.
"Why?"

Galloping horses is a simple child's game that involves
putting one foot in front of the other like a horse and
galloping round the room. William couldn't play it simply
because he had never mixed with any large numbers of
children in a classroom and didn't know the popular games.
Diana discussed the incident with Charles that evening and
convinced him, no matter what, William would benefit from
mixing with ordinary children of his own age. But what
school?

Young England, the Montessori-based kindergarten, re-
nowned for its wonderful school plays, was a bit too far away,
and all the children, ranging from two-and-a-half to five,
were taught in a large hall. After much deliberation and
discussion with her husband, her sister, and her girlfriends,
Diana found the solution: Mrs. Mynors school in nearby
Chepstow Villas, a quiet tree-lined street near London's
Notting Hill Gate. Several of Diana's friends had children
there, including Charles's newly appointed private secretary,
Sir John Riddell.

Remembering the fuss that had ensued when Prince Charles arrived at his first school, Hill School in Knightsbridge, twenty-eight years earlier, Charles and Diana composed a joint letter to be sent to all the Fleet Street editors. The letter politely requested that after the initial photo call William be left alone. Mrs. Mynors did her bit too and knocked on all her neighbors' doors to inform them the little Prince was coming to her school and to ask if they would be very kind and give him some privacy. She also spoke to the parents who had children at the £200-a-term kindergarten and explained that under no circumstances were any of them to speak to the press.

On a warm day in September 1985, 150 reporters and photographers, many of whom had set up their ladders hours earlier to ensure a good position, waited behind the crash barriers for the three-year-old Prince to arrive on his first day at school. William was used to cameras as he had been paraded in front of batteries of photographers on many occasions. But even for so sophisticated a youngster, the whir of the motordrives that sunny day was a bit much, and he seemed surprised. Diana confessed later that she had been far more nervous than William, who was terribly excited and longing to make some new playmates. To ensure he smiled for the cameras Diana let William choose what he wanted to wear—a pair of red shorts and a checked shirt. "It's best to let him do that if you want him to smile," she said, and he did.

Throughout his three short years, media attention had become commonplace to William, and during his time at Mrs. Mynors his classmates became as blasé as their rambunctious new friend and took little notice when banks of photographers stood outside while they rehearsed their school play.

"His classmates hardly know who he is," Mrs. Mynors commented. "Sadly that won't be the case at the next school he goes to." Mrs. Mynors was not entirely right, and Wills (one of William's nicknames) had discovered how a bit of pulling rank enabled him to get what he wanted. "My daddy can beat up your daddy," he is reputed to have said. "My daddy's a real Prince."

It was impossible to prevent a few tales of William's high-spirited behavior from filtering out of the classroom from time to time, and he was nicknamed "basher Wills." Some parents insisted these stories were untrue. "He's a charming little boy," said one, "and the most destructive thing he ever does is paint his face instead of the paper." Others claimed he was "rather a confused child, not unhappy, but increasingly aware he was in some way different from the others—something children hate."

This was the very thing Charles and Diana wanted to avoid. They insisted the policemen assigned to the Royal Protection Squad call William by his first name and make no reference to his title; the same rule applied to Mrs. Mynors and his classmates. If anything went wrong at school or if William misbehaved, Diana insisted she be informed immediately.

His bodyguard, always present in the classroom and as unobtrusive as possible, accompanied him to school and kept a watchful eye on his charge. If there were any tears or pushing in the playground, he soon sorted it out, gently but firmly. "Come on, William," he would say, "that's not a very nice way to behave." Both Charles and Diana insist that good manners are the most important aspect of their children's education. But any punishments doled out had to be administered by them, not by a bodyguard. They also insist that the bodyguards who watch over William and Harry should work on a rotating system to ensure that neither child becomes too attached to any one of them.

The Princess liked to deal with problems herself, however trivial, rather than letting Barbara Barnes dish out the discipline. Although both Barbara and Diana agreed that the nursery rule was no raised voices and no spanking unless absolutely necessary, Diana often took William or Harry's side against their nanny. "I'll always listen to both sides of an argument, then make my decision," she says, so each point of discipline was decided by a sort of committee. This often delayed any immediate action, and William had already forgotten what he had done wrong by the time the punishment was decided.

A few years ago at Highgrove William caused a major scare. One minute he was playing happily, and the next minute he was nowhere to be seen. Diana ran around the house shouting for him and instructed her bodyguards to search the garden, but to no avail. William was eventually discovered in the walk-in larder drinking from a large bottle of cherry pop, most of which had spilled all over him. Diana was so delighted to find her little rascal that instead of telling him off she grabbed the bottle and read the label. She was horrified to read the additive ingredients in the fizzy drink and requested the staff to remove all the carbonated drinks from the larder. She has always been a champion of additive-free food for her children, believing they can cause hyperactivity. Even when William was taken to Australia in 1983, the staff took along William's own provisions at Diana's insistence so that she could be sure his baby foods were additive-free.

By the time he was three William was well versed in the niceties of royal etiquette. He had mastered the Windsor wave, learned to shake hands and punctuate his conversation with plenty of pleases and thank-yous. But still Diana felt his public appearances should be kept to a minimum. Traditionally, royal offspring are trusted to behave themselves from an early age, but William's mounting indiscretions, harmless enough for any ordinary child, weighed heavily against him. She was forced to slap his bottom in public on more than one occasion, and when he crept into a policeman's car at Highgrove to play with the radio telephone, Diana was very annoyed, gave him a sharp spank, and made him apologize to the policeman for playing in his car while he was on duty. In 1986 he had his first of many outings to watch polo at Smith's Lawn, but from the moment he arrived he demanded attention. "Where's Papa? Can I have a drink? I want an ice cream." Diana, who had arrived alone, found William's whining impossible and was forced to bundle him into the

car and take him straight back to Windsor Castle and the
attentive arms of nanny.

William is better behaved now, and when he and Harry get
bored at the matches there are many other things to do—
feeding the ponies sugar lumps, playing doctors and nurses
in the ambulance car, treading in the divots (the lumps of
turf pulled up by the ponies' hooves) at halftime, and strok-
ing any one of the many dogs belonging to players and
spectators. At Smith's Lawn, in Windsor Great Park where
Charles plays most weeks, there is a wonderful character
called Ginger, whose duty it is to look after the Prince. He
enjoys looking after William and Harry too and, when nanny
isn't looking, will tempt them with sugar lumps and encourage them to stroke the ponies standing in the lines waiting to
play. William likes to go into the hospitality tent and help
himself to a plate of strawberries or raspberries, and then
both little boys will sit under the trees with their nanny and
tuck in.

If Diana sometimes finds handling an irrepressible toddler
as frustrating as other mothers do, she still takes pleasure in
doing the little things for them. Shopping for the children is
one such enjoyable task. In the early days she chose smocked
romper suits from the White House in Bond Street, and
William wore a frilly blouse that once belonged to Prince
Charles for a photo session with Lord Snowdon shortly after
Harry's birth. But these old-fashioned traditional children's
clothes are reserved for special occasions, and Diana likes to
see her young boys in practical, up-to-the-minute outfits.
Striped T-shirts by Jean Bourget from Harrods, sweatshirts
and corduroy trousers from Benetton 0–12, and Osh Kosh
dungarees form part of their wardrobe, and although Harry
has some of William's hand-me-downs, the two boys are
often dressed in identical outfits. For a photo session at
Sandringham in January 1988 they both wore their smart
pale blue coats, trimmed with white and fastened with
mother-of-pearl buttons. Diana had the same one copied for
her by Catherine Walker. It was one of her less inspired
fashion decisions: when she and William appeared in the his-
and-hers outfits one day, the world laughed.

Diana also patronizes fashionable children's boutiques such as Anthea Moore Ede's in Launceston Place, opposite one of her favorite restaurants, and is not averse to sending one of her staff into Marks and Spencer's children's department for an assortment of T-shirts and shorts.

In spite of the huge number of toys and other gifts presented to Diana for her children, she still loves to buy them—educational toys from the Early Learning Centre in Kensington High Street or something musical from Toddler Toys off Sloane Street. Then there are those special Christmas visits to Harrods toy department at 8:30 in the morning when Diana and the children have the whole store to themselves for half an hour. They enter by the side entrance in Hans Crescent, where they are greeted by the manager, who escorts them to the escalator, which takes them straight up to the toy department. William and Harry then spend half an hour of bliss running from one counter to another, squealing with delight. Diana ensures they have a hand in choosing gifts for their friends as well as deciding what they want themselves while she, with the ability of the seasoned shopper, selects toys for her sister's children and the other junior members of the Royal Family. Diana, unlike her husband, is very generous and gets great pleasure from choosing expensive presents to give to her family and friends. She is also very organized and admits, apart from last-minute purchases, "I do all my Christmas shopping in October."

Besides shopping for them and with them, Diana has always deemed it important to spend as much time as possible with her children, especially at bath- and bedtimes. Even if she was going to a film premiere or had an early-evening engagement, she would try to be the one to read them their bedtime story or sing nursery rhymes, rather than leaving it to their nanny or Charles. But try as she might to organize her day around the children, her official engagements prevented her from spending as much time with them as she wanted to. Some days she would leave early in the morning, return briefly in the late afternoon, only to have a bath, change, and go out again.

Charles had the same problem, but he was in a better

position to do as he wished, and it wasn't until his father, Prince Philip, pointed out he was neglecting his duties that Charles tore himself away from the nursery. Relationships between the two became very strained following the birth of Prince Harry, when Charles had just a dozen engagements in a four-month period and Prince Philip felt his son was not living up to his responsibilities. Philip made his feelings public by failing to visit Prince Harry until he was almost five weeks old.

Diana, who hates becoming embroiled in family rows between Charles and his father, kept in the background. Instead her irritation began to manifest itself against "Darling Baba."

In spite of rumors to the contrary, all of Diana's friends insist, "There is nothing pretentious about her. She is considerate, kind, and patient with everyone—especially her staff." But Diana has one overriding characteristic that she finds hard to control—jealousy.

It was in the summer of 1986, after the excitement of Sarah and Andrew's wedding—where William jiggled, fiddled, and was thoroughly entertaining as a sailor-suited page—that Nanny Barnes decided her role as the royal nanny was not working out as she had hoped. She was very fond of her little charges, especially William. But she was accustomed to living as one of the family, and after the initial excitement of living as the premier royal nanny she missed the more intimate atmosphere of a cozier environment. She decided working for the Prince and Princess of Wales was not a "forever" situation and she would wait for a suitable moment to leave.

In December 1986 she attended the birthday party for her former boss, Lord Glenconner, on the Caribbean island of Mustique, hobnobbing with the likes of Princess Margaret, Raquel Welch, and Jerry Hall. When Barbara Barnes's photograph was spotted among the group, people were intrigued. Why was Diana's nanny at this elite bash when she was supposed to be in charge of the heir to the heir? Diana asked herself the same question. She knew Barbara had been anxious to attend, but she didn't like the idea of a member of her staff—however close—socializing with her circle of friends.

Some would consider Diana's attitude a snobbish one, but she simply believed that this was not the order of things; she wasn't used to it. Her nannies would never have done such a thing. It would have been unthinkable for Mabel Anderson, Charles's old nanny, to mix with the "upstairs" set socially. Clearly having a "young, modern nanny" had its problems.

When Barbara returned to the calm of Kensington Palace with her West Indies tan, she was aware of a certain coolness between herself and her employers. William had completed fifteen months at his nursery school and was ready for his next step, pre-prep school, where he would remain until he was eight. It was, she thought, a good moment to give her notice. She could wait until her darling Wills started school and retreat quietly into the background. Harry would still have Olga Powell to look after him, and Barbara could stay on until a suitable replacement had been found.

Immediately after the New Year, when Diana returned to London from Sandringham, Barbara discussed the situation with her. They both agreed that William's first day at school, January 15, 1987, would be an ideal date to announce her impending departure.

"I thought no one would notice," Diana confessed later, "but I was wrong, wasn't I?" Just how wrong she had been was revealed the day after William's arrival at his new school. The front pages of most newspapers were devoted to Nanny Barnes and the inside pages to William's first day at Wetherby, his new school in Pembridge Square. Buckingham Palace refused to throw any light on the situation and merely stated that the move had been under discussion for ten days, Miss Barnes had no job to go to, and no replacement had been found.

No replacement had been found, but the feelers on the nanny network were already out, and the Waleses' staff at Buckingham Palace was preparing a list of possible applicants. Prince Charles, who hadn't joined Diana for William's first day at school because he was stuck in a blizzard at Sandringham, was not too concerned. He felt Wills needed more discipline, something he hoped Wetherby would provide quite effectively. One of the reasons Charles and Diana had chosen the £785-a-term school was that the headmistress, Frederika Blair Turner, who was educated at Diana's old prep school, Riddlesworth Hall, placed great emphasis on manners.

Diana and Charles had given William's future education a great deal of thought. "We're still learning the tricks of the trade," Diana admitted and, having drawn up a list of schools within a one-mile radius of Kensington Palace, narrowed the choice to less than half a dozen. It was not easy. Within a five-minute drive from the gates of Kensington Palace there were three excellent schools: Wetherby, Falkner House, and Norland Place. Security, of course, played a part in their considerations. William had to be driven to school every day accompanied by a bodyguard and a backup car in case anything went wrong. Police also had to be positioned outside the school, so the nearer he was to home, the easier it was for the Royal Protection Squad to do its job properly. This was something the Queen was most anxious for Charles and Diana to take into account.

"We're open-minded about William and his education," Charles said. "I would like to try and bring up our children to be well mannered, to think of other people, to put themselves in other people's positions. That way, even if they turn out not to be very bright or very qualified, at least if they have reasonable manners they will get so much further in life than if they did not have any at all." Wetherby, with its 120 boy pupils ranging from four-and-a-half to nine, and its smart gray uniform with red trim (available only from Harrods), fit the bill perfectly.

Lord Freddie Windsor, the son of Prince and Princess Michael of Kent, had been there and been extremely happy. He had sung in the choir, done well in exams, and above all, according to other mothers, "had the most perfect manners." More important to Charles than Princess Michael's son was that the nephews of his close friend, Andrew Parker-Bowles, Luke and Sam, had also been educated at Wetherby. Parker-Bowles was full of praise for the school, its educational merits, and its headmistress, Miss Blair Turner.

Most of the parents are affluent, upper-crust, and live locally, returning to their country houses on Friday afternoons when school finishes at lunchtime. William would not feel out of place in such company, although his Monday essays on what he did at the weekend would make far more interesting reading than those of the other boys.

When William arrived at Wetherby on a snowy January morning in 1987, he was greeted on the steps by Miss Blair Turner. Six feet tall and dressed entirely in blue with her long fair hair in a plait, she looked more like a Nordic figurehead than a schoolmistress, and it was all Diana could do to suppress her giggles. She told friends later that she had wanted to die laughing but wouldn't have dared to do so in front of William and so many members of the press. On his first day William left before lunch, but a staff member confirmed "he had fitted in immediately," with his former mistress, Miss Jane Ritchie, and his twenty classmates.

Diana, who had several official engagements to fulfill that day, told some old folks she was visiting in Islington she had no trouble packing William off to school and thought he looked sweet in his school uniform. She also admitted proudly her son was developing into a perfect little gentleman. "He's already opening doors for ladies," she said, "and he's calling men 'sir.' "

Barbara Barnes publicly agreed. She felt she was leaving behind a young prince who, as she says, "is a perfect little gentleman."

Bob Geldof was not so enthusiastic. When the disheveled Irishman called at Kensington Palace to discuss the famine problems in Africa with Charles, he was met by father and son.

"Why do you talk to that man?" William inquired, pointing at Geldof, attired as usual in jeans and sneakers, his face covered by his regulation designer stubble.

"Because we have work to do," Prince Charles replied.

"He's all dirty," William insisted. "He's got scruffy hair and wet shoes."

Geldof, true to form, retorted, "Shut up, you horrible little boy. Your hair's scruffy too."

To which the cheeky William replied, "No it's not. My mummy brushed it."

Mummy looked set to do her fair share of hair brushing, for finding a replacement for Barbara Barnes, who had left in February, was proving a problem. Several applicants were interviewed, but there was always something wrong. One girl was on the point of accepting the job, but when she was questioned about her religious beliefs she admitted she was a Roman Catholic. A polite letter arrived from Buckingham Palace informing her that her application had been unsuccessful. "I never thought about religion," she told her current employer, who had been aware of the secret interviews that had taken place. "How could a man who is one day going to be head of the Church of England employ a Catholic nanny?" her employer told her. "Of course you wouldn't get the job."

There were no such problems for forty-year-old Ruth Wallace, who finally took the sought-after job. She was working for Princess Michael of Kent on a freelance basis, looking after her two children, Lord Frederick and Lady Gabriella Windsor, and had often come across William and Harry within the confines of Kensington Palace. She had also spent some time working for William's godfather, King Constantine of Greece, a relative of the Royal Family who lives in exile in London. Ruth, a state-registered nurse trained at St. Bartholomew's Hospital in central London, was experienced with children and had worked as a freelance nanny since 1980.

On March 2, 1987, she started her new job, assisted by sixty-year-old Olga Powell, who was happy to teach her the ropes. Princess Michael, her former employer and next-door neighbor, was not quite so happy. This time Princess Michael decided there was no point in making a fuss. She was upset, but felt Diana needed all the support she could get, and anything she said would do little to change the situation. "Ruth is highly competent," she said, "and who can blame her for wanting to work for the Princess of Wales?"

It wasn't all work, as Ruth Wallace discovered. She had very comfortable quarters on the top floor of Kensington Palace, the use of a car, a chauffeur, and the invaluable assistance of Olga Powell, with whom she would share weekend duties so both had some time off. Before she accepted the job she had a long talk with the Prince and Princess on how they wanted and expected their children to behave.

The practical experience of parenthood was changing the Waleses' views. They all agreed the parents have the final say when it comes to discipline, but her new employers assured Ruth they weren't averse to her slapping the children if necessary. Charles reiterated his desire for them to be kept out of the public eye as much as possible and explained that from now on they would all travel separately. This was not practical when they were flying to Mallorca for their annual summer visit to King Juan Carlos's palace outside Palma but was a rule of thumb when going to Balmoral. Television was to be limited to certain programs, and above all, Charles explained, Ruth must be discreet.

"They're normal little boys," Charles said, "who are unlucky enough to create an abnormal amount of attention."

According to child psychologists, Prince Charles is quite correct. "Prince William appears to be going through a phase common in four- to five-year-olds. Their intelligence is developing rapidly at this age, and they need a lot of stimulation. Going to school full-time usually sorts them out. It occupies their growing mental and physical energies."

Going to school full-time certainly occupies a great deal of William's energy. Besides his ordinary lessons he takes weekly "Fun with Music" lessons at a cost of £50 per term. Every Wednesday he attends classes in a North London church hall, where teacher Ann Rachlin spins stories round classical music. And when he's not taking extra lessons, playing football, or swimming, he attends numerous children's tea parties, accompanied inevitably by nanny and his bodyguard. It was during one of these parties he was reputed to have thrown his food on the floor, screaming he hated the sandwiches, jelly, and ice cream on offer. When one of the other nannies made him clear up the mess, he shouted: "When I'm King I'm going to send my knights round to kill you!"

Tears of rage and frustration are natural in children William's age, as is liking to get one's own way. And whatever Charles and Diana may wish, it would be impossible for him to be completely unaware of who he is. Both Ruth and Olga are sensitive to this situation and try to deal out the discipline fairly, remembering the little boys are at a great disadvantage. Anything they do is newsworthy, and anything they say can be misquoted. Charles and Diana were particularly upset to hear of reports that William had been bossing around the guardsmen at Balmoral during the summer holiday of 1987 and decided he should not attend the annual Highland Games at Braemar. Only a few weeks earlier William had encouraged Harry to join in his pranks, and they hid in a horsebox at Highgrove. As the box was being driven out of the stable yard, taking one of Charles's horses to trainer Nick Gaselee's Lambourn stables, it was stopped and the two little Princes were discovered giggling in the back. Again Diana gave them a stern ticking off, for fear they might do it again and not be discovered.

Prince Harry, like many younger brothers, is an altogether gentler character than William. "Number two skates in quite nicely," Prince Charles said, and he did. In September 1987 he followed in William's footsteps and started school at Mrs. Mynors kindergarten. On his first day he was accompanied by his brother, who was not due to return to school until a couple of days later. William was only too keen to show him his old classroom and almost ignored the photographers in his haste to drag Harry down the basement steps.

The day before, Harry had celebrated his third birthday with a visit to London Zoo in Regent's Park, and he couldn't wait to tell his classmates about all the animals he had seen. Diana cut short an official engagement opening a dairy to dash back to Kensington Palace to meet her son when he returned shortly after midday.

"I was upset about leaving Harry," she said. "But now I'm going to meet him I can't wait."

Harry, shy in front of the assembled photographers, covered his face with a homemade pair of binoculars as he left the school just before lunch. He had enjoyed his morning and been far less upset than his parents. Prince Charles admitted it had been a wrench to leave their gentle youngest son behind. "It made me feel very sad," he said. "I had a big lump in my throat when we left Harry."

Leaving children behind is part of royal life, and Diana and Charles are accustomed to missing small milestones in their children's lives. They do, though, try to be around for Sports Day; Diana and Charles attended William's at the end of June 1987 and won the mother's 200-yard race. They also had front-row seats at Christmas to watch Wills perform as the little drummer boy in St. Mary Abbots Church, Kensington. Not to be outdone, Prince Harry took the part of a goblin in his Christmas play. And unlike his brother, who burst into tears when he saw his parents in the audience when he was at Mrs. Mynors, he acted his part well. Harry was so excited before the performance he couldn't resist sticking his tongue out at waiting cameramen.

Harry's first few terms at Mrs. Mynors elite nursery school proved he was quite a different character from William. He hid shyly at break time and refused to join in the playground games that his elder brother had so often instigated. At first he was embarrassed about using the two toilets and wouldn't put his hand up to be "excused," and he felt overshadowed by the ever-present competition with his brother. Psychologists explain this is quite normal with a younger child, who is dominated by an elder brother. In order to avoid failure the child tries not to do anything at all. But eventually Harry settled in and wasn't always longing to go home at the end of the morning.

Diana paid particular attention to Harry and tried to have lunch with him whenever she could, rushing back from her engagements in time for a plate of spaghetti or fish fingers in the nursery. On weekends she accompanied groom Marion Cox when she gave the two boys riding lessons on their little ponies, taking the leading rein of Harry's pony while William rushed on ahead. Harry's love of animals had encouraged his parents to give him a pony, and by the age of almost four he was competent enough to do without the leading rein. When Charles played polo and the boys came to watch, he showed Harry how to feed the ponies sugar by holding the lump in the flattened palm of his hand.

Diana and Charles's fervent wish for their children to have

as normal an upbringing as possible has not been entirely
unsuccessful. During the children's school holidays their
activities are planned carefully to be as diverse as possible.
They make unexpected trips to a North London play group,
where they mix with children from working families, as well
as their normal visits to the Queen at Balmoral, Sandringham, or Windsor and their annual summer holiday to Mallorca to stay with the King of Spain. They have plenty of
friends, as Diana explains:

"I have two sisters who have five children between them
and have lots of friends who have children." Since both boys
started school, Diana's circle has widened to include the
mothers of those children whom William and Harry have
befriended. Flicky Pleydell-Bouverie, whose son Nicholas was
a pal of William's at Mrs. Mynors and is following him to
Wetherby, is one such person. Flicky is over ten years older
than Diana, but the Princess sometimes used to pop into her
Holland Park house to collect William after tea. Diana's
friendly disposition endears her to everyone she meets, and
they are very protective of her and the children.

"The things you read about William being badly behaved
are simply not true," one young mother says. "He's a charming little boy with an inquisitive nature and the natural
boundless energy of any child his age."

"He's just like me," Diana says, but Buckingham Palace
staff find him more reminiscent of his uncle Andrew. Andrew was so naughty and cheeky he drove staff to distraction,
and they sometimes belted him when no one was looking.
His pranks were also well documented. He tied the laces of
the guardsmen together, poured bubblebath into the swimming pool, and teased the corgis (William got a walloping
from Nanny Wallace for teasing the gun dogs at Sandringham last November). Harry could also be compared to Edward as a child. He was quieter than his older brother and far
better behaved.

Norman Myers, who as Uncle Myers and his assistant,
Monty the monkey, have entertained two generations of royal
children, agrees: "William's like Andrew, extrovert and a bit

cheeky. But a happy person and utterly delightful. Harry's more like Edward, more shy and introverted."

At children's parties Myers leads his young charges through Pass the Parcel and Simon Says and games of musical bumps (the winner is whoever sits down on the floor fastest when the music stops). "William and Harry don't get singled out for special treatment," he says. "They love all the same sort of things as other kids." And they were always, he insisted, on good behavior.

However well they might behave at parties, there are occasions when, as Diana has remarked, they appear to have "grown into a couple of little thugs." And they can be exhausting. But still she tries to make sure they come first, as much as her work and other responsibilities allow. When they are unwell they climb into her bed, not nanny's, and although she may not be able to sleep, that is the way she wants it. If she has another child, which she most likely will, she very much wants a girl.

"I don't think I'd like to have three boys," she said, "but I'd love a girl." Even Diana cannot control nature, but at a party in early 1988 she told a friend who has two girls, "If I have another son and you have another daughter, we'll swap."

10

A Day in the Working
Life of a Princess

T *here is a routine* to the life of the Prince and Princess
of Wales. It is the routine of rush. It is a lifestyle very
different from that enjoyed by their royal predeces-
sors, whose lives were very much their own, to be enjoyed in
their own way, simply or extravagantly, but always self-indul-
gently. The role of the Royal Family has changed. Today there
is work to do. Life, as Charles says, is a job. And their job is
the life royalty imposes.

Says John Merton, the society artist who painted a portrait
of Diana in triplicate; "I saw her engagement book, which is
a terrifying thing. Every hour of the day is booked up for
nine months ahead." Diana's engagement book is not really a
book but a series of neatly printed pages in an embossed
folder, one day to a page and one line for every hour. These
are neatly filled in by her lady-in-waiting—appointments
every fifteen to twenty minutes and a strict timetable for
official engagements. Evenings and weekends are also inked
in with a line through the page to denote holidays.

John Merton and other portrait painters are allotted a
certain number of sittings. He had five, one at Kensington

Palace and four more at his studio near Marlborough in Wiltshire. Otherwise they work from photographs, and plenty of those are available.

Diana's schedule takes careful organization and rules out too many of the impromptu gatherings of which the Princess is so fond. "Imagine having to go to a wedding every day of your life—as the bride. Well, that's a bit what it's like," Diana confides.

Because her day is so full, she has to start early. The routine rush begins when butler Harold Brown knocks on the bedroom door, never later than 7:30 A.M. bearing a tray of weak coffee for Diana and Lapsang Suchong tea for Charles—he never touches coffee or sugar, preferring to sweeten his drinks with large spoonfuls of honey, which he takes with him everywhere. The breakfast china has a delicate pattern of butterflies and that typifies the taste of the Princess, who loves pretty, feminine things.

If her schedule allows, Diana then dons a tracksuit and heads for her early morning swim at Buckingham Palace. Her detective is already waiting in the car with the engine running, and they make the short drive to Buckingham Palace in record time, avoiding all the rush-hour traffic. If Diana has an early engagement or one of the children is unwell, she sacrifices the dip and does a few stretching exercises before sitting down to a frugal breakfast of pink grapefruit, müesli, and a piece of toast while glancing through the *Daily Mail* and the *Daily Express* gossip columns to see what her friends have been up to. She avoids reading stories about herself as she finds them too upsetting. But she knows what is being said: either her postbag of letters or her friends will tell her.

"If anyone mentions that story to me again, I will go mad," she said referring to her fit of giggles at the Sovereign's Parade at the Royal Military Academy at Sandhurst, where she represented the Queen. When she met the journalist responsible for the "giggling" part of the story, the *Daily Mirror*'s James Whitaker, she told him she had a bone to pick with him. Whitaker, who invented the job of royal watcher and followed Diana's romance with Charles right from the start, was concerned. He hated the idea of being blamed personally by the Princess for upsetting her. She then informed him she had not read his report but had received dozens of letters referring to his story in the *Daily Mirror*, so she knew he was to blame. Their conversation was very good-natured, and Whitaker questioned her as to why she had giggled in the first place—as a Princess, he observed, she should be used to such things.

"I was nervous, and when I'm nervous I always giggle," Diana said and then added endearingly, "There were so many princes and princesses there." There were two kings, four princes, and eight princesses—from the Jordanian, Greek, and Danish royal families. "It made me even more scared."

Diana's nerves are a real hazard when it comes to speech making, and she revealed that her "rude" royal relatives often tease her about her faltering attempts. Her own family members are her worst critics. Yet she still hasn't learned to adjust her voice tones, and her delivery sounds rather flat as she reads from her notes. In January 1987 she gave her first interview ever to Independent Radio News's court correspondent Dickie Arbiter. It was during a particularly harsh cold snap, and the Princess was visiting the headquarters of Help the Aged, of which she is patron, to see if there was anything she could do to help their plight. Dickie, an experienced interviewer, requested a few words with the Princess and much to his surprise and delight was invited to Buckingham Palace later in the afternoon to talk to her. He immediately put her at her ease and assured he was going to ask her only a few simple questions, but as soon as the tape was turned on she tensed up and her answers came back in the emotionless voice she adopts when nervous:

"I certainly feel that since I've come into public life I perhaps need a little more guidance," Diana said. "I know that my grandmother has got all the answers, purely because she's been through some of the experiences herself, and it's so important to listen to someone older. We, the younger ones, always think we know better, but we don't—we have to go through experiences to learn the ups and downs of life, and it's an enormous help to have a grandparent around who will say it in the nicest way."

Dickie was very pleased with the interview. Besides giving her views on the plight of the aged, Diana had added her own personal touch by mentioning the advice she received from her grandmother, Lady Fermoy. It was not rehearsed or preplanned (normally it takes several letters and a lot of patience to get an interview with a member of the Royal Family, and the only interview Diana had ever done before was a written reply to prepared questions about the charity Birthright). But he felt if Diana was willing to speak when she visited her charities, people would take far less interest in her clothes and appearance and concentrate instead on what she said.

Even recording a prepared speech onto a mini-tape machine and then playing it through the earphones of her Sony Walkman hasn't helped much. It was a method she tried before her maiden speech at the Guildhall in July 1987. It was not a notable success, but she did raise a laugh when she took a swipe at her critics, who had labeled her a "boozer" after reports that she went on drinking binges with her friend Fergie.

"Contrary to recent reports," she said, "I have not been drinking, and I am not, I can assure you, about to become an alcoholic."

When these stories start up, the people who work for her close ranks. Particularly protective is her hairdresser, Richard Dalton. He sees her every working day, passing on the news to keep her amused. He usually arrives at Kensington Palace at 9:00 A.M. to style her hair in the pastel green-walled dressing room with its kidney-shaped dressing table. He seldom sees Charles. The Prince of Wales is an early riser who listens to the farming report on Radio 4 at 6:10 A.M. Recently he has acquired the habit of being in his study and on the telephone, a breakfast tray of bran flakes and honey on his desk, before eight o'clock. He will read the papers, though newspaper games, it can be said, do confuse him.

One morning he lost his entry card for the *Times* portfolio game.

"Find it for me quickly," he instructed the butler.

"Don't worry, sir. I'll get you another," the butler replied.

"No, you can't do that—I must have mine," the Prince insisted in the mistaken belief that the card had been specially made for him.

As Charles wrestles with the sometimes unfamiliar ways of the modern world, Diana gets on with her own day. As a mother she is a light sleeper and unlike her husband, "who can sleep through anything," is wakened by the slightest sound. A pair of earplugs were once even found next to her side of the bed, by an amused member of staff who found it strange to think of Diana sitting through ear-shattering rock concerts, but going to bed with a pair of earplugs. (She does, however, also take them to concerts!) Diana may have had her night disturbed by a cry for a glass of water or complaints of a stomachache. The boys will always crawl into bed on Diana's side if they are frightened or unwell, and Charles seldom wakes up. But whatever Charles and Diana are doing during the day, they always kiss the boys good-bye before they go off to school in the morning. William has acquired an endearing habit of saluting his father by the front door—imitating some of the soldiers and officials who do the same. And amid much giggling Harry will imitate his elder brother.

If Diana doesn't have any pressing appointments, she will accompany the detective and the children to school in their Ford Grenada Estate car. She doesn't pick them up but tries to organize her day so she can be with them in the early evening.

Diana never forgets how her royal life also consumes that of her staff (the Royal Family never refers to its staff as servants) and, if they have been working particularly long hours, never forgets to thank them, often with a personal note written in her large rounded handwriting. She and Charles employ at Kensington Palace between sixteen and

twenty, including two valets for Charles, two dressers for
Diana, two cooks, two chauffeurs, a butler, a housekeeper,
an army orderly, a host of daily cleaners, plus the two nannies.

Diana is on first-name terms with all her staff at Kensington Palace but is not overly familiar with them as she was in
the early days of her marriage. She remembers their birthdays
and at Christmas chooses gifts with great care, having everything wrapped, tagged, and hidden well before the end of
December. Charles is happy to leave that "chore" to his wife,
just as before his marriage he left it up to his valet to do all
his shopping—at minimal expense!

Being a perfectionist herself, Diana does get irritated if
things are left untidy or dirty and won't hesitate to inform
them if she is displeased. At Highgrove one of the maids once
left some dirty fingerprints on the paintwork, and Diana,
who was feeling tetchy anyway, threw an angry fit. Normally,
however, she is never haughty or bossy and asks for things to
be done in the nicest possible way. "Would it be possible to
do this for me?" she says with a smile.

In their seven years of living at Kensington Palace, the
Waleses have had a rapid staff turnover. Diana is very sensitive about being blamed for this and even took the trouble to
defend herself publicly, explaining she was not responsible for
sacking any of her staff. She did however, feel insecure, in the
early days, surrounded by people who had known the Prince
throughout his bachelor days. She considered them a bunch
of "fuddy-duddies" and resented their interfering in her new
life with Charles. "It was as if he was married to them, not
me," she told one of her girlfriends, "and they are so patron-
izing it drives me mad!"

Because Diana's current schedule is such a busy one, it's
not surprising that the women in the royal employ find their
social lives curtailed to such an extent that their job, like that
of their employers, becomes their life.

Diana's chief lady-in-waiting, Anne Beckwith-Smith, is
one such person. For seven years she has held one of the most
demanding posts in the Waleses' household. She joined Di-

ana in September 1981 on the recommendation of the Queen Mother, who knew her father, Major Peter Beckwith-Smith, who is clerk of the course at Epsom where the Derby is run. Friendly and with sparkling blue eyes, Anne came with impeccable cultural and family references. She was educated at West Heath (the same school as Diana and her sisters) and Queens Gate and went on to study art in Paris and Florence. That led to a job in the English Picture Department of Sotheby's. But far more important than her connections and education was her personality. She had an exacting task in front of her, becoming an advisor and friend and general factotum to a young girl who barely knew what her own job was, let alone Anne's. But Anne, a mature twenty-eight-year-old when she took the job, handled it with easy grace. She successfully stayed in the background while encouraging Princess Diana to accept the foreground, which would always be hers.

Anne is very attached to the Princess, and the feeling is mutual. Diana calls Anne "Darling" and sees more of her than almost anyone else in her household.

Ordering clothes and liaising with designers is a small part of Anne's job. Her most important role is to assist Diana with her official engagements. The day before Diana is to make an appearance, Anne and Diana's equerry, Lieutenant-Commander Richard Aylard, will arrive at Kensington Palace to brief the Princess, having already briefed those at the site of her planned visit, informing them of her likes and dislikes if she is lunching and how to address her and, as vital to a princess as anybody else, checking on the availability of lavatories. It is a rule that the Queen and members of her family have to have a special separate loo provided for their visit. This can cause all kinds of problems, and new loos are often quickly installed, sometimes to no avail as the royal visitors might not feel any pressing need to use them. If they do, the lady-in-waiting will stand outside the door "on guard" to prevent any possible embarrassing intruders. Diana finds this very amusing and is far more embarrassed by the possibility of a new loo being installed especially for her than by the possibility of someone else wanting to use it at the same time.

"Absolute discretion at all times is the most important requirement for the job of lady-in-waiting," the Queen's assistant press secretary, John Haslem, says. "They will never discuss their role with outsiders."

The role of a modern lady-in-waiting is difficult. They have to be prepared to chat to anyone from a factory worker to a visiting monarch, provide an extra pair of hands to help with bouquets of flowers and gifts, and, if they see a member of the public holding the royal attention for too long, persuade him or her to move along to give others a chance to meet the Princess. They are paid very little, the part-time ones only out-of-pocket expenses, although the full-time ones such as Anne receive a proper salary. They also write hundreds of thank-you letters, which often means working late into the night.

In 1987 Diana carried out 175 official engagements, excluding overseas tours. She has five ladies-in-waiting, including Anne Beckwith-Smith, who work on a rota system. After the twice-yearly program meetings now held in the Waleses' larger offices in St. James's Palace, they decide among themselves who should do what and when. The other ladies-in-waiting are Mrs. George West, wife of the Comptroller of the Lord Chamberlain's office, Countess Campden, Vivien Baring, and Diana's old school friend Alexandra Loyd.

Alexandra, who is the youngest and newest of Diana's ladies-in-waiting, is the daughter of the Sandringham land agent Julian Loyd and lived virtually next door to Diana when they were children. She went to the same school— Silfield in King's Lynn, near both of their homes—and they have remained friends ever since.

"To be a lady-in-waiting you do not have to be a friend," one of them remarked, "but once you start working for the Princess, it is impossible not to become attached to her."

The role of lady-in-waiting is not the only difficult job that is part of Diana's typical workday. The royal protection

Summer fun means going to watch 'Papa' play polo, and visiting the refreshment tent for strawberries and ice cream, carefully carried by the Princess.

Behind the scenes at Buckingham Palace on the Duke and Duchess of York's wedding day. Diana cuddles an over-tired, over-exhausted Prince William as members of the Palace household and Royal Family go to the gates to see Fergie and Andrew off on their honeymoon. (The lady in white next to Diana is the Duchess of Kent.)

Schooldays can be fun. Prince William and his friend Nicholas Playdell Bouverie leave Mrs Mynors' school to perform their Christmas nativity play.

A couple of years later, Prince Harry is doing the same thing. Accompanied by his friend the wolf, Prince Harry, dressed as a goblin, sets out for his first acting performance.

The Windsor wave: Prince William on his first day at pre-prep school in February 1987 gives a coy wave to the photographers.

The Princess shows off her newly acquired ability with sign language in her role as Patron of The British Deaf Association.

Caring and thoughtful, the Princess chats with old folks at a Help the Aged centre during the cold winter of 1987.

Diana, talking to the nursing staff at the Middlesex hospital where she had held the hand of an Aids victim. In the background, holding the flowers, is her chief lady-in-waiting Anne Beckwith Smith.

At the Royal Ballet School, the Princess looks to see how the dancers are held by their partners, and reiterates her longing to have been a dancer herself.

The Princess demonstrates her warmth when 'working a crowd', and as hundreds of eager hands reach out to touch her, shares a joke with a well-wisher in Brixton.

Sometimes her good humour gets the better of her and she dissolves into giggles. Here at Sandhurst she was overcome by nerves and couldn't keep a straight face while inspecting the guard of honour.

Diana often presents the prizes at polo matches, and always gives her husband a kiss. On this occasion he was hot and sweaty and Diana got the giggles when his wet face brushed hers.

Dancing during their recent visit to Australia, Diana displays beautifully tanned legs (darkened with a little cosmetic help), and a stunning dress designed by Catherine Walker, as Charles twirls her around the dance floor.

In the early days of their marriage Charles was very tactile and here he gives Diana's backside a gentle pinch.

During their tour of Germany after the summer of discontent within their marriage, Charles stares at the ceiling while Diana looks moodily into the distance.

A warm welcome for his old friend and confidante, Lady Tryon, after an equally warm game of polo. If Charles's team is victorious he is always in a very good mood and will stay chatting after the match. If, however, he has lost he likes to get away as quickly as possible.

The glamorous Princess of Wales standing next to her husband at a reception in
Germany. Diana is wearing a deep-blue velvet dress designed by Victor Edelstein,
the Spencer tiara she wore on her wedding day, and thousands of pounds worth of
jewellery round her neck and wrist – a gift from the Sultan of Oman.

The many faces of Diana:
Anxious – as she waits for Charles while visiting the flood victims of Wales. It was the first time she had seen her husband for some weeks and as soon as the visit was over he returned to Scotland fuelling speculation that their marriage was in trouble.

Beautiful – in Thailand with her hair adorned with orchids, carefully pinned in place and colour co-ordinated by her hairdresser.

Giggly – as she hides her face with her hand after her best friend Fergie had cracked one of her wicked jokes.

Childlike – as she pulls a face of mock horror at the Bute Highland Games.

Movie star – Diana at her very best arriving at a film première in London. Her stunning gown is designed by Murray Arbeid and Diana has added her personal touches of one black and one red glove.

officers hold a demanding position as well. They have to be prepared to leave their families behind for long periods, have unsociable hours, and dress and act as courtiers while remembering their real role is that of armed guards employed to ensure the safety of their charges. They dislike being referred to as bodyguards or detectives, but most people find *royal protection officer* a bit of a mouthful, so they have to put up with it. Diana's senior detective is stern-faced Inspector Graham Smith, who keeps up the twenty-four-hour security by dividing his time with Inspector Tony Parker and Inspector Allan Peters and a couple of others, who also look after the royal children. They call the little Princes by their Christian names as requested by Prince Charles, and they refer to Diana as "Your Royal Highness" and then "Ma'am." She calls them by their Christian names or in some cases a nickname—Graham Smith is known as Smudger.

Diana resented for a long time having a member of the Royal Protection Squad with her wherever she went and even made a few late-night forays on her own. She has now, however, grown accustomed to the shadowy figures that follow her—if she goes out to dinner, they go too, sitting in an adjoining room until she is ready to leave.

Two members of Diana's staff that she has a good relationship with are her dressers, Fay Marshalsea and Evelyn Dagley. Diana attended the wedding of thirty-three-year-old Fay Marshalsea in 1987. But behind Fay's smiles on her wedding day was a tragic secret: she had recently learned she had cancer and could die. Only her husband-to-be, Steven Appleby, who is in the RAF, their immediate families, and the Princess knew. Fay continued to work for Diana after the wedding until she became too weak and was forced to stop. Diana insisted that she keep her flat in Kensington Palace as it would be easier for her to get the necessary treatment than if she had to travel from the home she shared with her husband at RAF Benson in Oxfordshire. Throughout Fay's illness Diana was deeply concerned and on one occasion even accompanied Fay to hospital for her daily treatment. The genuine concern and support Fay received from the Princess helped speed her recovery, and although she is still not out of danger she is back at work with nothing but praise for her employer: "She knew of my illness virtually from the start," Fay said in an interview with the *Sunday Express*. "She is very close to me, and I wanted to tell her. She gave me encouragement to carry on. She is a lovely person to work for and very special to me."

Diana is very caring with her personal staff, and nothing is too much trouble for her if something goes wrong in their lives. She also loves a romance within her household—as long as it's between two people of the opposite sexes. When Diana first appeared on the royal scene, she was shocked when she realized how many gays there were in royal service. But she has now come to terms with the "gay mafia" in royal service, realizing it isn't such a wonderful job for those with a wife and family they seldom see.

Diana's work and interests lead her outside the household as well. And that means hours and hours of charity work. The pursuit of such royal patronage for the many thousands of registered charities needs time, effort, and patience. First a letter from the charity has to be sent to the private secretary, in Diana's case Sir John Riddell, who has been with the Prince and Princess since 1985, replacing Edward Adeane. He will acknowledge immediately, either saying no or, if there is a chance that Diana will be interested, putting the request on hold in a large file, along with hundreds of others.

Usually the night before an engagement, Diana will do her homework, familiarizing herself with the names of the people she is going to meet and the part they play in the event. For example, when Diana attends a charity ball or film premiere, the charity will submit to her office in St. James's a list of those people they wish to present to the Princess. The people accorded this honor have usually put a great deal of time and effort into ensuring the evening is both a social and financial success.

This work brings her into contact with a wide and eclectic range of people. Some are interesting and intelligent; others inevitably are not. But they all want to shake her hand, and on her visit to Australia in 1988 she almost wilted away with the heat and the seemingly endless number of hands she had to clasp—many of them sticky.

It is a problem all members of the "Firm" have to face, and Diana admits she sometimes doesn't know what to do. She can't very well wipe her hand on the back of her dress, and she hates wearing the long white cotton gloves that the Queen wears to solve this problem.

Sticky hands are the least of Diana's problems with children. She dislikes having to deal with too many of them at once, explaining she doesn't have a chance to do anything beneficial when faced with a whole classroom. She prefers to meet each child individually or talk to children in small groups so she can walk from one to another. She experiences the same problems anyone would when faced with terribly handicapped children and often has to bite her lip to prevent tears from running down her cheeks.

On one occasion she was presented with an angelic-looking child who was both deaf and blind. The child had been told, through sophisticated methods of touch, that Princess Diana was coming to see her. But when Diana saw the child, she was so overcome with shock at her sad plight that she literally froze and couldn't touch her. When she returned home later in the day, she ran to her bedroom, shut the door, and wept, confused and upset by her inability to cope with the situation.

She experiences the same kind of emotion when visiting hospices, when she knows the patients she is talking to might be dead within a few weeks or months and comes home physically and mentally drained by such visits and invariably rushes up to the nursery to hug her own children.

"I'm so lucky," she says, "to have two healthy, strong boys. I don't know how I could cope if I had a child who was handicapped or mentally handicapped in some way."

A great deal of Diana's charity work involves children of all kinds, and as patron of the British Deaf Association she has taken the trouble to learn a number of words in sign language. The association sent her a video, and after a couple of weeks she mastered and performed her newfound skills in front of a crowd of people. To honor her, children at an East End school for the deaf invented a special sign for her name: you run your hand from the front of your hair to the back, referring to her famous swept-back hairstyle.

So conscious is Diana of trying to project an image as a hard worker, not an empty-headed fashion plate, that she goes to extraordinary lengths to do her homework and understand the complicated methods by which certain diseases or disabilities are treated. Equerry Richard Aylard writes all her briefs, but the Princess does a lot of her own research and refuses to be merely a figurehead for the charities of which she is a patron.

"I think it's important to show you're interested and that you're not just breezing in and out, having seen them for a morning," she explains. "I don't just want to be a name on a letterhead."

When Diana's love of dancing and childhood yearning to become a professional dancer became public news, she was inundated by requests from ballet companies anxious to benefit from her royal patronage. The London City Ballet, after many letters, was finally rewarded.

"We got the usual letter of acknowledgment, so we wrote several more times to let her know what we were doing," a member of the company explained. "We were delighted when she agreed to become our patron, and now she often pops in informally to watch us rehearsing."

Larger charities such as Dr. Barnardo's and Birthright have raised thousands of pounds from just one appearance by the Princess at a ball or film premiere. Diana however, takes care not to always be associated with the glamorous side of things. She makes a point to visit the charity offices and chat with the staff at least twice a year.

To watch Diana "work a room" is to witness a remarkable performance. There is something almost mystical in the way even the very ill respond to her presence. Eyes open, young and old forget their pain for a moment and smile.

In primitive societies kings and queens were believed to be blessed with magical powers, and it took the Civil War three centuries ago to dispense with the divine right of kings to rule. But the arrival of the Princess of Wales at a hospital or hospice can stir those atavistic folk memories. And even the more worldly among us rarely fail to respond to Diana's very natural charm, and I include myself.

She is an expert in the art of small talk and always looks directly into the eye of whomever she is talking to. She is very quick-witted, with an ability to respond to a question with a snappy reply, which stands her in good stead. I have seen hardened journalists walk away after speaking to her with a bemused look on their faces, muttering, "She's wonderful, so beautiful—and so much more intelligent than I thought." The old magic of royalty can still work its spell.

Both Diana and Charles play a valuable role with hysterical scares such as AIDS and national disasters such as the IRA's Remembrance Day bombing of Enniskillen in Ireland. They were criticized for not arriving on the scene immediately, but there was a very real personal danger to themselves, which they chose to ignore.

"If your name is on the bullet, there is nothing you can do," Prince Charles said, no doubt thinking once again of the death of his beloved Uncle Dickie at the hands of the IRA. So their visit to Enniskillen in November 1987, a week after the disaster, went ahead amid intense security. Their Wessex helicopter of the Queen's Flight was escorted by four other helicopters, and when they appeared out of the skies it was like the scene from the movie *Apocalypse Now*. They were then taken in an armor-plated car to the Erne hospital in Ulster to meet seven of the victims injured in the explosion. Mr. Gordon Wilson, whose twenty-year-old daughter had been killed in the explosion, slipped his arms out of his bandages to shake hands with the Prince.

"Their visit has helped me enormously," he said later. "Princess Diana is a really lovely girl."

It is a sentiment echoed by everyone she meets.

In addition to Diana's charity work and the daily responsibilities to her family, she and the Prince have embarked on several overseas royal tours nearly every year for the eight years of their marriage. For Diana, whose traveling had been limited to a few European resorts and one trip to Australia to see her mother, it has been very exciting. Her first Commonwealth tour, however, to Australia and New Zealand in 1983, was something of a shock.

"It was like a baptism of fire," Diana said. "But by the time I left I felt I'd actually been able to achieve something."

Tours may look glamorous, but they are very hard work. "Although you are tired, you just have to get on with the job," she says, and helped by her hardworking staff, that is exactly what she does.

During their most recent visit to Australia the Princess confessed to friends later she felt exhausted most of the time and was longing to lie in the sun instead of standing in a smart frock shaking hands. Diana suffers badly from jet lag, and that combined with the heat wiped her out.

Weeks of preparation are necessary to ensure everything runs smoothly, and Diana, helped by her two dressers, selects a wardrobe she hopes will be suitable for every eventuality. The dressers lay out all her clothes with color-coordinated bags and shoes to match, and when Diana has made her selection, often with the assistance of hairdresser Richard Dalton, who has an uncanny eye for accessories, they pack them into special trunks, all carefully labeled.

Packing and unpacking, entertaining and being entertained are all part of Diana's everyday life. In 1987 she spent 17 days abroad on official duties; attended 25 receptions, 7 official lunches, 19 film premieres, and 108 general visits; and performed 16 State duties that included garden parties, state banquets, etc.

Throughout all of this, Charles is always there advising her on what she should and should not do. He wasn't at all annoyed by her and Fergie's pranks at Royal Ascot last year and even offered to give her a piggyback ride over a puddle himself, which she wisely declined. But when it came to discussion as to whether or not she should be included in the royal It's a Knockout team, he put his foot down—quite correctly as it transpired. Prince Edward was annoyed. He saw his sister-in-law as a major pulling power to persuade Hollywood stars to take part. But Charles was adamant, and a family row ensued. The Princess Royal accused Charles of being a "stick-in-the-mud," and Diana felt once again she was missing all the fun. When the show came to be screened, she was secretly relieved she had not been allowed to take part; although she thought it a "jolly good giggle," she realized she would not have come out of it well.

While all the parties, receptions, official duties, and traveling keep Diana very busy, they leave her little time to relax and, more importantly, spend time alone with Charles.

"We're never alone," Diana frequently complains to Charles, and her moans are quite justified. When she is free, he is often busy, and if she is not visiting friends, she spends quiet evenings in her sitting room catching up on the TV programs she might have missed—she leaves a list with the butler, Harold Brown, of the programs she wants to see, and he arranges to have them recorded. Soap operas like "Dallas," "Dynasty," and "East Enders" are favorites, and she saw *Woman of Substance* starring Jenny Seagrove and *The Thornbirds* with Richard Chamberlain, but she doesn't always find time to watch the whole of the many current miniseries shown on television. Sometimes Diana will curl up with a book, but she finds it easier to read intellectually untaxing ones such as Danielle Steele, Colleen McCullough, and Barbara Taylor Bradford romances.

"My husband doesn't approve of the books I read," she admits, but she finds such novels easy to pick up and put down.

From her choice of books to her choice of staff to her determination to raise "normal" children, the Princess of Wales has come to recognize the things she wants in life. And in the years to come, the Spencer determination will ensure that she gets it.

11

Fashion

*T**he woman who,* almost single-handedly, has made the British fashion industry a multimillion-pound export business stands five feet, ten inches tall. Her long, slim feet take a size 7AA. Her bust and hips are thirty-five inches, while her waist regularly expands to a boyish, more than anorexic, twenty-nine inches. She wears a size 10 or 12, depending on the designer. It is not a conventional shape by any means. But put it all together and the effect is stunning.

As Princess Michael of Kent once remarked to me: "Princess Diana has such a beautiful figure she would look good in a sack."

It has never come down to that for the demure Sloane, who grew up to be one of the most elegant princesses in the world, and she has certainly come a long way from the little girl in her family's photograph album, who is pictured wearing a pair of old curtains.

"She has always loved dressing up," her father explains. It is a love affair that turned into a way of life, one that Diana now recognizes almost consumed her. Unlike the Princess Royal, Diana is not judged by what she does but by what she wears. Her true personality is lost in a swirl of silks and chiffons, lace and brocades. And that has depressed her for some time.

"My clothes are not my priority," Diana insisted in a television interview a couple of years ago. "I enjoy bright colors, and my husband likes to see me look smart, presentable, but fashion isn't my big thing at all."

When Diana first became engaged to Prince Charles and wore a blue off-the-peg suit from Harrods, chosen with her mother, fashion certainly wasn't her big thing. She has, however, always been interested in clothes, and even at Althorp, where there were a number of staff members to take care of such things as laundry, she did her own washing and ironing but couldn't afford the highest fashion, not in those early days. The £310 she paid for the engagement suit, designed by Cojana, may have seemed a fortune, but now Diana would pay that sum just for a handbag. When her new royal position took her from her life as a Sloane Ranger who did her shopping at Laura Ashley, Miss Selfridge, or Peter Jones, into the circuit of haute couture, she used it as a crutch. She wasn't allowed to say anything or do anything apart from smile and look pretty. Her freedom had been snatched, her personality engulfed. She began to express herself in the only available way—through her clothes and the newly opened coffers of her husband, the Prince of Wales.

Diana was right when she said her husband liked to see her looking smart. "It was one of the first things I noticed about her—her very good sense of style," he admitted. But being no great expert on womankind, Charles had no idea of the extent of the growing obsession or the reasons it came about.

Anxious, trapped, and insecure within the gloomy confines of Buckingham Palace, Diana was determined her future husband was going to continue to notice her, so she started shopping. It was also something to do.

Her sister, Lady Jane Fellowes, who had contacts with *Vogue* magazine, where she once worked as an editorial assistant, gave her some guidance. The two girls decided that it would be an excellent idea if they approached Jane's chums and entered the fashion world through the back door. It literally was through the back door that they entered the offices of *Vogue* in London's Hanover Square. Diana was always being followed by a posse of photographers, and back doors were becoming an everyday event.

At the time Beatrix Miller was editor of *Vogue,* and she thought that the soft-spoken Anna Harvey, assistant fashion editor, and beauty editor Felicity Clark, were the most suitable members of her team to help Diana create an appropriate image. They did an excellent job. While Diana was rummaging through the rails in the *Vogue* offices, looking at some clothes that were being used for a shoot, she came across a blouse designed by a young couple hardly heard of outside the fashion world—the Emanuels.

Diana liked it and got it, thus formulating the love-hate relationship she has had with that husband and wife team ever since. Recently they have been right back in favor and have even designed the odd frock for Fergie (the black-and-white outfit she wore in Mauritius, for example). Immediately after the wedding, however, they were right out. "We'll see about them," Diana remarked, referring to what she considered their cashing in on the publicity surrounding the famous wedding dress. She was still disgruntled when they presented her with the photograph album that showed the stages of making the dress and the final product. As she moodily flicked through the album she felt like tearing all the photographs out and using the white leather book for something else. But Diana doesn't bear grudges for long. It is not her nature, and besides, she likes the Emanuels' clothes. She considers them "dramatic."

From the black taffeta evening gown, which was so low-cut it caused a sensation when Diana wore it to the Goldsmiths Hall in March 1981, to the crumpling wedding dress whose hem they failed to weigh down, to the vivid green checked coat worn in Venice that reminded onlookers of a horse blanket, the Emanuels have been an important part of the Diana style. But they are not cheap. An off-the-peg ball gown can cost over £1000, and some of the fabrics they use can retail at over £100 a meter—with all the beading or sequins sewn on by hand.

However, the cost of the Princess's wardrobe is not as much as has been wildly estimated—and there have been some wild estimates. In April 1985 it was suggested that Diana had spent a staggering £80,000 on a new wardrobe for her Italian trip. She reacted by appearing at a gala evening at La Scala theater in Milan, the center of the Italian fashion industry, in an evening dress she had worn two years before in Canada. The 'old' dress—albeit a beautiful pink chiffon creation by Victor Edelstein—had the desired effect, and the ensuing criticism satisfied Diana's desire for revenge, although it must be said that for the remainder of the trip she produced some stunning new creations that did cost a considerable amount of money. However, when the Waleses are on royal tours and therefore representing the Monarch and their country, the cost of their official wardrobe is borne by the Keeper of the Privy Purse and Treasurer to the Queen, Shane Blewitt. The clothes are paid for out of a special fund that constitutes part of the Civil List—the only funds the Waleses take from the list.

The Prince of Wales's income is derived from his Duchy of Cornwall estates, which make him a very rich man indeed. Before he married in 1981, Charles took 50 percent of the net revenue from the Duchy and gave the other half to the Treasury in lieu of income tax. But once his bachelor days were over and he had the additional expense of two main residences, a wife, and two children, he made arrangements to take three-quarters of the revenue and pay a quarter instead of half back to the Treasury. As the annual income from the Duchy returns an income in excess of £1 million sterling, this leaves the Prince of Wales with at least £750,000 for his family and household needs.

"I have never heard them discuss the cost of her clothes," a member of their staff says. This might, of course, be partly to do with the fact that Charles seldom sees a bill.

Bills from designers and shops are signed by the lady-in-waiting and sent to the Waleses' office in St. James's Palace, or they are paid for immediately by a Duchy of Cornwall American Express card. Along with the elegant shopping bags and parcels, both Diana's lady-in-waiting and detective carry these American Express cards. Some cash is carried for smaller items, but the Coutts checks, where Diana has an account, are seldom used as people have a habit of not cashing them but keeping them as souvenirs, which confuses the household books.

Even before those handy and practical Duchy of Cornwall credit cards, Charles rarely saw bills and as a consequence had little idea of the cost of anything. He still doesn't and can kick up a terrible fuss if he thinks he is being overcharged, which he rarely is. Diana has tried to break her husband of this tedious habit. More generous, she is always buying him socks, ties, handkerchiefs, and sweaters.

Charles does not always reciprocate in quite the way Diana would like. At a dinner party she asked a girlfriend who had just had a baby what her husband had given her. Before the friend could answer Diana said, "Mine only gave me a boring old picture."

Charles would probably approve of the fact that Diana saves some money by shopping by catalogue, a habit she took up during the early years of her marriage when she was pregnant with Prince William and suffered from morning sickness and bouts of dizziness all day. Harrods sends her books from Laurel and Mondi—both German companies—and anything that takes her fancy is then ordered by her chief lady-in-waiting, Anne Beckwith-Smith. Her distinctive spotted skirt worn with matching ankle socks at a polo match a couple of years ago was a Mondi outfit, although Diana delighted the assistants in the separates department on the first floor of Harrods by purchasing this one herself. For the Highland Games at Braemar in 1986 her ensemble of a pink and green tartan skirt with color-coordinated tam-o'-shanter was straight out of the Laurel catalogue—ordered by telephone.

Avoiding furs is another way Diana saves money on her wardrobe. However much Diana might yearn to wear a beautiful fox or mink coat, she would not dream of doing so. She has not appeared in fur in public since the early days of her marriage when she wore a creamy fur jacket to a film premiere. Even on skiing holidays the Princess has to make do with a woolly headband instead of the popular fur headband that Fergie favors. If it's fur, it's fake, and Diana has a swagger coat designed by Arabella Pollen with a fake beaver collar and cuffs.

Whenever possible, Diana also asks her designers to revamp her clothes. A hemline altered, a pleat taken out, or a sleeve remade can make the outfit last for another season.

In addition, by paying wholesale prices (the cost of the fabric, labor, and expenses like light and heat), Diana manages to reduce the expenditure on the large number of outfits she needs. She also gets most of the clothes direct from the designer, which cuts out the markup the store is making, reducing the total cost to less than a quarter of the retail price.

It is a mutually beneficial arrangement and one that designers have with many of those favored clients who generate publicity. And there is no better publicity than having your clothes worn by the Princess of Wales.

These reductions, of course, apply only when Diana is organized about her shopping. An unexpected little foray into small boutiques or shops will result in the Princess having to pay the full price. It doesn't bother her. There is hardly a shop within the square mile of Kensington and Chelsea that hasn't had the excitement of the Princess of Wales walking through its door, to buy something for herself or for a friend, and more often than not these little shopping trips get reported.

"I can't win," Diana tells her friends. "They either accuse me of spending too much on my clothes or of wearing the same outfit all the time. I wish everyone would stop talking about my clothes. They are not my priority."

The Emanuels, Victor Edelstein, Bruce Oldfield, Murray Arbeid, Jacques Azagury, Catherine Walker—the list is endless—all have a great deal to thank Anna Harvey for. "She just went round and round," a fashion assistant said, "until she found the right clothes for Diana." Anna herself is understandably reticent to speak about the part she played in dressing the most famous face in the world and refuses to take any credit for turning Sloane Diana into mannequin Diana.

"She claims she just happened to be there at the time," a member of the *Vogue* staff says. "She's not at all pushy; she's very professional and very discreet."

It is Anna's discretion that has enabled her to remain friends with the Princess of Wales. Besides her job as fashion director of *Vogue*, she plays a very active part in charity work, especially for Birthright, whose patron is, of course, Diana. Always busy, Anna divides her time between her terraced house in Wandsworth, which she shares with her stockbroker husband Jonathan and their three children, and the *Vogue* offices. Slim, smart, and dark-haired Anna was recently offered the job as top fashion buyer for Harrods but preferred to continue her work at *Vogue*.

As the uncrowned queen of British fashion, Diana takes her role of ambassador very seriously. When she is at home she can wear Valentino, Ungaro, Chanel, or St. Laurent, but when she is doing official duties Diana seldom lets the side down. However, underneath all her British fashion she allows herself to splash out on extravagant Italian or French underwear. Courtenay in Brook Street stocks the Italian rage La Perla of which she is very fond. Its silk knickers are exquisite and very expensive as is its nightwear. When it gets cold, Diana wears thermal underwear by Damart because it enables her to wear dresses and thin coats in the middle of winter when most people might be protected by a fur or at least a fur-lined coat.

"Clothes are for the job," the Princess says. "They've got to be practical. Sometimes I can be a little outrageous, which is nice, but only sometimes."

If she can't be too outrageous, Diana will sometimes make a statement—one black glove and one red glove, for instance (at the suggestion of her hairdresser, Richard Dalton)—or pick a vivid color such as Rifat Ozbek's turquoise suit with gold embroidery, worn in Spain, or the cheeky "Sergeant Pepper" white suit, designed by Catherine Walker and worn to greet the King of Saudi Arabia.

Despite the restrictions put on her choice of clothing, however, Diana still harbors a passion for shopping. Indeed, it is not unusual for her to park her Jaguar on the double yellow lines outside shops like Night Owls in London's Fulham Road and rush into the store with her lady-in-waiting.

Sometimes a shop is cleared, but more often than not Diana will just browse through the racks with the other would-be purchasers. One young woman was flabbergasted when she spotted Diana in a boutique changing room with the curtain drawn aside so she could ask the opinion of her lady-in-waiting, who was standing in the shop. The gray silk underwear and the length of the Princess's legs reduced the surprised shopper to near paralysis. "I realized I was staring," she said, "but the Princess didn't seem to mind; she just looked at me and smiled."

Although Diana makes many forays into the boutiques she patronizes, when it comes to trying on clothes she usually has them sent to her or takes them home. This can cause some unfortunate results. Once when shopping in the popular Benetton chain she purchased a garment in the wrong size. Returning a couple of days later to change it, she was told by an assistant that she couldn't have a refund without a receipt!

Diana loves looking for new clothes, but as her workload increases, her forays outside her royal world decrease. She still finds time to go shopping, to play tennis, or to have lunch, but one of the things she most enjoyed—visiting the showrooms of her designers—has almost come to a halt.

Anne Beckwith-Smith would accompany the Princess on these visits, and as they entered the showroom (usually in the backstreets of London's West End) she would keep a wary eye on the time as the designer produced a selection of garments for Diana to try on.

"The Princess likes looking at people's collections in the

showroom if possible, but if there is not time we will go to her," Jan Vanvelden says. The designer, whether it's Victor Edelstein, Catherine Walker, Rifat Ozbek, or Murray Arbeid, will make an early appointment at Kensington Palace—usually around 9:00 A.M.—park the car in the gravel courtyard, and walk through the side entrance, under the old stone archway to the Waleses' back door, where butler Harold Brown will let the designer in. He takes the designer to the Princess's sitting room on the first floor, where he or she will wait until Diana is ready.

In the early days Diana could happily spend a morning, even a day, sifting through materials and discussing designs. No longer. As milliner John Boyd says: "She knows exactly what she wants." And there is a world of designers who would love to provide it.

Attractive Arabella Pollen, one of the youngest designers to have worked for the Princess, is one of them, and she has come a long way since Diana picked some outfits from her winter collection in 1982. "Bella" started business when Nicholas Coleridge, now editor of the glossy fashion magazine *Harpers and Queen*, spotted her potential and introduced her to publisher and entrepreneur Naim Attallah with the suggestion that Naim might finance her. He did so for a short time, and Bella has found her niche alongside many top fashion designers.

Bella isn't the only one to thank the Princess for putting her on the international map. Established designers such as Caroline Charles and Donald Cambell, Gina Fratini, David Neil, and Benny Ong, to name but a few, became household names when the Princess wore their designs in the early days of her marriage.

Even with the assistance of the *Vogue* team and such talented designers, Diana still made mistakes in those days. But she was getting used to the restrictions the royal dress code placed upon her and was not secure enough to be as daring as she is today.

Hats were one problem. They were something that Diana had worn only to weddings or the occasional day at the races.

It was Diana's mother, Mrs. Frances Shand Kydd, who introduced her daughter to her first real milliner, John Boyd. A few days after the engagement had been announced they both went to Boyd's London base—a tiny shop in the Brompton arcade at the time—and bought a sensible felt hat for Diana to wear to an event in the country.

While she was browsing through Boyd's collection Diana spotted a hat she loved—small with a curvy brim and a flowing ostrich feather. She asked him to reserve it for her, which he did, removing it from his summer collection, and Diana wore it on her wedding day as the finishing touch to her coral Belville Sassoon going-away outfit. The whole world saw that hat, and Boyd was firmly on the map.

Boyd remained discreet and faithful to his new royal client and was rewarded by being asked to make the hats for her first trip to Australia. However, the climatic conditions were not exactly what the royal party had expected, and Diana had a limited number of warmer clothes with her, so more dresses, suits, and hats had to be made quickly and sent out to the Princess by plane.

Boyd played his part by creating hats with only sketches and small swatches of material to match them to. It was a challenge, but one he relished. "It was hectic, but exciting to be able to see hats so quickly," he says.

Nowadays Boyd seldom makes hats for Diana, but the other milliners Diana patronizes—Graham Smith, David Shilling, and Philip Sommerville—usually find themselves invited to the Palace rather than having the pleasure of Diana popping into their shops. They are shown a selection of designs that their hats are meant to complement and must try to assess what the Princess will be doing in the hat. Milliners often complain Diana wears their hats the wrong way round, at the wrong angle, or even with the wrong outfit. She, however, remains silent if she doesn't like a particular hat.

"The Princess never says if she doesn't like something, but I always know," says Boyd. She just won't wear it, or she will have the offending creation returned by one of her ladies-in-waiting. "No one wants to make Diana something she doesn't like," says another milliner, "so we make sure we try and interpret her latest look."

"Hats give me confidence," Diana now says. And although she does not feel the necessity to wear them as much as she used to, they are still part of her style—the style which has given such a boost to the British fashion industry and created a look that is copied by millions of women around the world.

Wind was another problem—it ruffled Diana's carefully coiffured hair and has a habit of blowing up her skirts.

Says the Princess: "You'd be amazed what one has to worry about, from the obvious things like the wind—because there is always a gale wherever we go and the wind is my enemy, there's no doubt about that."

Her solution to that, ever since the day in Bristol a couple of years ago when the wind won and blew up her dress, has been to weight her hemline with lead.

"Then," she continues, "you've got to put your arm up to get some flowers, and you can't have anything too revealing. And you can't have hems too short because when you bend over there are six children looking up your skirt."

In fact, in those early days, as much fun as it was, everything was a problem.

"It's like getting dressed to go to a wedding every day," Diana moaned to a friend at the time, "and when you see yourself photographed in black and white, all the little mistakes show."

Diana is, by her own admission, a perfectionist. If something isn't exactly right, she feels unhappy and uncomfortable until it is. Normally punctual by nature, she has been known to stand for hours in front of her full-length mirrors discarding outfit after outfit because some detail was wrong. An exasperated Prince Charles would be waiting downstairs, pacing the floor, as the minutes ticked away.

Nowadays this happens very seldom. Her two dressers, Fay Marshalsea, who married in 1987, and Evelyn Dagley, are in charge of the vast and ever increasing wardrobe. In 1987 it was estimated to contain eighty-odd suits; nearly twelve dozen evening gowns; fifty-plus day dresses, many made up in the same style with different fabrics; seventy-two-odd hats; numerous blouses, sweaters, skirts, and trousers; and over 100 pairs of earrings!

Diana's clothes are stored in vast walk-in wardrobes in her dressing room, hung on padded hangers, and protected by plastic dressing bags from Eximious in London's Halkin Street, which holds a Royal Warrant (permission to use the coat of arms). The Royal Family members are great hoarders—at Buckingham Palace there are cupboards full of ancient clothing belonging to family members long dead, and Diana has relegated the clothes she seldom wears to a room downstairs at Kensington Palace.

With her appearance being such an important part of Diana's image, it is fortunate that her designers know exactly what her clothing needs are.

The restraints of royal dress code don't have to be spelled out to her designers. They know her taste, and they know what she can or cannot wear. So the meetings at Kensington Palace are very professional. The Princess is on first-name terms with all her designers, and they in turn are fond of her, though always careful to remember to address her as "Ma'am."

At Christmastime she remembers to send cards to them— usually a color photograph of the family on thick card with The Prince of Wales crest on the outside. In 1985 the photograph, taken by Prince Andrew, was one of them all at Highgrove. The following year it was a reproduction of a thirteenth-century map, found hidden among the possessions of the Duchy of Cornwall estate. But whatever the picture, Diana always includes a personal note such as "Thank you for designing my dresses," signed, simply, "Diana."

"The Princess is so friendly that it is sometimes hard to remember that you are not chatting to an old friend," one of her team says. "We have a good giggle about all the rubbish that is written about her clothes—although nowadays she seldom reads what is written about her."

Meanwhile, the clock set up on the table is ticking away the allotted twenty minutes, and Diana grimaces as she realizes she will have to go to her next appointment. Anne Beckwith-Smith will then finalize all the arrangements and organize the outfits to be picked up or delivered and further fittings booked.

Anne deals with Diana's many designers, setting up appointments and advising them on how much they can and can't say. "Her guidelines are very simple," Jacques Azagury explains, "we can claim an outfit that we designed, but never volunteer anything personal."

Anne also orders many of Diana's smaller items, such as tights, over the telephone and if she is very busy might send a driver to collect them. One of Diana's favorite shops for tights, Fogal in Bond Street, often receives calls from Anne. They inform her what they have in stock and if there is anything new the Princess might like. Anne has struck up such a good relationship with Diana's designers that she often buys their clothes for herself—at reduced rates, taking care to ensure they are neither too flashy or too obvious.

Shoes are also often brought to Diana at home. The samples from Charles Jourdan and Raine (the traditional royal cobblers) will be shown to her, and she will order what she wants. She prefers classic shapes with medium-height heels but might not like the available color. This is not a problem. If she wants some shoes that are produced only in red leather, she can have them in purple satin—as long as she orders in time.

She pays wholesale prices for these, but any shoes she might just see in a shop window, such as Pied à Terre, Midas, or Footloose, she will pay full price for.

Diana's unique style is also apparent in her jewelry. Since her marriage she has acquired a fantastic collection. She also has access to the Queen's, but she often prefers to wear costume jewelry.

"If it looks right, I don't think it matters whether it's real or fake," she says, a sentiment also proffered by the late Duchess of Windsor.

Prince Charles was in the bidding for a piece of the Duchess's jewelry in the Geneva sale two years ago. The piece, a fantastic brooch of diamonds set in the shape of the Prince of Wales feathers, finally went to Elizabeth Taylor for $567,000 or £350,000, certainly far more than Prince Charles would have wished to pay for any piece of jewelry, let alone something that, if his late uncle were still alive, he might surely have given to him.

In the autumn of 1987, the time when speculation as to the state of the Waleses' marriage was at its height, Diana declared that she wanted a cross. Garrard's didn't have one. Wartski's did, and the jeweler lent it to her. She wore it, rather to Garrard's consternation, to Garrard's charity evening in aid of Birthright. The effect of the cross and the Renaissance-style dress with its high collar especially made for *Harpers and Queen* by Catherine Walker and lent to Diana, was dramatic. If Diana was trying to make a theatrical point by inviting a comparison to that tragic Scottish queen, then she certainly succeeded.

Normally, of course, Diana will wear her own "rocks." And ever since that memorable Sunday night at Windsor when Diana was shown a large tray of engagement rings and "picked the biggest one," a sapphire surrounded by diamonds, the jewelry has been amassing. Charles bought her an art deco emerald and diamond bracement as a wedding present. The Queen gave her an emerald necklace.

It is not only Charles and the Queen who have given Diana such gifts. The Queen Mother presented Diana with an enormous sapphire brooch, surrounded by diamonds. It was so heavy that Diana found when she pinned it on a dress, even with the supportive backing specially sewn inside the material, it dragged the front down.

"Wear it as a choker," Princess Michael of Kent advised her. "It will look much prettier that way."

Diana took her advice and was seen wearing it fastened to a six-pearl choker for the Reagans' White House dinner in November 1985. Diana had never looked so lovely. In a midnight blue velvet off-the-shoulder dress, designed by Victor Edelstein, with the choker glimmering round her neck, she had the devastating effect of making every other woman in the room appear badly dressed. The Washington elite, including a large number of imported movie stars, were suitably impressed. And when John Travolta took to the floor with the Princess, you could hear a pin drop. While the band played a medley of disco tunes the couple did a series of spins and twirls. Travolta, later hounded by the British press, admitted that Diana was a good dancer and then added with relish, "My greatest moment was when I put my arm around her waist—she's so tiny."

That night Diana didn't wear a tiara, and she avoids doing so whenever possible. They are difficult to hold in place, and the family heirloom—the Spencer tiara—falls forward over her head. On her wedding day her then hairdresser, Kevin Shanley, admitted it did just that, creating the effect of an even fuller fringe. "It was a humid day, and the style dropped completely," he said. The bowknot pearl and diamond tiara, which the Queen gave to Diana as the formal gift that marked her entry into the Royal Family, is mounted on a velvet headband and gives her a headache. Diana caused a sensation by wearing the emerald and diamond necklace, another family heirloom given to her by the Queen, as a headband in place of a tiara while in Australia in 1986. But it turns out this was not because she wanted to avoid a headache, but for the simpler and more worrying reason that the tiara had been mislaid in the luggage.

Besides gifts from her immediate family, Diana has received some of her most spectacular jewelry from the Arab sheikhs. They are often too flashy for her liking, but out of politeness Diana is obliged to wear these pieces without usually having them remounted or reset. She does, however, add her individual stamp. A suite of sapphires, a wedding gift from the Crown Prince of Saudi Arabia, was given the Diana touch when she wore the bracelet as a choker on a narrow velvet ribbon around her neck.

During a visit to Germany in 1987 she displayed another spectacular gift, a suite of diamonds and sapphires in a modern setting, this one a gift from the Sultan of Oman.

As the Princess of Wales, Diana will continue to receive heirlooms and gifts, but one of her most treasured is something quite simple: a watered silk ribbon pinned to which is a miniature painting of the Queen surrounded by diamonds. This is the Queen's Family Order, and it is not given to all the royal ladies, so when Diana received it a year after her marriage she knew it was a very special honor.

Sometimes she is even tempted to buy her own jewelry. She was very taken by a £16,000 Cartier watch she saw in Zales. Then she exclaimed, "Oh, it hasn't got any numbers—I couldn't manage a watch without numbers."

She also, like many people, is worried about the stones she wears. "I don't particularly like expensive jewelry because I am frightened of losing it," she says. It is for this reason that she often wears costume jewelry.

Butler and Wilson, who have shops in London's Fulham and the West End, are her favorites. Earrings, brooches, in the shapes of large lizards or stars, set with diamanté, often adorn her person. She likes to mix a frankly fake brooch or pair of earrings with her most elegant ball gown, and it works. It's part of the Diana style.

Although Diana no longer has to call on the assistance of the *Vogue* team to advise her and knows all the designers personally, she is not averse to accepting a little advice. That advice comes from one of the people she spends a great deal of time with, her hairdresser, Richard Dalton.

A soft-spoken Scot in his late thirties, Dalton used to work at Headlines with Kevin Shanley. But when Shanley broke the royal rule and talked to a newspaper about his life as the Princess's hairdresser, Diana turned to Dalton to tend her locks. Dalton, whose loyalty to his illustrious client is unswerving, decided that he could no longer continue to work with Shanley and left to work freelance. (He has now opened his own salon in Claridges Hotel.)

It was a sensible decision, for Dalton has the complete trust of the Princess. And, besides doing her hair most days, he accompanies her on royal tours and acts as unofficial advisor on the royal wardrobe. It was Dalton who suggested that Diana wear the chiffon scarf slung round her neck, à la Grace Kelly, when she attended the Cannes Film Festival in 1987.

It was Dalton who suggested it might be fun to wear one black and one red glove—thus setting a fashion trend. And it was Dalton who gives the Princess that little bit of encouragement when she decides to wear something just a little more daring than usual.

He also has fixed ideas about the Princess's designers. He can spot the ones who are good and professional and is scathing of those who he thinks charge far too much money and produce substandard goods. The old favorites like Bruce Oldfield, Jasper Conran, and Victor Edelstein have never failed the Princess, and she continues to support the newer designers like Rifat Ozbek, but it is Catherine Walker, who works from a small shop in Chelsea—The Chelsea Design Company—who now produces the majority of Diana's clothes. Catherine, an elegant dark-haired Frenchwoman in her early forties, is quiet and unassuming. She started her business in 1977 after she had painstakingly taught herself to sew as therapy after the death of her husband. From a hobby she built up a thriving business and now has over forty people working for her. Her clothes range from £500 to £5,000 for her special couture range, and they are beautifully designed and made.

Although Diana still loves to shop, developing her own unique style has been no easy task. Fashions change, but a sense of style does not, and Diana's is part of her. It's not just in her clothes and the way she wears them, but in her personality as a whole. And it's a style that many admirers—from near and from afar—would like to emulate.

Diana sometimes gives clothes to her sister Lady Jane Fellowes, who is a similar shape, but as Diana's clothes are so visible, her sister is reluctant to take anything too dramatic.

Just before Fergie's engagement was made public, Diana lent her one of her old coats—a black and white check—which she wore when she visited Andrew's ship HMS *Brazen*. It wasn't long before everyone noticed it was one of Diana's castoffs, and that useful idea had to be terminated. They do, however, swap sweaters and designers. For her trip to Thailand, Diana wore several Alistair Blair outfits and has privately borrowed some of Fergie's prepregnancy Yves Saint Laurent couture frocks.

And Diana is not the only member of the Royal Family to

wear Catherine Walker's creations. Fergie has called into her Chelsea boutique, and the Duchess of Kent often arrives demanding outfits identical to Diana's—down to the last button. This can be awkward, and Catherine has to dissuade her, pointing out it would be most odd if she turned up at an official function wearing something exactly the same as Diana.

"She has the best image we could possibly hope to have for this country," says David Sassoon, who has made well over fifty outfits for the Princess, including her pink going-away suit. "We are very lucky to have someone as glamorous and as pretty as she is. For us she is a miracle worker."

Having the body of a top model is a great help, of course, and Diana, the most famous clotheshorse in the world, is fascinated by the possibility. During a photographic session with fashion photographer Terence Donovan, Diana asked, "How much would a girl earn if she was sitting here like me being photographed by you?"

"Oh, 'bout £800 an hour, luv," the Cockney snapper replied. Diana giggled and asked, "I wonder how much I could earn?"

Donovan's reply is not recorded. But *Life* magazine photographer Harry Benson, when asked to consider the question, replied, "She could retire after a day."

12
Fit to Be Queen

A *s a teenager Diana* was never part of the high-living set. She was too unsophisticated to relish wild nights on the town, druggy parties, or anything more daring than the odd bottle of wine. She hated smoking and was not born of the age that thought it smart and clever. And in those days she could eat as much as she liked without putting on the pounds. She also had a perfect English complexion, her only problem being the occasional spot and a tendency toward high coloring when she was excited or nervous.

Nerves were, and still are, a problem for Diana. She is highly strung and sensitive, and if she feels people are hostile toward her, she will "freeze them out" rather than have a direct confrontation.

The restrictions of Diana's new life were making her increasingly tense. In her bachelor days she had always been the one to wash up, empty ashtrays, and water the plants, and when she first moved into Buckingham Palace she had no domestic distractions to occupy her time and energy. So it was in the early days of her marriage that she decided to renew her love affair with dancing and took tap-dancing lessons in the Music Room.

Royal dance teacher seventy-seven-year-old Lily Snipp came to the palace twice a week with Diana's teacher, Wendy Vickers. Together they took the young Lady Diana through energetic hour-long sessions. "She just lived for ballet and was completely dedicated," Miss Snipp said. "The two days a week we taught her were the times she most enjoyed. Her lessons helped her get away from the pressures of being a member of the Royal Family."

When the two teachers arrived at Buckingham Palace, they were shown to the Music Room by a footman, who informed Diana they were waiting. Diana, dressed in a black leotard, always insisted they start the music straight away. First it was ballet, and then ten minutes of tap dancing in the circular mirrored room. One morning when they arrived Diana was upset; her new tap shoes with studded heels had marked the parquet floor. An official from the Department of the Environment—responsible for the upkeep of all the official royal residences—was sent for but seemed unperturbed.

"Don't worry," he said. "We have another room, and the floor in there doesn't matter." He then showed them into the Throne Room where the Queen does all her investitures. The Throne Room has a balcony at one end where there is an upright piano.

"It was a wonderful setting for a ballet lesson," Miss Snipp remembered, "but I wasn't too keen on playing an upright piano, so the official simply ordered some footmen to manhandle a grand piano into position. So we had our lessons in the Throne Room."

As a schoolgirl Diana would never miss a dancing class and was "mad keen" on ballet. Her name was always at the top of the list for school outings to the ballet, and she saw all the favorites like *Swan Lake* and *The Sleeping Beauty* several times and used to wait outside the stage door to get the dancers' autographs. When she met Russian ballet star Mikhail Baryshnikov, at the White House in 1985, she confessed to him she had once been one of the eager fans waiting outside Covent Garden after his performance.

Nowadays, as patron of the London City Ballet, Diana

goes to rehearsals to watch the dancers and chat to them about their work and their exercise routines, some of which she follows herself at home. The thirty-strong company is underfunded with no local or Arts Council grant, and Diana sees herself as something of a fairy godmother to them. The company's spokeswoman, Marian St. Claire, explains Diana's personal involvement:

"She certainly loves her dancing. She really enjoys the nitty-gritty of the rehearsal studio. She's always asking what it feels like to be lifted high into the air. What thrills us is how relaxed she is with us. She has fits of giggles when we tell her about our dressing room picnics. She's more than our mascot—she's one of us."

As much as the Princess might have liked to have been one of the young dancers, she readily admits: "I actually wanted to be a dancer but overshot the height by a long way."

Instead Diana concentrated on being a teacher. She didn't concentrate hard enough, however, and after a term at Miss Vacani's School of Dancing, where she taught two-year-olds and upward to dance to nursery rhymes, she abandoned the idea. She has, however, persisted with evening classes in Latin American jazz and tap.

Today those classes are held in the sitting room at Kensington Palace. "I do it once or twice a week," Diana says. "It's a combination of tap, jazz, and ballet."

The Princess also attends outside classes with other dancers and in 1983 arranged six weeks of lessons at the South London studio of Royal Ballet director Merle Park. And, before her surprising debut on stage at the Royal Opera House, Covent Garden, in December 1985, she took lessons from dancer Wayne Sleep—over the telephone.

No one was more surprised than thirty-nine-year-old Wayne Sleep when he received a call from the Princess of Wales suggesting that they both do a dance routine for the Friends of Covent Garden Gala on the day before Christmas Eve. They had discussed the possibility of her dancing on stage when they had met through Wayne's company, the London City Ballet, but because of her position he hadn't taken the idea seriously.

"It was all her idea," Wayne explained. "For her the excitement of doing it was to keep it from her husband more than anything else. Our biggest problem was going to be rehearsing in complete secrecy."

Diana sent Wayne a tape of her current favorite record, "Uptown Girl" by Billy Joel, and he went round to Kensington Palace to choreograph the number. In tracksuits they both danced around the sitting room, with Diana collapsing into giggles when she thought of how Prince Charles would look when he saw them on stage. But Wayne was impressed by her genuine ability: "She had rhythm, she can do high kicks, and she has a real feel for jazz dancing, which was great, so the rehearsal was amazing."

As both Wayne Sleep and Diana were very busy, they continued their lessons over the telephone, Diana speaking in a breathless whisper to prevent anyone from overhearing her and telling Charles. Their second and last rehearsal was on the day of the gala, when Diana arrived at the Opera House in the morning, for two hours of rehearsals. She even practiced her curtsy to the Royal Box, and the idea of Diana bowing to her own husband caused Wayne great amusement.

Throughout the performance that evening Charles suspected nothing and hardly noticed Diana leaving his side two numbers before the end. She dashed backstage, changed into a flimsy dress, and calmly waited in the wings until Wayne beckoned her on stage.

The sophisticated, elegant audience at Covent Garden could not believe what they were witnessing when the Princess came on, and they let out a collective gasp of amazement. "The only time I've had a reaction like that is when I've fallen over on stage," Wayne said. "It was astonishing."

There was no one more astonished than the Prince of Wales as he watched his wife of just over four years do her routine, which went from classical steps to the Charleston. They were called back eight times before a still nervous Wayne Sleep noticed Prince Charles laughing and clapping with delight as Diana turned for the carefully practiced curtsy to the Royal Box. He was greatly relieved to see this reaction, and when he came face to face with Charles at the party afterward he had a short chat with him.

Charles admitted he had been "absolutely amazed" when he saw his wife appear on stage with Wayne and had known nothing about it. As for Diana, she was so thrilled with the reaction from the Covent Garden audience that her original thrill of surprising her husband was almost forgotten.

Unlike Diana, Charles dreads what he calls the "awful exhibition" they are obliged to make of themselves as a royal couple, when they start the dancing during the many gala dinner dances they attend. Diana enjoys it, and she has had some very glamorous and powerful partners. At the White House dinner in 1985 Diana started the dancing with Ronald Reagan and after a couple of minutes John Travolta, the star of *Saturday Night Fever*, tapped him on the shoulder and asked if he could dance with Diana.

"Mrs. Reagan told me," Travolta recalls, "that when the President was finished dancing with Diana I should go over and ask her to dance. I was worried it wasn't appropriate, but she assured me it was."

Travolta and Diana jived for eight minutes to a medley of songs from *Saturday Night Fever* and *Stayin' Alive*, while the other guests retreated from the floor to watch the spectacle. Diana confided to Travolta she was suffering from jet lag and might not be at her best. Travolta assured her she was terrific and said: "My cure is exercise and sleep, and based on my theory, this is the beginning of your cure."

Dancing is one area where Diana knows she can excel, but according to her former flatmate, Carolyn (née Pride) Bartholomew, swimming is another:

"Diana was an excellent swimmer at school and won the diving cup three years running. She was also a very good dancer and a superb tap dancer."

Dancing and swimming are not Diana's only forms of exercise, but they consume a large amount of her nervous energy. She still avails herself of the heated indoor swimming pool at Buckingham Palace usually in the early morning when no one else is around. "I'm quite disciplined," Diana says. "I swim regularly—once a day if possible."

Diana finds these sessions so therapeutic that during royal tours a swimming pool is always made available for her use.

Few of the embassies where the Prince and Princess stay have a pool of their own, so the nearest one is made available. Accompanied only by her detective, Diana will go to the pool, swim her regulation twenty lengths, dry off, and head back to base in time to have her hair done and get ready for the day ahead.

And once Fergie arrived on the royal scene, Diana's sporting life expanded—to her benefit. She started to mix with Fergie's friends, some of whom seemed much more fun than her own. They played tennis twice a week at the exclusive Vanderbilt Racquet Club in London's Shepherd's Bush, and Diana, who had always been a good player, started to improve rapidly under the coaching of the club's managing director, Charles Swallow. Always conscious of her legs—as a schoolgirl she found them too thin, too fat, or too knobbly— Diana was annoyed at discovering photographs of herself in a tennis dress appear in the press, but that didn't keep her from enjoying the game, and afterward she would cool off in the cocktail bar with a glass of orange juice. It was exactly the kind of physical and mental therapy she needed to relieve the stress of royal life.

The Princess's encounters with equestrian sports have been more fraught—and more controversial. To please the Queen, Diana has gone riding, although she has never liked horses or the horsey set. Talk of the day's eventing or hunting and analysis of the merits of various horses bores her to tears. But as many of the Royal Family circle are of that ilk, she has been obliged to put up with it. The royals feel at ease in the company of horsey folk; they share a common ground where class, money, and breeding are all secondary to their knowledge of horseflesh.

Diana is too nervous to feel comfortable on a horse, and she used her minor fall from her pony at the age of eight as an excuse to avoid riding whenever she could. Such excuses simply don't hold up, however, when confronted with a request from the Queen. The Queen didn't pressure Diana into going riding; she merely suggested she might give her some lessons to get her confidence back. Diana could hardly refuse. But in spite of this encouragement and further help from Fergie during the long summer and winter breaks at Balmoral and Sandringham, Diana looks as uncomfortable as ever on horseback.

It was therefore all the more surprising when she went out hunting in 1987. Encouraged this time by her sister, Lady Sarah McCorquodale, with whom she was staying on her Lincolnshire farm, she followed the hounds with the Belvoir, reputed to be one of the toughest hunts in Britain. Although Diana went at a gentle pace on her sister's horse and didn't tackle any large fences, she was obviously making an effort to please Charles, who is mad keen on hunting and loves everyone to indulge in the sports he enjoys. She might have pleased Charles, but she didn't please the League Against Cruel Sports and was predictably criticized for her action.

A similar outcry had occurred when Diana was accused of shooting and wounding a stag during her honeymoon in October 1980. She was livid when the story appeared in the press, and Charles could do nothing to appease her. He spent the following day on the telephone to his London office, deciding what course of action to take. Finally, as is the usual royal way, he did nothing and hoped the story would just fade away. It did, but Diana remained thoroughly miserable. It was not her first taste of unpleasant press—she had also been accused of spending the night on the royal train before their marriage—and it certainly wasn't going to be her last. At the time, however, she couldn't understand why her husband didn't do something, and she felt let down.

Not that Diana minds shooting. The Royal Family has been stalking deer at Balmoral since Queen Victoria purchased the place in 1848, and Diana first went stalking in Scotland in her early teens. She is a good shot, and a gillie from the Balmoral estate clearly remembers "blooding" Diana after she had shot her first stag there. Blooding is the traditional, if barbaric, practice of smearing the blood of a dead stag on the face of the man or woman who has killed it.

Diana is in a no-win situation. If she refuses to join the traditional stalking parties—the Queen shot her first stag at sixteen, but no longer shoots—she will appear rude, but if she goes, she runs the risk of unwelcome publicity from animal campaigners. Apparently she has decided to compromise. Although she joins the royal shooting parties for pheasant, partridge, and grouse, she has never been spotted with a gun. She has even been credited with persuading Prince Charles to give up shooting for a short period.

Actually, Charles was simply going through one of his phases, as when he turned vegetarian for a short time. He felt that killing anything, especially the overfed pheasants at Sandringham, was not good sport, and he gave his priceless pair of Purdy guns to his brother Andrew. After some pressure from Prince Philip, who rightly pointed out that Charles was the mainstay of shooting parties on the royal estates, he started again.

It has been eight years since Diana was first spotted with Prince Charles on the banks of the river Dee in Scotland and seemed to have the makings of a keen fisherwoman. It was not to be. In spite of fly-fishing lessons from her mother in the Highlands of Scotland and instructions from one of the Balmoral gillies, Charles Knight, Diana never took to her husband's favorite pastime. She even had to put up with him fishing on the river Test on the first evening of their honeymoon at Broadlands. Charles still goes fishing and most years joins his friends Lord and Lady Tryon at their fishing lodge in Iceland. Charles goes alone. Diana will sail with him and ski with him, but fishing is something she has abandoned.

Childhood holidays, a later spell at a finishing school, and subsequent chalet parties in Switzerland with her contemporaries left Diana an adept skier. But she has never liked skiing furiously down the black runs like Prince Charles or the Duchess of York. And she hates skiing when it is very cold.

This lack of bravery on the pistes does have a medical justification. The Princess enjoys good health, which is just as well for one who says, "I don't like needles or drips." But she did once break her leg skiing, and she suffers from a painful back. Physiotherapists have little doubt that her problem stems from her habit of holding her children on her hip, thus causing her back muscles injury. When they act up, she has a physiotherapist visit her at home to give her treatment. Standing for long intervals in high heels doesn't help, and Diana admits to getting "backache, not tired feet." When her back is bad, the only exercise she does is walking. With her Sony Walkman clamped firmly to her head, she goes for long solitary strolls.

"I'm a great believer in having music wherever I go," she says. "And it's just a big treat to go out for a walk with music still coming with me." Diana also has a special hard mattress to help her back.

Like her husband and most members of the Royal Family, including the Queen and Queen Mother, Diana has become a champion of alternative medicine, whenever possible using herbal remedies as cures rather than the antibiotics of modern medicine. It was not always so. When she was being courted by the Prince, she didn't know what the word *homeopathic* meant. A friend pointed out, "If you're going to become the daughter-in-law of the Queen, you'd better find out."

She went away and tried a homeopathic cure for the flu she was suffering from. It worked for twenty-four hours. "But when the effect wore off, I think my cold was worse than ever," she reported. Encouraged by Charles, however, her faith has increased, and she tries herbal remedies such as diluted traces of arsenic for stomach complaints, deadly nightshade for sore throats, and feverfew plant, a type of chrysanthemum, to relieve symptoms of migraine.

When Charles or Diana is really unwell, they will consult a doctor, but for a cold or headache Charles finds a game of polo just as good. "If I have a game of polo," he says, "I feel five hundred times better."

Because the children pick up all types of childhood ailments at school, including colds and flu, Charles and Diana suffer during the winter. If Charles has a cold, he will sleep in another room to try to avoid infecting Diana and keeping her awake with his coughing. All the Royal Family members avoid each other when they have colds—an illness might mean canceling an engagement and disappointing hundreds of people. Even during the uncomfortable times of her pregnancies, when the Princess was suffering from morning sickness that went on all day, Diana seldom canceled an appointment, preferring to suffer the discomfort rather than the guilt she felt at letting so many people down.

Diana couldn't bear the extra weight she gained while carrying William and was determined to lose it as quickly as possible, "I want to fit into my jeans," she said and did the vigorous aerobics made fashionable by Jane Fonda at the time. She didn't do them after the birth of Harry, however, which led to another bout of rumor. But then there are always rumors about Diana's weight gain and loss.

Diana doesn't have very good circulation, and she suffers from extremes of temperature and jet lag, which can make overseas tours difficult for her too. Unlike her husband, who has the ability to catnap anywhere and has even been known to fall asleep over dinner and wake ten minutes later, refreshed, Diana will lie down for a rest only to discover she is unable to sleep. Combating jet lag with plenty of water and very little food has not helped, and she now resigns herself to staring at the ceiling or half-watching any program on television while she tries to relax. The breathing exercises that Betty Parsons taught her during her pregnancies sometimes help, but they don't put her to sleep, and she dislikes sleeping pills.

Despite her determination to meet her commitments, Diana's discomfort is sometimes obvious, and it leads to much speculation about her health and, especially about whether she is pregnant again.

Another strange rumor started when Diana, who gets slightly claustrophobic in large crowds, suffered a dizzy spell during a tour of Expo '86 in Vancouver and appeared to faint. That led to speculation that she subsequently visited the clinic of Swedish homeopath Gudrun Jonsson and underwent sessions encased in a white plastic barrel that electronically neutralizes the harmful ions that build up in the body.

Gudrun's treatment, so the story goes, was designed to counteract Diana's fainting spells. Gudrun, whose treatment—a mixture of homeopathy, reflexology, and biopathy—is designed to bring the body back to its correct balance, has many society patients, including the Duchess of York, but has never treated the Princess.

Even the most seasoned travelers suffer such discomfort of course. But Diana, because of her exhausting schedule, does have to take care, and she doesn't always take enough. When she is very busy, her eating habits become erratic, and her weight starts fluctuating.

It has fluctuated so dramatically since the birth of William, in fact, that during the early years there were suggestions that she had anorexia nervosa.

"I can tell you for a fact, Diana did *not* have anorexia nervosa," her former hairdresser, Kevin Shanley, says. "The more people worried, the more annoyed she became."

She has even been suspected of having bulimia, another eating disorder characterized by binging and purging. It was reported that Diana was caught in the kitchens at Windsor Castle by a footman just as she was cramming a feast of meat pie into her mouth. And one story has it that she consumed an entire chicken meant for a dinner party.

Diana's friends deny all this. Diana, they say, eats normally, but she still does not like official banquets. Says Kevin Shanley, "Diana told me how she cuts up her food, moves it around her plate, and brings her fork to her mouth a couple of times without taking a mouthful." To make up for this calorie deficiency, Diana will grab a sandwich or a piece of chocolate afterward. She does not throw up. Nor does she binge.

She takes the same precautions with alcohol, realizing that if she drank all the booze offered to her at official functions Prince Charles would have to carry her home on his back.

Last year, while the Waleses were on holiday with King Juan Carlos and his family in Mallorca, a snapshot revealed Diana's considerable stomach and sparked rumors of another pregnancy. Nothing could have been further from the truth.

Diana had gained her stomach as a *result* of her pregnancies—her abdominal muscles had collapsed, doctors explained, due to lack of postnatal exercise. Diana had lost weight easily after the birth of Harry and therefore did not feel the pressing necessity to embark on a special exercise program at the time. However, she is still insecure about her looks and worries about her weight, so she has installed an exercise machine in Kensington Palace to combat the problem.

And although she still tucks into her favorite sweets or any form of chocolate, because she finds it gives her energy, Diana, partly under the influence of her husband, is obsessed with healthy eating. All their vegetables are grown organically at Highgrove and transported to London on Monday mornings. Charles has been an advocate of the low-fat, high-fiber diet since 1978, sparked off by a visit to an agricultural center. He was disturbed by the environment in which the pigs were kept to produce maximum output. "I shall become a vegetarian," he declared. "I'm glad I'm not a pig."

Both Charles and Diana admit they feel much better if they don't eat much meat, so their meals consist mainly of fish, chicken, eggs, and fresh vegetables. Diana once took a cooking course, but describes herself only as an "average cook." That doesn't stop her from appreciating good food; however. She loves to tuck into pasta, homemade soups, and quiches. "I'm so busy," she says, "I never put on an ounce, and I can eat as much as I like."

Even when on a skiing holiday the Waleses are fussy about their diet. Chalet girls are dispatched to all the neighboring villages to find fish, vegetables, and fruit suitable for the royal palates. And when Charles is off powder-skiing with the Duchess of York and a guide, Diana is quite happy to give her rusty cooking skills a whirl while she waits for the more adventurous in the party to return.

Diana's healthful diet and faithfully followed exercise regimen are largely responsible for the glow of her natural beauty, but she has other assistance as well. "I'm a perfectionist with myself," she says, And as a perfectionist she always wants to look and be at her best.

One way she does so is by being able to command the services of the best people in the British beauty business.

One of the best things about royal tours, Diana admits, is having her own hairdresser. Richard Dalton visits Kensington Palace most mornings when the Princess has an official engagement, and depending on the timing, she sometimes washes her own hair in the shower and is ready in her dressing room listening to Capital Radio before he arrives. If they have very little time, he will brush her hair through and restyle it with curling tongs. As it is lightly permed on the top, Diana's hair holds a style well and doesn't need to be washed every day, unless she has been swimming. Whenever necessary, Dalton streaks her naturally fair hair, and they sometimes experiment with new styles—but nothing too outlandish, just a change in the length. Nowadays Diana reserves the more outrageous hairstyles she longs to have for private photo sessions.

Both William and Harry also have their hair cut by Dalton, and if Prince Charles is around, the hairdresser will shape his thinning thatch too.

When the princess is on holiday, she finds her hair a problem. Heat and humidity frizz it, so she often wears a scarf or just pins it back. She admits "lots of lacquer" helps keep her hair in place between sessions, but she is not very good at handling it herself. So she is relieved to have Dalton accompany her on royal tours, available to do her hair whenever she needs him. Then he will also do the hair of the Princess's lady-in-waiting, and Anne Beckwith-Smith has a hairstyle suspiciously like her employer's.

During Ascot Week in the summer and big shooting weekends in the winter, Dalton spends a couple of nights at Windsor or Sandringham to ensure Diana's hair is perfect. Then the entire party—apart from the Queen, who has her own hairdresser, Charles Martyn—can benefit from Dalton's expertise and have their hair done before the evening's entertainment. It is hard work for him, but he readily admits the advantages far outweigh the disadvantages.

"I once dreamt of being Elizabeth Taylor's hairdresser," he said, "but I never thought I would end up doing the hair of the future Queen."

Ever since Grace Coddington, the beauty without cruelty cosmetics champion and her team at *Vogue* introduced her to Barbara Daly, Diana has remained with Britain's top makeup artist. Barbara did Diana's makeup for the wedding and, until she became adept at it herself, for important engagements. When Diana first saw the effect the television cameras had on her simple makeup, she implored Barbara to help her. It was, however, impractical for her to do Diana's makeup all the time, so the Princess, through trial and error, devised her own methods. Sometimes she got it wrong and wore too much, but increasingly she got it right. She has learned to accentuate her startling blue eyes with liner drawn just inside the lower lid, and to combat her high coloring she uses peach, not pink, blusher and has literally hundreds of different cosmetic brushes to blend color on every part of her face. Many of the products she uses are hypoallergenic, such as Clinique, or from Daly's extensive Colourings or Body Shop range.

"I'm a fan of Body Shop," Diana says. She even insists that her husband use the shampoo and picked up some special mud shampoo from Barbara Daly, inquiring whether it would help the thinning. She likes experimenting with different-colored eyeshadows and wears Christian Dior's Sailboat Blue mascara. A couple of years ago she was brave enough to wear body glitter and sprayed it on her hair and shoulders for the British fashion banquet, where she knew it wouldn't cause any comment.

To combat the small blemishes she gets on her cheek she uses a concealer stick from the Colourings range. She also uses the Colourings leg makeup in the summer, though not always applying it as expertly as she might wish. It does, however, have the effect of making slightly tanned legs look "holiday brown" and saves the necessity of wearing tights.

"Tights are great," Diana says, "but I hate them in the summer and prefer tanned legs." So much so that during a Buckingham Palace garden party in the early part of her marriage Diana turned up with bare legs, shocking the establishment, who considered appearing without them the equivalent of appearing undressed.

The pencil-slim, suntanned Diana is almost a thing of yesteryear. No longer desperate to stretch out by the pool or rush up onto the roof garden at Kensington Palace the moment the sun appears, Diana has opted for a paler, though still athletic, look.

All in all, since she became the Princess of Wales Diana has become more polished, more poised, and possibly even happier. Prince Charles has educated his wife to believe in the Kurt Hahn (the founder of Gordonstoun) philosophy of the "platonic ideal" of a healthy mind in a healthy body. He feels the pressures of living in the royal goldfish bowl can generate problems that directly affect the body: stress, loneliness, anger, and frustration—all regular features of royal life.

"I'm a great believer in having friends to whom you can talk about anything that bothers you," Charles says. "I'm against bottling it up. If you haven't got someone to talk to, it's vital to get rid of what's bothering you in some way or another."

In the early days, Diana really didn't have such a friend. Fortunately, those days ended with the arrival of one Sarah Ferguson.

13
Sisters-in-Law

W hen *Prince Andrew became* engaged to Sarah Ferguson, Diana drew an almost audible sigh of relief.

"You don't need me anymore," she told waiting newsmen. "Now you've got Fergie."

That will never be quite true. The Duchess of York is vibrant, adventurous, and unstuffy. And as the newest daughter-in-law of the Queen, she has inevitably attracted the flock of photographers and reporters who make their living following the Royal Family.

But Diana will one day be Queen, a status Fergie—the wife of a younger son—will never attain. For all the attention she now attracts, her life will always be played out in the shadow of the younger woman.

In a very real way, however, Sarah's arrival has eased the pressure on Diana.

"It's nice for Diana to have a friend to talk to that really understands what it's like to be watched whenever she sneezes or coughs," former Highgrove housekeeper Joan Boardman says. "I don't think she's jealous that a new face on the scene will steal the limelight from her. In fact, I am sure she is quite glad to have someone to share it."

Most important, she now has a real friend she can confide in. For no matter how outgoing and informal she may be— and Diana is both—there is always the barrier of her royalty between her and even her oldest friends.

For it is a royal rule—and one emphasized over and over again by her husband, who is constantly warning her to be on guard against people whose motives for courting her friend ship may not be unconnected to the fact that she is the Princess of Wales—that problems are never discussed outside the immediate family.

With Fergie that regal precept does not apply. The two have been friends ever since they met at polo ("And doesn't everyone meet at polo?" as Fergie's mother, Mrs. Susan Barrantes, exclaimed from the ivory tower of her own inter ests) when Diana first started walking out with Charles. "Look after her for me," Charles told the friendly redhead. And she did.

It was a natural friendship that drew on a common back ground. Both had spent their childhood in the company of the royal circle. Diana's father, Lord Spencer, is a former equerry to the Queen and was her frequent guest at lunch and dinner at Sandringham. The Queen also would occasionally call by for tea at Park House on the Sandringham estate where Lord Spencer lived until moving into Althorp, the fifteenth-century ancestral home. Diana grew up calling Andrew and Edward by their first names.

Fergie has also known the Queen's younger sons for al most as long as she can remember. But not in quite the same way. Her father, Major Ronald Ferguson, had once com manded the Sovereign's Escort, the cavalry detachment that accompanies the Monarch on ceremonial occasions. It brought him into close contact with the Queen, and there was the time when, riding a trifle too enthusiastically, he got ahead of her coach. "Come back, Ronnie," the Queen or dered. "It's me everyone has come to see—not you."

The Major did not succeed in emulating his own father,

Andrew, who had risen to the rank of colonel commanding the Life Guards. His association with the Royal Family did not end, however, when he left the army. A fine horseman and a finer polo player who had acted as military advisor on the film *Charge of the Light Brigade*, the Major remained a close friend of Prince Philip. They played polo together and socialized within the elite polo crowd.

When Philip was forced to give up the game because of arthritis of the wrists, Ferguson was placed in charge of Prince Charles's polo interests.

"It just sort of happened," the Major says. "When Philip was playing, the chairman of the Guards Polo Club was Colonel Gerald Leigh—he looked after Philip's affairs and organized his matches. As deputy chairman I do much the same thing for Charles.

"I'm not employed by the Prince of Wales. I do it as an act of friendship, and it's worked terribly well. I don't have to refer to anybody except him."

It is a role that puts him on first-name terms with the future King, but only in the environment of that tough, hard, equestrian sport. Away from the polo field, he says, "I don't see very much of the Royal Family."

Nor did his daughter Sarah.

There were, it is true, the occasional picnics at polo that Fergie was invited to. But that was really as far as it went. An independent young woman, Fergie had set off at an early age to make her own life and her own set of friends.

While Diana's premarital experiences were confined to brief employment as a cleaning lady and then at a nursery school, plus a rather innocent social life, Fergie had pursued a much more worldly path.

After school, where, like Diana, she had not exactly distinguished herself academically (though, unlike Diana, she did manage to garner enough "O" levels to give her the British equivalent of junior high school graduation), she had taken a bus ride through South America down to Argentina where her mother now lives.

She had had two serious love affairs. One was with Kim

Smith-Bingham. She had also stayed in the Swiss ski resort of Verbier with Paddy McNally, a motor racing entrepreneur almost old enough to be her father.

And while Diana had a family trust to fall back on, Fergie had had to work for a living.

The Fergusons own an eight-hundred-acre estate called Dummer Down in Hampshire. But as a retired army officer from a family of army officers and without any great family fortune behind him, Major Ferguson was not able to give his daughter more than a small private income—"And when I say small, I mean small," he insists.

For all those differences—and as slight as they may seem to the untutored eye, they constitute the finer nuances that make up the class divisions in Britain—the two women hit it off immediately.

There was, for instance, the similarity in their childhoods. When Diana was six years old, her mother, Frances (who, by one of those ironic coincidences not uncommon in the small, claustrophobic world of society, had once been proposed to by Ronald Ferguson), had left the marital home and moved in with wallpaper heir Peter Shand Kydd.

When Fergie was thirteen, her mother, Susan, had done likewise and run off with the Argentine polo player Hector Barrantes. "It was a trauma," their father recalls, for both Sarah and her sister Jane.

It would be stretching the psychological truth, however, to say that these early upsets provided the foundation of the empathy Fergie and Diana felt for each other. Rather it was the way each had reacted to the upheavals in her life that opened the way to a friendship that has changed the face of the Royal Family forever.

The departure of her mother had left Diana diffident and insecure, a woman whose shyness had only been emphasized by her entry into the most isolated family in the world.

Fergie, on the other hand, had responded to the change in her domestic circumstances by developing into a buoyant, outgoing personality, always willing to join in and always eager to please. In Verbier she had always made it her duty to ensure that all who came to McNally's "castle"—the sixteen-room chalet up the hill from the notorious Farm Club (*the* nightclub in Verbier) that she retreats to for weekends and school holidays—were put at their ease, no mean feat in the acerbic, conversationally savage McNally set.

It was this quality Fergie brought into her relationship with Diana. She knew how to put the Princess at her ease. She had been accustomed to talking to royalty and courtiers since she was a child. She had refined that ability to draw the best out of people without losing sight of her own personality in the hard school of jet-setters she had mixed with in Switzerland and the south of France and on the holiday island of Ibiza.

She was outgoing and friendly, and she made Diana laugh. They giggled together at some of the characters they observed on the polo scene.

Also, and most important, Sarah represented no threat. For in those early days of her marriage Diana was noticeably on guard if any attractive "rival" ventured into the vicinity of her husband; Lady Tryon and Camilla Parker-Bowles, for instance, quickly found themselves on the outside of the royal circle they had once been so close to the center of.

No one was surprised when Diana asked Sarah to her wedding at St. Paul's Cathedral. And there was even talk that Diana would make her a lady-in-waiting.

Her father discounts that. "She'd only known Diana for a year at the time," he points out. That would not have mattered except that she was a little too inexperienced and, more significantly, a little too exuberant for such a job.

Fergie, was however, asked to Diana's twenty-first birthday lunch at Buckingham Palace—the only non–family member to be so invited.

This was a difficult time for the new and terribly young Princess of Wales. She had married a Prince, but in this fairy tale the Princess found herself increasingly confined in the ivory tower that constitutes royal life. The royal machine had cut her off from the few friends she did have and was slowly but inexorably starting to swallow her up.

Into this void had come Fergie, who, as the daughter of her husband's polo manager, belonged ostensibly to Charles's circle. It was on Diana's insistence that she was also invited to join the Royal party at Windsor Castle for Royal Ascot, which is where Fergie's romance with Andrew began over the profiteroles.

Diana did not push Andrew and Fergie together. But she did encourage their friendship. She invited them to tea at Kensington Palace and Highgrove and Gloucestershire.

She and Fergie started having luncheon together, sometimes at Kensington Palace, often (to Diana's greater enjoyment) out at places like the restaurant at the Harvey Nichols department store in Knightsbridge.

And when romance developed into marriage, Diana was there to help Fergie with the ropes that she had had to learn through hard experience herself.

"She talked to Sarah about her life, and that helped her enormously," says Major Ferguson.

But if Diana was involving herself in the life of her new "BF" and offering her what advice she could, Sarah, in her turn, was also having a considerable effect on Diana.

The Princess of Wales had come into the Royal Family a maiden barely out of her teens, gauche and immature. "She came straight from the nursery school to the Palace," Prince Charles's former valet, the late Stephen Barry, remarked.

Fergie's case was very different. She was twenty-six years old when she married. She had been around—geographically, emotionally, sexually. Her personality had been formed and glazed in a wider world than Diana had ever known. She was, her father was fond of saying, "streetwise."

At first there was a reserve in her public approach to her new public role as a member of the world's most scrutinized, most public family. Being in their company and being one of them are very different things, and the change from friend to Duchess in her own right, was, as her father observed, "daunting."

Like her father, however, the Duchess of York has a character even the rigors of protocol cannot smother. Tall and attractive, with a gruff exterior that only emphasizes a wicked sense of humor, the Major has never been anything less than outspoken. "I am not bound by any rules or regulations, only by common sense and loyalty to my daughter," he says.

Unlike the family Sarah has married into, which makes it a rule never to answer the criticism and speculation that shower its way, Ferguson—like the proverbial cavalry and in conscious rejection of Windsor protocol—is always ready to ride in to her defense. When she visited Canada in 1987, for instance, the local press accused her of being, among other things, "a fat and frumpy, giggly disco queen."

Said the Major, "I should think those reports annoyed her intensely. But there is spunk behind Sarah's bounce, and those reports made her go all out to prove to them that she is not what they said she was."

It is an attitude that meets with father's approval. For it was Major Ferguson who turned to his daughter as they drove down the Mall in her wedding coach on her way to Westminster Abbey that morning in July 1986 and reminded her, "Always be yourself."

It is advice the Duchess of York has followed. She remains as friendly, outgoing, and spontaneous as she ever was in those far-off days in Verbier. She is still just as anxious to put people at their ease—a trait that has endeared her to the Royal Family in a way that Diana has never quite managed.

The Queen Mother, who can be quite cantankerous, adores her. "She is so *English*," she keeps saying, adding that she is free of those airs and graces "we can't stand."

She has also established a rapport with the Queen. It would not be accurate to say that the Queen and the future Queen do not get on. They do. But it is not a particularly close relationship. Fergie, however, has a great deal in common with her mother-in-law. They are both countrywomen by inclination, with a mutual interest in dogs and horses. And the Queen knows very well what it is like to be married to a young naval officer who is away much of the time, as Andrew is. That is how she started her own married life, after all.

When Andrew is on duty, Sarah sometimes sees the Queen alone. They dine together, official engagements permitting, often on the card table in front of the television.

It is on occasions like these that Fergie's absence of those "airs and graces" comes into play. If, for instance, the Queen offers her a glass of that sweet white German wine she likes so much—a taste few share—Fergie will drink it. Her more modern palate—like Diana's—much prefers the crisper sparkle of Champagne or Chablis or an Italian Orvieto, but that is not the point—not for Sarah, that is. She wouldn't dream of asking for a glass of Champagne or even a glass of Perrier.

Yet if this latest recruit to the Royal Family has won herself a high approval rating within the Firm, not everyone approves of the subtle but penetrating wind of change she has brought to the dusty recesses of royal life.

Some will argue, and argue forcefully, that the changes she has wrought have not been all for the good. Indeed, the critics claim, her influence on Diana, the woman who will one day be Queen, has in fact been positively harmful.

Princess Michael of Kent once told me, "She is strong, she is independent. You watch—Fergie will change us all!"

And the person who has changed most is the Princess of Wales. The Shy Di of yesterday has gone, to be replaced by a woman who seems increasingly determined to enjoy herself even if it means going against the traditions of conservative decorum that the British have come to expect from their reigning family.

In one sense the metamorphosis was, if not inevitable, then at least not unexpected. Diana never really had the chance to get out with people her own age and enjoy the things most other young people take, naturally and healthily, for granted. She has lived a life without dates or carefree holidays in the sun. Friends never simply "drop round" to Kensington Palace for a cup of tea, and when Diana went out it was always with a detective and, certainly in the early days of her marriage, only to places her husband had decided she should go.

If there was going to be a breakout, it was going to come now. Her sons had started school, and for the first time in her marriage she found herself with time on her hands—and an understandable determination to get out and enjoy it.

Sarah showed her the way. She introduced her to a new and wider range of people drawn from her own age group and so very different from the conservative and intellectually intimidating circle Charles prefers. She showed Diana that, notwithstanding her position, it is possible to have fun.

The fun started almost straight away. For it was Fergie who persuaded Diana to make a foray into Annabel's disguised as a policewoman.

It was the night of Andrew's stag party, and Fergie was convinced that he was holding a dinner party in the private room of that most exclusive nightclub in Mayfair's Berkeley Square. She was wrong, but it was a reasonable guess; Annabel's has built its reputation on discretion, and for twenty-five years the rich and the famous have sought their relaxation there, secure in the knowledge that any word of their indiscretions would remain safely within the confines of its basement walls.

Opened by Mark Birley in 1963 and named after his then wife, the sister of the Marquis of Londonderry, who is now married to international corporate raider Jimmy Goldsmith, Annabel's is where the younger members of the Royal Family go when they want to relax and let their hair down.

To call Annabel's a nightclub is something of a misnomer. It is really an old-fashioned club with music and a dance floor at the back if you want it—a place to drop into to see friends and to dine on some of the finest food in London.

The style is English country house, but on the grandest and most luxurious scale and much warmer than any of the Royal Family's homes. Annabel's style recalls an earlier era. From the moment Nando the doorman takes your car keys— he never gives you a ticket; he *knows* who you are—you are back in an age of elegance and service.

In the ladies' cloakroom, Mabel rules. She has been the confidante and romantic advisor to three generations of gentlewomen. Fergie, who has been going to Annabel's since she was nineteen, introduced Diana to Mabel.

Then it is to the bar, an elegant wood-paneled room covered with the works of Sir Edwin Landseer and Augustus John and Mark's own father, royal court painter Sir Oswald Birley.

This is not a place for gold chains or bleached blonde bimbos. At Annabel's the men wear suits. There has always been a Duke, a Cabinet minister or two, perhaps the heir to the Throne gathering for a drink before moving on into the dining room where Louis reigns. The finest of maitre d's, Louis has an elephant's memory for faces and names.

This of course was no mean hurdle for the two young women to overcome. The club servants know Fergie. Diana is hardly unnoticeable. To get through the club and into the private room to the right across from the restaurant bar was clearly going to prove no easy matter. This, however, is exactly the kind of merry jape Fergie had always enjoyed and still does. And this was exactly the kind of night out Diana wanted to join in on.

Diana, Fergie, Pamela Stephenson, and Renate, Elton John's wife, had been dining with Jane, the Duchess of Roxburghe. At about 10:30 Diana was ready to head off home for bed but Fergie had other ideas. She and Pamela had "borrowed" some police uniforms from their friend Billy Connolly's theatrical outfitters.

With a great deal of giggling they dressed up and Pamela drove Diana's dark green Range Rover to Berkeley Square.

They left the Range Rover on the other side of Berkeley Square and walked across it and into Annabel's, under the awning, down the stairs, and into the club. City financier Paddy Dodd Noble, whose wife, Julia, is an old friend of Fergie's and once (in yet another circle within a circle that so marks London society) walked out with Andrew, signed them in.

As disguises go, policewomen's outfits are not the most unnoticeable in Annabel's. This is no speakeasy; the only police ever to be found here are very senior members of the force, and they arrive not in uniform but in well-cut Savile Row suits.

Louis, the manager, was annoyed and told them to leave. "You're upsetting the other customers," he said as they retreated to the front bar. But if the costumes did not for one moment fool the club servants, they certainly confused the members clustering in the outer sanctum. They looked and they stepped back, leaving the three women to make their way up to the bar, where they dissolved in a most unpolicelike fit of giggles.

Even that failed to provide the clue to one well-known Fleet Street journalist, a large bumptious man much the worse for alcoholic wear, who, oblivious to the scoop swimming before his eyes, staggered over to demand to know what a nice WPC like her (Diana) was doing in a place like this. He then proceeded to pinch the bottom of the Princess of Wales. Greater men have paid dearly for lesser crimes in times past, but in 1986 the covey of royal women simply giggled.

Then Fergie, who was wearing a wig and glasses, recognized two friends on the opposite side of the room. She winked. They stared blankly. She winked again. In confused disbelief the couple made their way through the crowd and offered them a drink.

"I don't drink on duty," Diana said and dissolved into another fit of giggles, but both the girls finally accepted a Buck's Fizz.

By now the club's servants were in a state of some anxiety. A few members now knew the Princess of Wales and Sarah Ferguson were on the premises. Others believed they were kissogram girls. Most, however, were convinced that three policewomen were on the premises—an unheard of intrusion in a club where good behavior is a requisite of membership. The joke was now perilously close to the precipice of farce.

By now Diana, Fergie, and their "minders," Pamela and Renate, knew that whoever else might be there, Andrew and his stag party were not. (They were in fact several miles away in a private house in Holland Park.) It was time to go.

They drank the last of their champagne and orange juice. They said a whispered farewell to the few who had recognized them. And then, still dissolved by the laughter that makes little sound but convulses the body, they made their way back up the staircase, past the trelliswork, and into the night. No nightingales sang; instead the air was rent with the sound of the giggling women.

Diana was last seen waddling across Berkeley Square— doing her impersonation of Charlie Chaplin—to the Range Rover and the drive back to Buckingham Palace and a confrontation with the very real policemen on the gate who, unaware of their identities, at first refused to allow them in.

Within twenty-four hours the story was front-page news. The account of the royal party's nocturnal meanderings had sprinted down society's telegraph and into the social columns. As it was bound to. And the reaction was just as predictable.

The sanctimonious mounted their high horses. Several MPs, their eyes focused firmly on their press cuttings, demanded to know what action the police intended to take against two young women who had impersonated police officers in violation of the law (the answer was none). Forests were felled as newspaper pundits, dipping their pens into the ink of lighthearted controversy, scribbled their way into the debate, some to defend the highjinks of youth, others to condemn.

Fergie took the brickbats in her stride. It had, she would say later, just been a bit of harmless fun, the kind of prank she had always indulged in and always enjoyed. And why not? she would ask.

Diana was not allowed to dismiss the incident quite so easily, however. The public, brought up to expect the Royal Family to set a standard of stolid bourgeois propriety, might excuse a bouncy twenty-six-year-old her bit of fun on the eve of her wedding. But Diana is different. She is the mother of two small boys and the future Queen. The suspicion was laid that the Princess of Wales was traveling dangerously close to the edge of the rails.

But if the public was concerned, Diana most decidedly was not. Early in 1987 she joined her husband on their annual skiing expedition to Klosters in Switzerland. The Duke and

Duchess of York were there too. And one night in their chalet the two women put on a cabaret act for their friends.

They put on head scarves and dark glasses and whatever other unlikely items of clothing they could find, and in between fortifying gulps of *gluwein*—the potent mulled wine—they danced and sang and kicked their legs high in the air.

Prince Charles was not there that night. A young man called Philip Dunne was.

Once again Major Ferguson rides to his daughter's defense. "I am not aware," he says, "that Sarah has encouraged her [Diana] to meet anybody who is dubious. Why should she?"

As far as Diana was concerned, it was all good clean "hooray" relaxation. "It was a wonderful holiday," she said. "And Fergie is such fun to be around."

Prince Charles agreed—up to a point. He was thoroughly bored by that sort of impromptu entertainment and much preferred to devote his energies to a hard day's skiing on the slopes with his friend Charles Palmer-Tomkinson and take it easy afterwards with a hot bath, a book, or a video. Nor did nightclubs hold much attraction for him, and he let Diana go off dancing at Casa Antica with friends like brewery heir Peter Greenall and his wife Clare, while he stayed behind in the chalet, explaining that when he did go out, "I get too tired as I like to start skiing early in the morning."

"Sarah is a marvelous girl," Charles has always insisted. But of all the members of the Royal Family, the Prince is the most muted in his praise of the extroverted redhead who is now his sister-in-law. Her jolly hockey sticks approach to life can grate on a man who is falling fast into a premature middle age, and the tetchiness showed when the two royal couples gathered on the slopes one morning for a photo call.

Charles has always disliked the staged informality of these moments, and as his relationship with the traveling press corps that accompanies him everywhere continues its deterioration, he dislikes them even more. At best it is a duty, but usually it is a chore. Diana, conversely, and despite her occasional moods, quite enjoys looking into a camera lens. It is one way this woman, who dreads public speaking and has given only one interview (and that one on television with Sir Alastair Burnet was carefully rehearsed), has to communicate. This morning she was in fine fettle, laughing and joking and clowning about with her new sister-in-law—her friend.

They started screaming at each other and trying to stuff snowballs down each other's ski suit. They started pushing, and as their skis began sliding away from underneath, the photographers poised themselves for a money-earning picture of the Duchess and the Princess on the piste, collapsed like two melted snowmen.

Charles was not amused. "Come on, come on," he barked tetchily. Diana, for a moment, looked as if she was about to ignore her husband. Fergie did not. She took one look at the future King and promptly straightened up. She may be the life and soul of the party, but she also knows where to draw the line.

But if Fergie's sense of "correctness" reined Diana back that day, they both crossed it at Royal Ascot some months later.

As an "incident" it was harmless enough. Diana and Fergie were walking back together from the paddock, where they had been to see the horses being paraded before the next race, to the Queen's box in the Royal Enclosure. In front of them was Lulu Blacker, a cousin of Yorkshire landowner Earl Peel. She has been a friend of Fergie's since they were at Danes Hill School together and was once the companion of re-formed drug addict the Marquis of Blandford, son and heir of the immensely grand Duke of Marlborough. She is now a friend of Diana's and was invited to join the royal party at Windsor Castle for Ascot Week.

Without thinking, Fergie and Diana started prodding Lulu in the backside with their umbrellas. They also prodded the Queen's former equerry, the late, dashing Hugh Lindsay. Both with the inevitable consequences. The photographers poised on the press balcony on the first floor of the grandstand had had their cameras trained on the royal twosome from the moment they left the enclosure and all the way back again. Their shutters clicked, and yet again the Duchess of York and the Princess of Wales found themselves on the front pages in a situation that many—Prince Charles included—deemed less than proper.

Again Major Ferguson rode forth to his daughter's defense. "It so happened that the person they jabbed was a very great friend of theirs," he says. "He was just in front of them, and it was a very natural reaction to have a bit of fun."

In an interview in an American magazine he added, "The press say you can't behave like that, which is ludicrous."

Not everyone is so convinced. "Look, Fergie's wonderful and great fun and all that," says an advisor to the Royal Family. "But I am afraid that there are different rules in force when it comes to the Princess of Wales."

That carefully weighted remark carries the implicit accusation that in some direct and specific way the Duchess of York is responsible for whatever changes have taken place in Diana over these past couple of years.

At a casual glance there might appear to be some truth in that. It is only since Fergie arrived on the royal scene that Diana has started behaving in such a lighthearted and, to the deeply conservative, frivolous way. It is also true that the more notable breakdowns in regal dignity have occurred when the Duchess of York has been in attendance.

To suggest, however, that in some bewitching way Fergie is the cheerleader egging Diana on is to overstate the influence she exerts over the future Queen.

For above all the Duchess of York is a team player, and even in the intimacy of the Royal Family she always knows how far she can go. It is something she learned from her father, who may resort to barrack language in the royal presence but never forgets to call the Prince of Wales "Sir."

So it is with his daughter. If the Princess wants to sing or dance or get dressed up in funny clothes and hide under the sofa, Fergie is delighted to join in. If the Princess decides to start a snowball fight, Fergie will throw one back. But she will always curtsy to the wife of the future Sovereign when she comes into her presence. It is the protocol, and the Duchess of York knows the rules.

Fergie does not compete with Diana in the fashion stakes, either. For one reason, she does not have the money. "Everyone thinks that because you're married to a member of the Royal Family you are rich beforehand and automatically become even richer," says the father. "That is ridiculous."

Nor does she have the same model's figure. In real life she is in fact quite trim and well groomed. And, with the help of St. Laurent's French fashion house, which free of charge provided her with a dozen haute couture outfits (one evening gown alone cost $21,000), and that magnificent mane of red hair, she can look stunning. In the distortion of photographs, however, a figure that until she started dieting was Junoesque and even now could not be called svelte tends to inflate—leading to those charges of dumpiness.

That is something Diana can never be accused of; even on a bad day, when she is making a deliberate effort to dress down, she still carries herself with the kind of style that one can only be born with.

Says a friend of the Duchess, "Sarah always treads carefully. They are genuinely the best of friends, but Sarah knows when to stop fooling around; she never forgets that Diana is the Princess of Wales. It does not interfere with their friendship—it is so subtle that an outsider would never really notice. But it is there."

But if the Duchess of York, out of breeding, protocol, and an innate sense of what is right, makes it her business not to be seen to compete with the Princess of Wales, one cannot help but sense that Diana is in subtle competition with Fergie.

Before Sarah arrived on the royal horizon, Diana held unchallenged the high ground of attention. Now she finds herself constantly being compared to a woman who is at least her match in most things and her better in many.

It must be galling to the Princess to see how well and without any apparent effort Sarah has slipped into the rhythm of the Royal Family and the easy, unaffected way she has won the approval of her royal in-laws—something she herself has never quite managed to achieve.

And while Diana is an excellent swimmer and a superb dancer, Fergie is a black-run skier, a fine horsewoman, and "can swim like a mermaid," and recently she qualified as a pilot in both fixed-wing planes and helicopters.

She can tell risqué jokes that have her husband and her father-in-law, Prince Philip, roaring their heads off, while Diana's attempts at humor all too often fall on the fallow ground of bad taste. That was the case—so the story goes—the day she asked her husband, who was deep in conversation at the time, what the definition was of "confusion."

When no reply was forthcoming, she gave the answer, "Father's Day in Brixton." The "joke," needless to say, went down like a lead balloon.

Nor can the obviously tactile, physical nature of the Yorks' relationship and the obvious interest they have in each other have escaped Diana's notice.

Perhaps most irritating of all, even if only at a subconscious level, is the independence Fergie continues to enjoy. The Duchess can go around rapping with the press, cheerfully advising a motley crew of paparazzi hiding behind a fence not to get "too sunburnt." She can pull faces. She can burst into tears, as she did when faced with a snake. She can put on a fur coat. Yet whenever Diana tries any of these things, she finds herself buried in criticism.

When the Duchess of York's pregnancy was first announced in January 1988, the situation was reversed. She was criticized for flying a helicopter and continuing to go skiing. But unlike Diana, who suffered terribly from morning sickness throughout her pregnancies, Fergie felt terrific and wasn't going to be told what she could and couldn't do.

Motherhood will, however, also bring the two women even closer. Diana adores children and is very fond of Fergie. There are other advantages in having a pregnant sister-in-law. It meant that Diana could wear some of Fergie's clothes. Before her engagement to Prince Andrew, Sarah sometimes borrowed Diana's clothes, but as her figure swelled the situation reversed. Diana was seen wearing one of the Duchess's Yves St. Laurent couture ball gowns at a private party.

"Fergie lent me this because she can't fit into it anymore," Diana explained jovially to friends. But that choice of friends again underlines the different standards by which the two women are judged.

Fergie still keeps in close contact with the people she knew before her marriage—an eclectic group of well-heeled, upper-class socialites. She has introduced many of them to Diana. But while it is acceptable for Sarah to dash out to lunch with a girlfriend and drop into Annabel's for a nightcap, it is not all right for Diana.

To argue that this is because Diana is the future Queen is an oversimplification. More than the roles marriage assigned to them, the real difference lies in the characters of the two women.

Fergie is doing what she has always done, behaving in the boisterous way she has always behaved. She is, as her father says, simply being herself. And why shouldn't she be? She was twenty-six years old when she got married, old enough to know her own mind. And while her exuberance can occasionally get the better of her, it leaves no feeling that anything untoward is lurking in the psychological background.

Diana is different. Plucked unripe from the tree of her life, she has grown up in a cosseted, unexciting world, hidden away from modern life by a curtain of advisors and retainers and a protocol that can be frustrating and emotionally stifling.

That, she had come to accept, was the price she had to pay.

Then along came Fergie, full of pluck and spirit and determined to live her own life to the fullest, in her own way, and getting away with it. It proved to be the catalyst in Diana's life.

14

The Throne Rangers

They drive through the gates in their Ford Escorts, Porsches, BMWs, and Range Rovers. They are the Di-set, the Throne Rangers, that group of well-heeled upper-class men and women who attend Diana's dinner parties at Kensington Palace, usually when Prince Charles is away. They escort her to the cinema, to lunch on shopping expeditions, and sometimes back to their own homes in Fulham, Chelsea, or Knightsbridge. (Throne Rangers seldom live north of London's Hyde Park, though they do sometimes venture south of the river Thames into Battersea and Clapham.)

Some of them have known Diana since her bachelor days. Many belong to the new crowd, people who have known the Duchess of York for years and now know Diana. The men, some married, are mostly army, ex-army, or "something in the city." Many have double-barreled names—Wentworth-Stanley, Twiston-Davies, Holland-Martin—and they address the Princess of Wales by the sobriquet "Duch," short for Duchess, the nickname her graces earned her as a child.

But even if the hairstyles have changed from the simple

cuts of yesteryear, and the low-heeled Gucci court shoes and Cacherel shirts cuffed with gilded bracelets have been replaced by Bruce Oldfield and fine jewels, Diana remains the "Sloane" she always was. And Diana, for all her rank and privilege—and in a significant way in spite of them—still values the friendships she forged long ago in a flat near Earl's Court where she would wait, hour after hour, sometimes for days on end, for a telephone call from the man who would one day make her a wife and Princess.

"She's incredibly unpretentious," says her old flatmate Carolyn Bartholomew. "I can pick up today where I left off with Diana." Carolyn, a godmother to Prince Harry, is now married to William Bartholomew, who owns Juliana's mobile discotheques, and is forging a career for herself as an opera singer.

Diana, to supplement the allowance she received from her trust funds, washed shirts and baby-sat and worked as a daily maid (a lowly occupation for an Earl's daughter, perhaps, but quite acceptable for those who did not have a proper job—provided of course, they were doing it for the right people). One person she worked for was Phillipa Whitaker. She employed Diana as a temporary nanny at her home in Hampshire and remembers, "If there was a job to be done, she'd do it."

And once it was done, there were dinners in local bistros and supper parties at home and rowdy skiing parties in Switzerland. And there were boyfriends to keep Diana company—men like Old Etonian Simon Berry, who took her to the tennis championships at Wimbledon and was a member of the chalet party during a skiing holiday in the French resort of Tignes, and George Plumptree, son of a Kent landowner. George, who is now happily married with two children, writes books about gardening and cricket and was supposed to take Diana to the ballet the day she got engaged to Charles. He didn't, of course, but was invited to the wedding.

She no longer sees him—he was a regular escort for almost a year—but still keeps in touch with many others of the group, including Phillipa Whitaker's brother, Willy van Straubenzee, whose shirts she once washed.

Diana was very popular. "There was nothing hoity-toity about her," Simon Berry remembers. "We were all just friends together."

There was a time, however, when she hardly saw anyone. Those early days in Buckingham Palace were lonely ones. With only a set of Walkman headphones for company, she would roam the Palace corridors waiting for Charles to come home—and too unsure of herself and her new position to invite her old friends round. Suppose Charles didn't like them? It was worry based on reason. The Prince had little in common with Diana's easygoing friends, almost a generation his junior. Usually only when Charles was out did she invite them in, for small lunch parties, but her life was not her own. She wasn't even allowed to spend the night before her wedding with her friends.

Diana had wanted to invite her flatmates Carolyn Pride, Ann Bolton, and Virginia Pitman to a small supper party. She was staying at Clarence House that evening, and for all her pleadings the Queen Mother refused her request, explaining gently there were some royal rules that could not be broken. Diana was told she must spend the last night of her spinsterhood with her family, not friends. Diana felt trapped. She was used to getting her own way, and it had been a long time since she had been told what she could do or whom she could see. Her father had seldom denied her anything. Out of a feeling of guilt that in some way he had been responsible for the departure of their mother, he had tried to compensate by allowing his children a very free rein. And when Diana was told none of her flatmates could be bridesmaids, she was even more upset. The only thing she could do was to ensure they had prime seats in St. Paul's on the wedding day, which she did.

It all came down to a question of confidence, and in those early days Diana quite simply did not have enough of it to claim vital territory as her own. She was not even mistress in her own home; it was Charles who organized their occasional dinner parties. And without a ready-made "Royal Blooms-bury Set" of interesting people to call upon, she found herself coming face-to-face, time and time again, with the same old collection of people whom Charles knew but with whom she had little in common.

If dinners at home were difficult, official functions were worse. Her throat would dry up, and she would find it impossible to eat. Her position prohibited her finding release in alcohol (she hardly drank anyway, because booze made her cheeks flush), so formal, public luncheons and dinners, she said, were "yuk."

It is not surprising she felt trapped. Understandably, she has started to break out. For Diana, for all that early demure-ness, is not the kind of woman to subordinate herself indefi-nitely to her husband, no matter how princely that husband may be. It is not her character. And as Diana settled into her royal role that character started to reassert itself.

We have seen her grow in confidence, and she has felt it herself. She has achieved her modest ambition—to be a wife and mother—and she is tackling the heavier task of being herself. The process, because she is who she is, has caused ructions and unhappiness and concern. It has generated rumor and invited scurrilous speculation. But Diana, per-haps too isolated in the ivory tower of royalty to at first realize the reaction her behavior would generate, has pursued her goal—of a life of her own filled with friends of her own choosing. She has now achieved it. And if Charles prefers not to be around when she entertains her own friends at "KP" as she calls Kensington Palace, then so be it.

"We can't always find a date to suit us both," she says diplomatically.

When Diana decides to have a dinner party, she will telephone friends like Mervyn Chaplin, who works for Ge-rard Holdings in the city of London, and invite them around. She calls herself "Diana" on the telephone, and the switch-board operator will put her through, unaware of the identity of the voice on the other end of the line. Mervyn has been caught out on more than one occasion when friends, deciding to have a bit of fun with him, have telephoned imitating Diana's flattened vowels.

"Hi, Duch," he will say. "Thought you looked wonderful in the papers this morning. But that dress—I nearly saw everything you had!"

Diana makes no fuss when her friends tease her, which they constantly do. It is what she wants. She finds all the adoration heaped on her shoulders very tiresome and embarrassing.

"There's far too much about me in the newspapers, far too much," she says. Her friends agree, and it is but rarely that her private entertainments make the popular print.

When her friends dine at Kensington Palace, they are secretive about it, never mentioning where they are going. These suppers are usually very informal and served in the small dining room or Diana's sitting room. The menu is equally simple: pasta and salad or lobster. Occasionally they will go to a movie first, but this is not easy for the woman with the most photographed face in the world. More usually they stay in Kensington Palace and watch the latest videos, or Diana sometimes shows them the home movies she and Charles have made of their children. She claims she is not much good at photography (not true; she is very good), but she has hundreds of excellent snapshots, carefully pasted into leatherbound albums, which she will show to her guests. Wallace Heaton in Bond Street develops all the royal snaps, including those taken by any of Diana's friends during skiing holidays or weekends at Windsor Castle or Highgrove.

During the 1987 skiing holiday in Switzerland, all the guests dutifully gave their film to the'royal detectives at the end of the holiday and had it returned processed but without negatives. The precaution is a sensible one; the daring snaps of Diana and Fergie dressed up in head scarves and T-shirts doing a risqué cabaret act is not the image the Royal Family wants to project. Informal pictures of Diana therefore are always at a premium, and although the tiara and ball gown photographs no longer command the vast sums they once did, many magazines and newspapers will pay a great deal for off-duty snaps, a situation that caused Diana and her friends a great deal of aggravation in the latter part of 1987.

Diana had organized to go to a bridge party given by one of her friends, Kate Menzies, the heiress to a newsagent chain. As usual the weekly bridge party had been planned carefully; Kate had telephoned Diana and spoken with her secretary, who agreed on a suitable date with the Princess and, for security purposes, a list of the other guests. Accompanied only by her detective, Diana drove to the South Kensington mews house Kate shares with her sister Sarah.

As the evening progressed, the players, who dined off Marks and Spencer lasagne, were unaware that a photographer was positioned outside the house, waiting for them to come out. Her detective that night, Sergeant Ken Wharf, was in an adjoining room and also unaware. The photographer's long, cold wait did not go unrewarded, and eventually Diana, wearing a satin bomber jacket and tight purple trousers tucked into boots, emerged from the house with Kate Menzies to say good-bye to one of the guests, Major David Waterhouse, a young officer in the Household Cavalry and an old friend of Diana's.

Stupidly perhaps, they started fooling around outside the house with masks and rubber noses and tried to put a rubber balloon over the exhaust of Waterhouse's car. Their howls of laughter drowned the click of the photographer's camera, and he got the shot he wanted—the Princess of Wales larking about with a young man who clearly wasn't her husband. The photographer, who was hiding behind another car, was suddenly spotted, and Diana leapt back onto the doorstep and shouted to David Waterhouse to drive off and let her detective handle the situation. Grabbing the photographer, twenty-two-year-old Jason Fraser, Diana's bodyguard swiftly removed the film from his camera and told the photographer in no uncertain terms what would happen to him if he didn't leave immediately.

Brushing aside tears of frustration and rage, Diana explained to the young photographer that he and his sort were making her and her friends' lives a misery and he had to give her his film.

"I've been working hard all week," the Princess said. "Katie fixed up a nice evening for me. She laid this whole thing on. It's very sweet, and it's the only time I've been out all week. I've got so few friends left, and this will only make things worse for me."

The following day the photographer, who had given his name and address to the bodyguard, Ken Wharf, was handed back the film, fully processed but without the negatives of Diana. It was an unfortunate incident, and it highlighted the Princess's loneliness and frustration at not being able to keep her private life private. It also affected the Menzies sisters, who were hounded subsequently by photographers after the story broke. Far from dropping Diana, her close-knit circle of friends rallied round and determined the press should not ruin her life—or theirs. But the situation worried them. It also worried her security advisors. What if instead of a camera the man had been carrying a gun? Her bodyguards and their superiors much preferred it when she confined her nocturnal outings to more conventional activities.

While Charles loves the opera and will often go to Covent Garden with the minimum of fuss, accompanied perhaps by Lady Susan Hussey, one of the Queen's ladies-in-waiting with whom he is very close—whose husband, Sir Marmaduke Hussey, chairman of the BBC, is not an opera buff—Diana and her friends prefer to go to the theater. They will drive to Kensington Palace and transfer to her car, arriving at the theater with the detective a few minutes before the curtain goes up. The cast members are informed of the Princess's arrival by the theater manager, and if any of her show business friends like Wayne Sleep or Michael Crawford are in the show, she might dine with them afterward.

Dinners are never completely impromptu, as the restaurant is always informed of her impending arrival. If the venue is new, it is checked out by a couple of detectives the day before. The detectives also dine in the restaurant at a couple of tables to either side of the Princess and her party. It does, however, not always work out that they can be seated exactly this way. A sneaky snapshot of Diana sharing a table with Lady Tryon, nicknamed "Kanga," on the occasion of their reconciliation lunch at San Lorenzo in Knightsbridge resulted when the photographer discovered Diana was lunching and managed to secure the adjacent table and take the clandestine shot without anyone noticing. Lady Tryon, however, was not displeased to be so publicly back in the royal fold from which, Diana, jealous of the closeness of Kanga's friendship with her husband, had banished her. The friendship has not developed. Diana was not exactly delighted that the Australian Kanga spent so much of the autumn of 1987 at Balmoral with Charles, while she remained in London. The pair are no longer seen together in San Lorenzo, though Diana is often there with another of her girlfriends.

It is one of her favorite lunchtime haunts. She loves the food, which is Italian, and the hustle and bustle of the three-tiered restaurant. There are always plenty of "faces"—a Sloane expression for famous people—and Diana sits with girlfriends like Caroline Twiston-Davies, who works in interior design in nearby Walton Street, gossiping about who is there and what they have both been doing.

Another of Diana's favorite restaurants is Launceston Place, situated close to Kensington Palace and almost next to Lord Snowdon's London home. After lunch there Diana will sometimes go shopping in the maze of smart boutiques and children's shops nearby. She often lunches with her sister Jane Fellowes at Launceston Place or La Fontana, an unpretentious Italian restaurant in Pimlico. For show business friends Diana chooses haunts like the Groucho Club in Soho, where she ate monkfish with Wayne Sleep, or Luigis in Covent Garden, where she joined Wayne and a crowd of ballet dancers for a pasta dinner.

Apart from Wayne Sleep with whom she once danced at Covent Garden and shares a love of the ballet, her lunches are strictly for the girls. Young men are in attendance only in private houses or one of the royal residences. The men, for their part, are understandably delighted to entertain the Princess to dinner, even if their homes are not particularly smart. Mervyn Chaplin lives in a mansion block of flats above an arcade of shops on Fulham Road. It is not grand, but boasts a dark green dining room decorated with hunting prints. Together with Humphrey Butler, who works at Christie's, and Willy van Straubenzee, who works at Morgan Grenfell & Co., Ltd. Bank, they will invite Diana to dinner. The conversation is jovial, and Diana entertains her fellow diners with risqué jokes and anecdotes about her children. She seldom mentions Charles but doesn't mind being teased about her latest nickname, hairstyle, or outfit. When the press called her "Disco-Di," a reference to her late-night dancing in a Swiss nightclub, she would ring up and announce, "It's Disco-Di from KP."

In return she will invite them to Windsor for Royal Ascot, where officially they are guests of the Queen. Humphrey Butler, Willy van Straubenzee, and several girls from the set—including, of course, Sarah Ferguson before she was Duchess of York—have all been invited to Windsor at Diana's suggestion. So has Philip Dunne.

The Queen loves having young people to stay during the racing week. They make a good foil for some of her husband's "boring" German relations, and every evening each guest has a card in his room informing him whom he will be escorting into dinner. After dinner the men swap stories over port while the ladies retire to an anteroom and decide on the silliest party games they can play. Dancing games such as Twister, which involves trying to return to your original spot when the music stops, are popular because everyone can understand the simple rules. The Queen usually retires early, followed by the Prince of Wales—Ascot is a busy polo week for him, and he practices in the morning and plays every afternoon after the races. Those who don't go to the polo return to Windsor Castle and have a swim or play tennis before dinner.

The Duchess of York and Viscount Linley, Princess Margaret's son, who runs an extremely successful furniture business with his partner, Matthew Rice, have been almost entirely instrumental in enlarging Diana's circle of friends. Before Sarah got married in July 1986, her father gave a large party on the polo grounds at Smith's Lawn, Windsor. It was an eclectic gathering mixing the Royal Family and Nancy Reagan with Paddy McNally, Sarah's former boyfriend, and his jet-set group of friends. Diana had the time of her life; she boogied in the mobile discotheque organized by another of Fergie's mates, the dashing Angus Gibson, and danced with a host of attractive men she had never met before.

Financier Charlie Carter was one. He had several dances with the Princess, and when he returned to his table she invited him to dance again, which he duly did. They made an attractive couple as they are both excellent dancers, and he found Diana "charming and a terrific dancer." They met again several months later at a charity ball, and Charlie, who is happily married, asked Diana to dance. This time, however, a pair of mischievous press people were watching, and the story found its way to the newspapers. For the next few weeks Charlie and his wife Tita had to put up with the press camping outside their Belgravia home, hoping to "snatch" a picture of Charlie as he left for work. They didn't go unrewarded and caught him one morning when he left his house with a terrible hangover, his hair in his eyes and his tie askew.

"I can't understand them," Tita exclaimed. "All they had to do was ring on the doorbell and ask us if we minded posing for a picture." She added: "Both Charlie and I think the Princess of Wales is terrific but hardly know her apart from being Charlie's dancing partner on a couple of occasions."

Charlie Carter is not the only one whose name has been linked with the Princess merely because they shared a shimmy on the dance floor. Peter Greenall, who was in the 1987 Klosters chalet party with his wife, Clare, was another. He escorted Diana, who was dressed in sexy black leather trousers, to a local disco (where the Princess delighted the disc jockey by requesting Diana Ross's "Chain Reaction").

"I asked if she still liked Duran Duran, but she wanted Diana Ross's hit 'Chain Reaction,'" DJ Martin Melsome explained. "I obliged, and she did a fantastic rock-and-roll solo to it. Then I had her in stitches by playing 'Oh Diana.'"

Diana was with a group of friends and being carefully

watched by three British detectives and two Swiss policemen. Charles was not part of the party, but, said Melsome, "she didn't look lonely or sad that her husband wasn't with her. In fact, rather the opposite. She drank red wine and seemed to have a marvelous time."

Diana's friends claim that there was nothing unusual about Charles letting Diana dance the night away without him. He loves skiing hard and starts early and therefore doesn't particularly want to spend his evenings in nightclubs. Unlike Diana, Charles hates making an exhibition of himself on dance floors, as he revealed during their trip to Australia:

"I assure you it makes the heart sink to have to make an awful exhibition of ourselves," he explained as they started the dancing to the strains of Glenn Miller's "In The Mood." "Having had a certain amount of practice in the last few years, each time I keep meaning to try to take lessons to learn the finer points of the tango, or the paso doble, or even break dancing."

They began by doing a formal quickstep and then launched into their own medley—a personal jive in which Prince Charles threw Diana to one side while keeping hold of her with one hand. He then spun her around and around while he stood on the spot, causing her to call out, "Steady, please slow down."

Diana often gets the giggles when she dances with Charles and, like many women, prefers to dance with almost anyone other than her husband. At the wedding ball after "Bunter" Worcester, the Duke of Beaufort's son and heir, married actress Tracy Ward, Diana never left the dance floor. She danced with Gerry Farrell, who runs a mail-order art business, and David Ker, who owns an art gallery near Sloane Square. And she danced with Philip Dunne—again and again and again.

"It's all so innocent," she told friends, "and I don't intend to act like the guilty party."

The gossip columns, which take a more cynical view of life, were not convinced. The speculation, however, only served to draw her circle tighter than ever. They included her in as many dinner parties as possible, and Julia Dodd Noble, known as "Crown Jewels" because of her royal connections, and Antonia, Marchioness of Duro, encouraged Diana to join the Vanderbilt Racquet Club and play tennis with them. Diana is godmother to Antonia's daughter, and both she and Charles spent a long weekend on the estate owned by her father-in-law, the Duke of Wellington, in Spain. She attended a David Bowie concert with Viscount Linley and a group of friends including Major David Waterhouse. Photographers mistook the major for Philip Dunne, and the ensuing publicity forced the gallant Major, who was at Eton with Dunne, to speak up in the Princess's defense, as did Kate Menzies.

Kate, who once enjoyed a brief liaison with Viscount Linley (they remain good friends), was introduced to Diana through Susannah Constantine and Fergie. She is in a perfect situation to be able to gather all Diana's friends together and provide the Princess with the normal social scene so lacking in the early years of her marriage, and she does so. But unfortunately for Diana, who loves giggling at the risqué jokes that fly around the dinner table and being teased about her wild dancing or sexy clothes, her position as Princess of Wales has to come first. Any breath of scandal, however unjustified, is harmful to her, her husband, and the Royal Family.

Entertaining royalty is not easy, as Diana realizes. When she took a breather from the Royal Box at Ascot last year and went for tea with her friends Clare Wentworth-Stanley and her husband in the Turf Club, she was criticized because she herself was not a member of the elite gentleman's club. And when she returned with Prince Charles the following day, she spied her friend Ben Holland-Martin holding a table she assumed was for her and Charles. Much to Ben's consternation, it wasn't—he was holding it for Princess Margaret, who was due to appear, and the Prince and Princess were forced to move to another already crowded table. To make matters worse, Princess Margaret changed her mind and never appeared, leaving a red-faced Ben sitting at the empty table he had refused to the Prince and Princess of Wales!

When the pressure gets too great, Diana will retreat to the sanctuary of Highgrove and her husband. Charles and Diana

do have a few mutual friends, and they will occasionally
invited for weekends in Gloucestershire. (Charles is too b
with business dinners or official royal duties during the
week to socialize much.) Sir Laurens van der Post sometimes
visits so he can see his godson, William, and so do a group of
Charles's hunting cronies, like "Milo" and Penny Watson.
Miles, Lord Manton's son, is the brother of one of Charles's
old flames, Fiona Watson. He and his wife, Penny, get along
very well with Diana and love her wicked sense of humor.
Catherine Soames, who in the spring of 1988 separated from
her husband Nicholas, is also a regular guest. So is her
brother-in-law, Rupert, who is now engaged to Philip
Dunne's sister Millie.

Now that the Duke and Duchess of York have their own
home, they are not such regular visitors, but during Andrew's time at sea and Fergie's pregnancy Diana did her best
to persuade her friend to spend as many weekends with them
as possible. She is Diana's "BF," and if Charles is in one of
his tetchy moods, Fergie can usually chide and tease him out
of it—something Diana cannot always do, and she and
Charles often find themselves rubbing each other the wrong
way. If Diana really wants to irritate her husband, she will
crack a stream of childish jokes about sex and social background—guaranteed to drive Charles into a fury. He then
refuses to speak to her, and no amount of flirting and teasing
will pull him out of his mood. Eventually, however, he will
give in and sigh, "Anything for a peaceful life"—one of his
favorite phrases.

Charles may yearn for the peaceful life and Diana for the
bright lights, but they have an amicable agreement to do their
own thing. Charles is long suffering, but he is also selfish
and doesn't like his life being disrupted. After much consideration he allowed Palace officials to give Philip Dunne a
gentle telephone call and inform him it would be far better
for everyone concerned if he were to leave the Princess of
Wales alone. By way of setting up a smokescreen, several other
people also received the call so that Dunne could not claim to
have been singled out. It is the royal way of coping with a
problem; Richard Meade, a one-time boyfriend of the Prin-

cess Royal, received a similar call when Mark Phillips appeared on the romantic scene. He agreed to leave Anne alone, and it was not until several years later, when they were both married to their respective partners, that they became good friends again.

Obviously neither Diana nor Anne was happy with this kind of forceful alienation, but there was little either of them could do at the time, apart from sulk. Diana chose not to take this course of action and threw herself into her family life and socializing.

She also had her brother, three years her junior, to turn to. Since Viscount Althorp has been working for the American television network NBC, Diana hasn't seen so much of him, but they are close. She cared for him as a baby, found him a "pest" when he was a "spotty ten-year-old creep" who spent his days following her and her friends around, but grew closer again when he matured. Today they are united by the love of their frail father, Earl Spencer, and contempt for their stepmother, Raine, who has gradually removed their heritage by organizing the sale of certain family treasures.

Althorp is reluctant to discuss his favorite sister with anyone, and when he was originally hired by NBC to do commentary on the wedding of the Duke and Duchess of York in 1986, the only thing he let slip was that Major Ronald Ferguson had once proposed to his mother. He swallowed their referring incorrectly to his sister as Lady Diana and during all the speculation in 1987 when the major American networks ran stories on the state of her marriage he refused to comment.

"I'd never let her down in any way," he said.

Intelligent and hardworking, he is highly regarded by his American employers. It took him a long time to shake off his "Hooray Henry" image of the champagne-swilling hooligan who liked to sit around in nightclubs hurling abuse at those not so fortunate as he, but he has finally succeeded, and Diana is proud of him.

She is, he claims, a good mixture of both his parents—she has his father's gentleness and his mother's single-mindedness: "I think the combination's pretty good," he says. "And it's most obvious in Diana. She is exceptionally kind and thoughtful, but she's nobody's fool. She weeded out quite a few of the hangers-on that she found around her husband and his family in a subtle way."

For all that and for all her insistence on developing her own circle of friends, Diana does do her best on occasions to include her husband in her activities. She was delighted when he agreed to host a pre-Christmas party for the stars who had worked so hard for his pet charity, the Prince's Trust, as a thank-you for their various appearances. Among the guests at the Kensington Palace bash were ex-Beatle George Harrison and his wife, Olivia; Elton John and Renate; Paul Young; Kate Bush; and Howard Jones. Diana had the carpet in their large reception room rolled back and persuaded Labi Siffre to play the piano. As always, Elton John gave a rendering of some of his hit songs, and everyone danced and sang. Diana was ebullient and danced with as many of the famous guests as she could.

Both Diana and Charles, stars themselves, are attracted to show business folk and like to count them among their friends. Diana might prefer pop stars and TV heartthrobs like "Miami Vice" hero Don Johnson, while Charles favors pretty actresses such as James Bond heroine Maryam D'Abo, whom he sat next to at the Cannes Film Festival dinner in 1987. It is a real affinity the Waleses feel with people who are in the public eye almost as much as the Royal Family and know what it is like to be stared at all the time.

"You musn't believe what you read in the papers," Charles told Maryam D'Abo. "I don't believe any of it. In fact, I avoid reading them whenever I can."

Ex-Goon Spike Milligan is a great friend of the Prince and they exchange a zany correspondence. "He wrote to me by hand recently," Spike explained, "because he was het up about the plans for Paternoster Square near St. Paul's, saying, 'I need your support.' I wrote back that I wasn't wearing one." Spike loves what he calls "loopholes" in the English language that enable him to play with words, and he receives equally witty letters back from the Prince of Wales, whom he sometimes entertains to dinner.

"Charles is a very ordinary person," Milligan says. "I wrote to him and asked if he and his wife would like to come for dinner. He turned up with an aide—I presumed she had another engagement. I was disappointed. I would like to have met her properly."

One entertainer that both Diana and Charles love is Barry Humphries, who created the outrageous saliva-spraying slob, Sir Les Patterson, and Dame Edna Everage. At his charity show, Charles and Diana were both in fits of laughter at his blue jokes. After the show, dressed as Dame Edna Everage, Barry Humphries made an unabashed reference to the "tip" of his gladioli being the most sensitive part.

The world has indeed changed. It would have been unthinkable a few years ago for anyone—even an entertainer such as Humphries—to make such a lewd remark to a member of the Royal Family. But then Diana too has changed. Marriage may have made her a Princess, but it deprived her of the irresponsible good times that are part of growing up. Instead of parties and dates and nightclubs, Diana had marriage, motherhood, and the confines of royal responsibility.

She could not linger for hours in restaurants, dance the night away with a series of unlikely partners, or do anything quite mad and bad, just for fun. She had hardly experienced a normal life. Instead she had been wrapped in royal cotton wool. But then she started to break out, to lead her own life away from Charles and the confines of court. It led to gossip and speculation and reports of a serious rift in her marriage.

"I feel sorry for the Princess," one of her girlfriends admits. "She can't do anything without running into a mountain of criticism."

But as Prince Charles says, "The moment people have put you up on a pedestal, along comes a separate brigade that like knocking you off. It's human nature."

The foundations of Diana's pedestal have taken a fair knocking recently. But she is determined to survive them and keep her seven-year marriage alive—with a little help from her friends.

Epilogue

It was nineteen minutes after midnight (French time) on Sunday, August 31, 1997, when Diana, Princess of Wales, tightly holding on to the arm of her lover, Dodi Al Fayed, emerged from a private entrance at the rear of the Hotel Ritz in Paris and climbed into the back of a waiting car. Fifteen minutes later, that car was a tangle of twisted metal in the middle of an underpass that runs beside the River Seine; Diana was crumpled in the back seat, her life ebbing away. And as she lay dying, the sound of the clicking cameras could be heard—cameras that had followed and pursued her, given her fame and identity, but in the end proved too obtrusive for this highly publicized and analyzed, fragile and naïve woman who had captivated a generation.

Ironically, it was almost exactly ten years since her former husband, Prince Charles, had retired—wounded—to Scotland, thereby giving the first clear public indication that the "fairy-tale marriage" was tearing itself apart at its emotional seams.

By then, of course, Prince Charles had revived his relationship with his old love, Camilla Parker-Bowles. And Diana, by her own admission, was "in love" with a handsome cavalry officer named James Hewitt.

Had Charles and Diana been an ordinary couple, they probably would have ended their union at that time. But royal marriages—because of the attention they generate and the expectations they elicit—are bound by their own set of rules. Another nine years would pass before this royal marriage was finally dissolved.

The initial phase of the royal separation was a particularly painful time for Diana. There were adjustments, problems, struggles, and disappointments that she could barely have imagined when she agreed to separate from the man who had made her a Princess.

Clearly, she had found it impossible to realize her full potential as a woman within the confines of the Royal Family. She quickly discovered, however, that life outside its protective cocoon was even more frightening. She was grittily determined to make her own way and, in the process, to create a new role for herself—on her own terms—free from the restrictions that are an integral part of Britain's reigning family.

At first she was not certain which way to turn or what path to take. In December 1993, for example, she announced that she was retiring from public life. Eleven months later she changed her mind and was appointed Patron of the Red Cross on the occasion of its 125th birthday celebration, only to relinquish the post again when she gave up all but six of her charities.

Her private life was equally confused—and hardly private at all. No sooner had she entered into an ill-considered relationship with art dealer Oliver Hoare than she began another with the England rugby captain, Will Carling. Since both were married men, Diana found herself once again the center of exactly the kind of media attention she insisted she was so anxious to avoid. It was not until almost the end of her short glittering life, when she took up the campaign to outlaw land mines, that she found a real sense of purpose.

It had been a struggle—and the greatest struggle had been with her own demons.

Diana's unhappy childhood had a profound effect on her,

which manifested itself in her eating disorders. They came to the forefront even before she was married. Shortly after her engagement was announced, Diana moved into Buckingham Palace. It proved to be a lonely time for the beautiful but insecure young woman.

She found the Palace routine stultifying and resented the way the old courtiers tried to tell her how to behave. She continued to act as if she was still living in a bachelor girl apartment, not a palace, and shocked the crusty members of the staff by running down the corridors to the swimming pool wearing nothing more than a swimsuit and a beach robe. Confronted with their disapproving looks, she retreated into herself and took solace in solitary eating and purging. Many years later she would tell me that it was the Palace system as much as Camilla Parker-Bowles that had ruined her marriage.

Camilla certainly played a part, however. Prince Charles kept in touch with his old girlfriend. He would insist that their relationship was open and aboveboard until his marriage had "irretrievably broken down," but the very fact that he continued to talk to Camilla in an intimate and confidential way was enough to incur Diana's understandable jealousy. That triggered her insecurity and contributed to her emotional instability. As Diana explained in her now-famous television interview, the effect was "pretty devastating. Rampant bulimia, if you can have rampant bulimia, and just a feeling of being no good at anything and being useless and hopeless and failed in every direction."

Asked if Mrs. Parker-Bowles was a factor in the breakdown of her marriage, she replied, "Well, there were three of us in this marriage, so it was a bit crowded." Her remarks struck a chord with millions of women everywhere. By then, of course, public sympathy was already moving in Diana's favor. Diana's unhappiness had been an ill-kept secret for years.

Her bulimia had been compounded by a severe case of postpartum depression following the birth of her eldest son, Prince William. "You woke up in the morning feeling you didn't want to get out of bed, you felt misunderstood and very, very low in yourself," she explained.

At that stage Prince Charles was still trying his best to do what he could to help his troubled wife. Telltale signs of Diana's unhappiness had been there almost from the beginning. On their honeymoon at Balmoral, for example, Diana had been unable to face the traditional family picnics eaten on the hill wrapped in tartan rugs and surrounded by midges. Instead she insisted on staying in her room and gorging on candy bought from the local town of Ballater. So concerned was Prince Charles that he sent for a psychiatrist from London to give medical counsel to them both. The doctor said that what Diana really needed was female company of her own age, and one of her old roommates was duly invited up to Scotland. It did little good, however, because the Princess was already convinced in her own mind "to the point of obsession" that Charles had already renewed his association with Camilla.

Coming to terms with being a member of the Royal Family was never easy for Diana. Self-contained to a fault and wary of outsiders, the Windsors had never embraced her in the manner she expected. She was left very much to herself, to get on with life as best she could and deal with her own problems in her own way. When she proved incapable of doing so, she could feel herself become increasingly isolated. Princess Margaret, who had been so supportive of Diana in the early days, was one of the first to turn away from her.

Charles's sister, Princess Anne, was notably colder. She had never taken to her sister-in-law and had as little as possible to do with her since Diana had declined to attend the christening of Anne's daughter, Zara, two days before Diana's wedding in St. Paul's Cathedral. Anne, in turn, refused to attend the christening of Prince Harry on the insulting grounds that she had a rabbit shoot that day.

That left the Queen. She at least tried to see Diana's point of view. The affairs of state permitting, she always made herself available when Diana wanted to see her and spent many hours with her daughter-in-law in the months leading up to the final separation. Diana would pour her heart out, tears flowing down her face. She would explain to her bemused monarch that nobody understood, nobody liked her, nobody cared for her.

It was not true. Diana had very quickly established herself as the most popular member of the Royal Family. Her openness, her obvious vulnerability, had struck a chord. Paradoxically, her contradictions made so many people identify with her. She held up a mirror to this fractured age and allowed people to project onto it their hopes and ambitions, their fears and resentments. Because she was so obviously troubled, many people were willing to forgive her almost any transgression.

Diana met James Hewitt, an officer in the elite Life Guards, at a party in London's Mayfair in late summer 1986. He was twenty-eight, she was twenty-six; their attraction was mutual and immediate. She told him she wanted to learn to ride again, and he offered to teach her. They started riding together in the early mornings and evenings in Hyde Park.

After one evening ride, Diana asked Hewitt to join her for dinner at Kensington Palace while Charles was away. It was the beginning of a relationship that lasted for almost four years, during which time she wrote him love letters and bought him handmade shirts, a diamond tiepin, and gold cuff links. Given the security surrounding members of the Royal Family, it was inevitable that Prince Charles would hear about what was going on; it was the reason for his retreat to Scotland in the autumn of 1987. Looking back on their affair, Diana said: "He was a great friend of mine at a very difficult time and he was always there to support me."

When asked if their relationship went beyond a close friendship, Diana replied, "Yes, I adored him. Yes, I was in love with him."

The romance came to a bitter end when Hewitt assisted in a book detailing their affair. "I was absolutely devastated when this book appeared because I trusted him and because again I worried about the reaction of my children," Diana said.

Hewitt was not alone in resorting to print to get his story across. Prince Charles collaborated with author and broadcaster Jonathan Dimbleby to produce an authorized biography (and, in the process, confessed his adultery to Dimbleby during the television program that accompanied the book). And, even more famously, Diana allowed her friends and family to cooperate in producing *Diana: Her True Story*. It was a bleak and spiritually desolate tale. It contained a detailed account of her eating disorders, her attempted suicide, and her ongoing depression. It upset the Queen, further strained her marriage, and brought her into direct conflict with Sir Robert Fellowes—who, in addition to being the Queen's private secretary, was also Diana's brother-in-law.

A faxed copy of the newspaper prepublication serialization of the book arrived at Charles and Diana's country home, Highgrove, very early on a Sunday morning and was placed at the head of the dining table for the Prince to look at. Breakfast that morning was a stilted affair. Diana remained in her room while the Prince read through the faxed pages. The atmosphere was made even more tense by the presence of houseguests who were staying with the royal couple that weekend. After seeing the guests off, Charles walked upstairs to the Princess's bedroom. Diana emerged a few minutes later. Crimson-faced and with tears in her eyes, she ran down the stairs. She got into her car and told the staff that she was going back to London.

It was several weeks before Diana returned to the country home she had grown to hate. By then husband and wife could hardly bring themselves to exchange a civil word.

Another blow fell in August 1992 with the publication of the so-called Squidgie Tape, the unauthorized recording made on New Year's Eve three years before of a conversation between Diana and her friend, car dealer James Gilbey. On the tape Diana recounted how she had almost started crying at lunch. "I just felt really sad and empty, and I thought, after all I've done for this . . . family. I am going to do something dramatic because I can't stand the confines of this marriage."

It was a situation beyond Charles's experience or understanding. By opening her heart, albeit by proxy, Diana had broken the royal code of *omerta*, which dictates that, no matter what the problem, royal decorum must always be preserved. The monarchy is governed by what has gone before, and there was simply no precedent for a Princess of Wales going public with her woes.

But then Diana had never been one to play by the rules. Free-spirited and ungovernable, she was determined to forge a life for herself unfettered by the constraints of royal protocol. Attempts were made to paper over the gaping cracks in the royal marriage, but no amount of cosmetic dressing could disguise the fact that the Waleses had reached the end of their marital road. Henceforth Diana refused to spend any more Christmases with her in-laws, preferring to be anywhere else, even alone, than at Sandringham.

On December 9, the couple bowed to the inevitable and announced their formal separation. But if ending her royal marriage had been hard, making a career for herself was even harder. Prince Philip had summed up the royal attitude when he declared, "If she wants out, she can get out—and stay out!" Diana started to flounder. Unsure of where she was going or even who she now was, Diana turned inward. She gave up many of her old friends and looked more and more to her sons for emotional support.

The one thing that united Charles and Diana throughout this very tense time of separation was their shared concern for the Princes William and Harry. Diana had tried to diffuse the boys' intense concern at what was happening to their parents by explaining at each step what she thought was going to happen, thus preparing them for the emotional shock of the divorce. She continually reassured both of them that their lives would remain very much the same, and because of this she decided to remain at what had been the marital home at Kensington Palace while Charles moved into new quarters, across London in St. James's Palace. She explained how much her sons loved Kensington Palace and felt secure there, and she placed great importance on their having what she called a "relaxed routine"—including free time to be with her and to be without too much pressure to perform and achieve.

It was hardest for William to come to terms with the change in his parents' domestic arrangements. More sensitive than his buoyant younger brother, he became withdrawn and introspective. Diana worried about the effect her personal traumas were having on William, but that did not stop her from burdening him with her problems. She always treated William as a friend and would whisk him upstairs with her to watch television when her rows with Prince Charles became overheated.

There is no doubt that Diana would have seen her sons as the most important legacy of her extraordinary life. She was the mother who taught them to care for others, who took them from their palace homes to visit the terminally ill, the homeless, and the sick; it was she who underlined the need for compassion. She taught them never to shout at anyone who could not answer back. She introduced them to the "modern" world and injected fun and excitement and thrills into their otherwise royally regulated lives. She took them white-water rafting in Colorado and to Disney World in Florida, fed them hamburgers, and dressed them in jeans and baseball caps.

Her sitting room in Kensington Palace was a shrine to William and Harry. Photographs of the two—individually and together; laughing, playing, fooling around, and joking; in black and white and in color; in simple leather frames and in ornate silver frames—decorated every available space. Her boys, she told me, were part of her very being. They were the reason for her existence, and she was determined that whatever she might do with her own life it would come second to them. She went on to say that whatever her personal feelings were, she would never taint her children's relationship with their father or anyone else in the Royal Family.

"I have no wish to upset what is essentially part of William's inheritance, whether he likes it or not," she told me. "I always tell my boys what I am doing and ask their advice," she added.

It was William, for instance, who advised her to sell her vast collection of dresses in aid of charity. It was William who had pushed handkerchiefs under the door of her bathroom where she had sought sanctuary at some of the worst moments of her breakup with Charles.

Diana's reliance on her son was sometimes so overpowering that it worried the Queen, who felt it was unfair to place such weighty emotional responsibility on the shoulders of one so young as William. Charles was more ambivalent. His arguments with Diana had deeply upset him, and he was reluctant to enter into further verbal combat. He had once remarked, "Anything for any easy life," and it had become something of a motto for him. Only when William was sent to Eton, the five-hundred-year-old prep school across the River Thames from Windsor Castle, was some sense of pre-breakup equilibrium restored.

Surrounded by boys of his own age and protected from the intrusions of the paparazzi, William was able to develop at his own pace and in his own way, away from the scorching glare of publicity and the emotional upheaval of his royal home life. He also started seeing more of his grandmother, who would invite him over for tea on Sunday afternoons. Her eyes would light up when he entered her private sitting room for an hour of talk and discussion. It was very much a learning process for William because the Queen would recount to her eventual heir what she had done and whom she had met that week. The best way to learn about monarchy and its duties, she explained, was to see it in operation.

The one topic they never discussed was Diana. Never one to show her emotions, the Queen was determined not to trouble her grandson with her own concerns. Her refusal to speak her mind and say what was worrying her most was in the royal tradition. She had been brought up to keep her feelings to herself. That had always been royalty's way. It certainly was not Diana's. And that is precisely what endeared

Diana to so many millions of people both in Britain and around the world, yet at the same time brought her into such dramatic conflict with the family she had married into.

"I always follow my instincts," Diana once told me. But where did those instincts lead her? For a long while it looked as though the last person who had any idea where she was heading was Diana herself. She had challenged the power of one of the world's most venerable institutions, and though she declared, "I won't go quietly," it was clear to all that her position was a precarious one.

For example, there were long and fraught arguments over money during which it was made quite clear to Diana that while she would enjoy all the comforts befitting the mother of a future king, she was not going to get a multimillion-dollar payoff. In the end she settled for $25 million. This was not cash in hand, however; the money was bound up in trust funds, which have now reverted to her children.

When her divorce finally and formally came through in 1996, she was stripped of the right to be addressed as "Her Royal Highness" and, at least in theory, forced onto the sidelines. According to the rules, that was where she should have stayed.

What the Royal Family had not reckoned on, however, was Diana's enormous popularity. She had won the affection of people around the world, and everywhere she went she was assured of a grand and glorious reception.

"I want a monarchy that has more contact with its people," she declared. And she was as good as her word. Without regard for prejudice or protocol, she visited the sick, embraced the dying, and gave comfort to victims of diseases with historical social stigmas, such as AIDS and leprosy. Other members of the Royal Family have devoted themselves to charity but never to the same effect as Diana. She became a touchstone of hope for the sick and the despairing. Her effortless charm won over world leaders such as South Africa's Nelson Mandela and U.S. President Bill Clinton. Her secret was in her willingness to take people into her arms with no thought about how dirty or ill they were. She would climb onto hospital beds and crouch beside wheelchairs, smiling and joking all the time. When someone once called out, "Can I kiss you?" she answered, "No, but you can kiss my hand, though you never know where it may have been."

In his powerful funeral address Diana's brother, Earl Spencer, summed up her universal appeal. "Diana explained to me once that it was her innermost feelings of suffering that made it possible for her to connect with her constituency of the rejected," he said.

Diana was personally captivating, and this quality won her an army of admirers. Furthermore, it made her royal relations look stiff and inhibited, out of touch, and emotionally cold. No one suffered more in comparison to her than her former husband. Charles simply could not compete with her. Thus, ironically, it was Diana who—more than the Prince of Wales, more even than the Queen—increasingly came to represent the British Royal Family to the world at large.

There was still an emptiness at the heart of Diana's life, however. She longed to have more children, but finding the man to have them with seemed beyond anything her celebrity would allow. Although it was the camera that had made her a star, she eventually came to see it as an instrument of violation. Where years before the attention of the ubiquitous cameras had given her emotional sustenance, it now terrified her. She saw the lens as "a sexual predator." Every time a paparazzo pointed a camera at her it was physically interfering with her; she went so far as to describe it as "mental rape." It threatened her well-being and had a detrimental effect on her romances, all of which faltered and then collapsed under the relentless media attention she had come to command. What man, she asked, could put up with the scrutiny a date with her entailed? She had almost given up looking altogether when she set off in July 1997 for a holiday on the French Riviera as a guest of Mohamed Al Fayed. All she was looking for was a relaxing break after tiring visits to Angola and Bosnia. What she found was a romance with his son, Dodi Al Fayed, which very quickly developed into love.

Her relationship with Dodi was certain to be controversial. His father, the Egyptian-born owner of Harrod's department store in London and the Hotel Ritz in Paris, was one of the most contentious figures in British politics. He admitted to paying Tory members of the British Parliament to ask questions in the House of Commons in return for cash; the ensuing scandal played a significant part in the electoral defeat of Prime Minister John Major's Conservative government.

Dodi, too, was saddled with a less than regal past. His late mother was the sister of Saudi arms dealer Adnan Khashoggi, which seemed to be at odds with Diana's campaign to ban land mines. After a brief spell in the armed forces of the United Arab Emirates, Dodi entered the film industry, coproducing the Oscar-winning movie *Chariots of Fire*. He then moved to Los Angeles, where he confirmed his reputation as a rich playboy. As a young man in London in the late seventies, he frequented all the notable nightclubs. In Hollywood he was seen with a succession of actresses including Brooke Shields, Winona Ryder, Cathy Lee Crosby, Julia Roberts, Mimi Rogers, Frank Sinatra's daughter Tina, and Prince Andrew's ex-girlfriend Koo Stark. In Britain the inevitable question was asked: Is this a suitable potential step-father for the future king of England?

The one person who seemed unconcerned by the controversy was Diana. Like Jackie Kennedy before her with Aristotle Onassis, she appeared to have found in Dodi the instant security she craved. He offered her all the material trappings she could have wished for—three yachts; a chalet in Gstaad, Switzerland; a castle near Invergordon, Scotland; apartments in New York and London; a house in Los Angeles; and a private jet to ferry her from one to another. But more significantly, there was the emotional protection that Dodi, a wordly, well-mannered forty-two-year-old accustomed to celebrity, was able to give her. Suddenly there was a bounce in Diana's step and a self-confidence that showed in her frequent smiles. We will never know where her relationship with Dodi would have led. What is clear is that she had discovered the companionship and affection that had been so notably absent for so long. She was, she told friends, "having a lot of fun."

Her happiness was destined to be tragically short-lived. Only eight weeks after the start of her summer romance, Diana lay fatally injured in the mangled wreckage of a chauffeur-driven car, her lover already dead beside her. The crash occurred at 12:35 A.M. (French time), and although Diana received medical attention while still in the car before being taken to the Petit Salpetriere Hospital in eastern Paris—where surgeons massaged her heart for two hours—she was declared dead at 4:00 A.M.

The reaction to her death was one of stunned disbelief followed by a worldwide flood of grief unprecedented in its intensity. On Saturday, September 6, millions lined the streets of London as the cortege bearing her body was drawn by horse to Westminster Abbey for her funeral service and then, by hearse, north to her final resting place on an island on her family's estate in Northamptonshire. She was, as Britain's Prime Minister Tony Blair declared, "The People's Princess."

Bewildered by Diana in life, the Royal Family was equally bewildered by her in death. The Queen, Prince Charles, sons William and Harry, and the rest of the family were far away in Balmoral. There they had intended to stay. The force of public opinion was such, however, that they were forced to travel south to London to share publicly in the remarkable outpouring of anguish over the death of this exceptional young woman.

Had she remained married to the Prince of Wales and settled into comfortable middle age, Diana would never had shone so brightly. The canopy of royal protocol would eventually have smothered her and her star would have diminished with the passing of the years.

In death, however, she was poignantly able to accomplish everything she wanted. She has reshaped the British monarchy and ensured that henceforth it must show more compassion. She has given unforgettable impetus to the causes she so cherished. She has won the public love that she so privately and earnestly desired.

She has become in death what she always wanted to be in life—"the Queen of Hearts."

Index